T0330013

CHINA
AND THE
PERSIAN GULF

CHINA
AND THE
PERSIAN GULF

The New Silk Road Strategy and Emerging Partnerships

Mordechai Chaziza

sussex
ACADEMIC
PRESS

Brighton • Chicago • Toronto

2 4 6 8 10 9 7 5 3 1

First published in 2020 in Great Britain by
SUSSEX ACADEMIC PRESS
PO Box 139
Eastbourne BN24 9BP

Distributed in North America by
SUSSEX ACADEMIC PRESS
Independent Publishers Group
814 N. Franklin Street
Chicago, IL 60610

British Library Cataloguing in Publication Data
A CIP catalogue record for this book is available from the British Library.

Library of Congress Cataloging-in-Publication Data
To be applied for.

Hardcover ISBN 978-1-78976-040-8

Typeset & designed by Sussex Academic Press, Brighton & Eastbourne.
Printed by TJ International, Padstow, Cornwall.

Contents

Acknowledgments

I would like to acknowledge the support and encouragement of my beloved kids, Hillel, Agam and Yarden, and especially my dear wife, Revital, for her constant support and understanding. I particularly wish to thank my colleague and friend Professor Zaki Shalom for his encouragement and support. Finally, the work on the book was supported by the Ashkelon Academic College, Israel.

List of Abbreviations

Asian Infrastructure Investment Bank (AIIB)

Arabian Travel Market (ATM)

Belt and Road Initiative (BRI)

China–Arab States Cooperation Forum (CASCF)

China Central–West Asia Economic Corridor (CCWAEC)

China's Ministry of Commerce (MoC)

China National Petroleum Corporation (CNPC)

China Nuclear Engineering Corporation (CNEC)

China–Pakistan Economic Corridor (CPEC)

Foreign Direct Investment (FDI)

Gulf Cooperation Council (GCC)

International Energy Agency (IEA)

Jebel Ali Free Zone (JAFZA)

Joint Comprehensive Plan of Action (JCPOA)

Khalifa Industrial Zone Abu Dhabi (KIZAD)

Liquefied Natural Gas (LNG)

Memorandum of Understanding (MoU)

Middle East and North Africa (MENA)

Mohammed bin Salman al-Saud (MBS)

National Bureau of Statistics (NBS)

One Belt, One Road (OBOR)

Organization of the Petroleum Exporting Countries (OPEC)

People's Republic of China (PRC)

Qatar Investment Authority (QIA)

Shanghai Cooperation Organization (SCO)

Sea Lines of Communication (SLOC)

Silk Road Economic Belt (SREB)

Special Economic Zone (SEZ)

The 21st-Century Maritime Silk Road (MSRI)

United Arab Emirates (UAE)

Introduction

Opportunity and Strategy

In recent years, the People's Republic of China (PRC) has significantly increased its engagement in the Middle East and in the Persian Gulf in particular. Their involvement spans multiple dimensions, including trade and investment, the energy sector, military cooperation, and diplomatic activity. Outside of Asia-Pacific, the Middle East (West Asia) is likely the most critical region of the world for China.[1] Connecting China through the Suez Canal to the Mediterranean and Europe, the Middle East is a unique geostrategic location for Beijing, a critical source of much-needed energy resources, and an area of expanding economic ties. In turn, Middle Eastern countries see Beijing as the most important world capital after Washington because of China's considerable economic power.

China's economic relationship with the Middle East gained a higher profile with the official launch of its One Belt, One Road Initiative (OBOR) in 2013 – a name changed in 2016 to the Belt and Road Initiative (BRI). At the Third Plenary Session of the 18th Central Committee of Communist Party in China, Beijing designated the Middle East a 'neighbor' region, which indicates that the Middle East now falls into China's top priority geostrategic zone.[2] Most of China's trade and investment in the region involves the Gulf countries, focusing on energy, infrastructure construction, and investment in nuclear power, new energy sources, agriculture, and finance.

In the past two decades, substantial changes have been seen in the global economy and geopolitical trends, with the rise of PRC on the global and regional stage. These developments are creating new opportunities for the Gulf countries, as they look to diversify their economies, increase trade, and seek investment opportunities in emerging markets. They also want to promote the BRI and incorporate it into their national development plan. This is a growing tendency among the regional countries that want to benefit from China's favorable business conditions, expertise, and experience, in its rapid path to economic development.

The relative decline of US hegemony and power in the Persian Gulf and the emergence of a risen China that seeks significant roles in the region might affect the stability of power balance.[3] Within this context, the Gulf countries have started seeking ways to invest in stronger ties with the PRC, as well as with other powers, to strengthen their position in an increasingly vulnerable geopolitical balance of power. The Gulf countries are determined to preserve their strategic alliance with the US but are also seeking to hedge themselves against the threats that are emanating from regional crises or power competition in order to guarantee their security in the future.[4]

Since the announcement of China's Silk Road Economic Belt and 21st Century Maritime Silk Road, the Gulf states have become a crucial hub in the successful implementation of the BRI due to their geostrategic location links China to Middle Eastern, African, and European markets, while their vast hydrocarbon reserves are an essential factor in driving the development projects that comprise the Silk Road. Sino–Gulf states cooperation can, therefore, be expected to expand as China's footprint expands across the Indian Ocean. At the same time, the BRI cooperation builds upon bilateral relationships that China and the Gulf countries have been developing over decades.

This book explores the significance of China's strategic partnerships with the Gulf states in its BRI framework, as well as the increasing mutual interdependency between both sides in various sectors, such as energy, construction, and infrastructure building, political ties, trade and investments, financial integration, culture and tourism, and defense ties. A stable Gulf region is vital for China's sustainable growth, and with the completion of the Gulf Pearl Chain, PRC can achieve effective management and control the flow of its energy needs. This will open new markets and trade routes for the Gulf countries as the BRI would connect Gulf economies with the Southeast and East Asian economies, which will enhance economic integration and co-operation.

One Belt, One Road Initiative (BRI)

China's most significant twenty-first century diplomatic and economic activity is the launching of the Silk Road initiative that has become the flagship foreign policy of the Xi administration. China's Belt and Road initiative (一带一路) is comprised of two components: the Silk Road Economic Belt (丝绸之路经济带) and the 21st century Maritime Silk Road Initiative (21世纪海上丝绸之路). The different sub-branches of the Silk Road Economic Belt (a series of land-based infrastructure projects including roads, railways, and pipelines) and the 21st-Century Maritime Silk Road (made up of ports and coastal development) would create a multi-national network connecting China to East Africa, the Middle East, and Europe. This will facilitate trade, improve access to foreign energy resources, and give China access to new markets. The two schemes are inseparable, and the PRC has set as its goal their parallel implementation.[5]

The Belt and Road Initiative is a developing economic trade network planned to stretch from China to Europe. The BRI provides two pathways for connecting China with Eurasia. The Silk Road Economic Belt (SREB), the one garnering the most attention, is an overland route that begins in Central China, moves through Xinjiang and China's western region into Central Asia, across the Middle East, and terminates in Europe. The SREB will have two main corridors, with several offshoots and hub cities. It would begin in Xi'an, capital of Shaanxi province in western China, and continue west crossing Central Asia, the Middle East, possibly Russia, and finally end in Europe. The 21st-Century Maritime Silk Road (MSRI) has one primary sea corridor, also with many hubs and offshoots. The MSR would start in China's southeastern ports, travel along the coast of Southeast Asia, around India, connect with the Persian Gulf, and end in the Mediterranean Sea.[6]

The Belt and Road will require cooperation and agreements with over a dozen states along the route, greatly expanding not only China's economic connections to these regions but also its political relationships. This, in turn, will expand China's sphere of influence into areas traditionally under the purview of other great powers. The plan progresses through a multitude of projects in stages, including roadways, bridges, telecommunication networking structures, pipelines, etc. The BRI emphasizes certain countries, namely Pakistan, Myanmar, Iran, and Kazakhstan, but includes virtually all of the countries that are considered part of China's Eurasian west.[7]

China's Belt and Road Initiative (BRI) – previously called 'One Belt, One Road' – has been designed by China as its new guiding economic and foreign policy framework with a focus on its direct neighborhood at its southern and western borders, but also reaching out to the Persian Gulf, Africa and Europe. However, the BRI is not just a strategy to enhance China's commercial, trade, and other economic interests. The BRI was designed as a multipurpose umbrella for the PRC's comprehensive economic, domestic and foreign policy development in order to increase its geo-economic and geopolitical influence and is a vehicle to open markets, expand export overcapacities, generate employment, reduce regional inequalities, promote political stability and security through development as well as prosperity, and to restore Chinese spheres of influence in the Eurasian landmass and beyond.[8]

The scope of the BRI is large, covering more than 72 countries along six economic corridors. The Belt and Road initiative covers two-thirds of the world's population, 40 percent of the global gross national product, and an estimated 75 percent of known energy reserves.[9] Thus, this great ambition will require significant resources – technological, human, financial and political – that must be garnered globally to realize the vision as the BRI will run through Asia, Africa, and Europe and will directly link the East Asian economies to the West Asian and further to the European economies.[10]

The global infrastructure investment needed to support the currently expected rates of economic growth is between \$3.3 trillion and \$6.3 trillion annually.[11] According to the chief economist of the Bank of China, Beijing's outbound direct investment in the Belt and Road Initiative will reach \$300 billion by 2030.[12] Furthermore, BRI has the potential to establish a new order not only in Eurasia but in the entire international system as well.[13]

The BRI fits China's economic, security, military, and diplomatic strategy as well as its long-term strategic requirements. In the 21st century, the PRC has emerged as the world's top trading nation; hence it needs to ensure that it has timely, efficient, and secure access to markets and resources, and therefore facilitation of trade and investment is one key focus. Also, it should not be surprising that securing conventional and renewable energy and resources is another focus for China. Once completed, the BRI will provide land-based and sea-based alternatives not just for China accessing the continents, but also access for other countries to China. Transport link is a critical consideration for China, as it is vulnerable to choke points along its sea route. Such threats would be mitigated once land-based alternatives, including railroads, highways, and communication links, are in place.[14]

The PRC has reportedly invested more than \$148 billion already, while the total value of projects funded by China in its Belt and Road initiative partners in the past four and a half years reached \$256 billion;[15] the total volume of trade between China and other Belt and Road initiative countries has exceeded \$3 trillion.[16] Chinese firms have also established more than 50 economic and trade zones in more than 30 countries.[17] In the past five years, nearly one hundred Chinese state-owned enterprises carried out a total of 3,116 investment projects in Belt and Road countries.[18]

According to data provided by China's Ministry of Commerce (MoC), the trade volume between the PRC and countries along the

Belt and Road Initiative totaled $1.3 trillion in 2018. This marked a year-on-year growth of 16.3 percent, 3.7 percentage points higher than China's trade growth in 2018. That is, China exported goods worth $704.73 billion to Belt and Road countries last year, up 10.9 percent year on year, while importing goods from them worth $563.07 billion, increasing 23.9 percent year on year. Chinese firms invested $15.64 billion in non-financial sectors in Belt and Road countries last year, up 8.9 percent year on year, while receiving investments from them totaling $6.08 billion, up 11.9 percent.[19]

The Belt and Road Initiative and the Middle East

The Middle East is the region bringing together the land and maritime Silk Road, coupled with its unique geographical location and diverse and complex humanitarian, religious, and ethnic factors, notably with an increasingly significant role played by the energy sector. As an energy-rich zone, it plays a decisive role in the process of building the BRI. This region also plays a prominent role in security coordination, economic cooperation, and cultural exchanges under the BRI framework. Thus, the Chinese government should pay close attention to the role of the Middle East region in the construction of its Belt and Road vision.[20]

In the second decade of the 21st century, the Middle East represents four major priorities for China's foreign policy. Foremost among these priorities is the criticality of the region as a source of imported energy and an important region for Chinese trade and investment. As the world's largest consumer of energy overall and the second largest importer of crude oil, safeguarding a stable flow of crude oil from the region is a paramount concern.[21] Second, the region is also a key part of China's Belt and Road Initiative, especially for its 21st-Century Maritime Silk Road component. In the past, the Middle East was considered by Beijing a peripheral and relatively insignificant region of the world, whereas now the Middle East is considered a vital geostrategic global crossroads, and the PRC's most important region beyond its own Asia Pacific neighborhoods for the realization of the BRI. Third, Beijing views the Middle East as an arena of great power competition in which a rising power such as China must be seen as a player.[22]

Finally, China has vital security interests in the Middle East: concerns regarding the spread of terrorism and extremist ideology from the Middle East and its impact on Uighur separatism.[23] China fears that Chinese Uighurs fighting alongside al-Qaeda and ISIS in Syria may leave the fighting and attempt to return to China. As they return, they may bring a newly Islamized narrative and motivation, which will pose a challenge to Xinjiang's social stability and economic development.[24]

The Middle East is also situated at the heart of China's BRI where not only do the three continents of Asia, Africa, and Europe meet but the five seas of the Mediterranean, Red Sea, Arabian Sea, Caspian Sea, and the Black Sea also converge there; and it is adjacent to the four maritime strategic channels of Bosporus, Dardanelles, Bab el-Mandeb, and Hormuz. The Gulf countries can be referred to as the core of the region since they are the most influential countries in the Middle East. The advantageous location, the unique endowment of natural resources, and the huge industrialization potential make the Gulf regions of supreme strategic importance to the implementation of the Belt and Road Initiative.[25]

This initiative called for "policy coordination, facilities connectivity, unimpeded trade, financial integration, and people-to-people bonds to make complementary use of participating countries' unique resource advantages through multilateral mechanisms and multilevel platforms".[26] The BRI is at the core of China's diplomatic encounter with Middle East countries. Chinese officials have repeatedly emphasized that through the BRI, China and countries of the region will be able to develop mutually beneficial relations.

The Belt and Road Initiative and the Persian Gulf Region

In March 2015, the Chinese government published a report: "Vision and Actions on Jointly Building the SREB and the MSRI". This report describes plans for how the SREB will link the PRC with the Persian Gulf and the Mediterranean Sea through Central Asia and West Asia, and how the MSRI will connect China with Europe through the South China Sea and the Indian Ocean. This means the Persian Gulf region will serve as a hub of the two routes, entailing many added economic benefits. Furthermore, Gulf countries could benefit not only from the BRI's focus on improved transportation across Eurasia, providing an alternative route for exports to Asia that avoids the bottlenecks of the Strait of Hormuz, but from greater affluence and stability in Central Asia.[27]

The BRI has become the main focus of strategic and economic engagement between the PRC and countries in the Gulf region. The Gulf countries, the Gulf Cooperation Council (GCC) countries (Saudi Arabia, UAE, Qatar, Kuwait, Bahrain, and Oman), plus Iran and Iraq, are 'natural cooperative partners' in the Belt and Road construction in an essential geographical area which is difficult to bypass.[28] Thus, the Gulf countries are important key partners and will play significant roles in the successful implementation of the Belt and Road Initiative due to their geo-strategic location, vast reserve of oil and gas, the fast and steady growth of the economy of the region with the rapid expansion of the market for consumer and merchandise goods, of which China has plenty. Chinese companies are investing in building infrastructure and construction projects under the framework of the Belt and Road Initiative that has become a key theme of diplomatic relations and could create new opportunities for energy and economic partnerships in promising new sectors between Chinese companies and the Gulf countries.

China increasingly attempts to engage with the Persian Gulf through two multilateral mechanisms. First, the China–Arab States Cooperation Forum (CASCF), which was launched in 2004 in Cairo. In June 2014, at the sixth Ministerial Conference of the CASCF, President Xi Jinping proposed the establishment of a '1+2+3' pattern of cooperation: energy cooperation as the core; then infrastructure construction plus trade and investment facilitation as two wings; and three new areas of high-tech cooperation (nuclear energy, space satellites, and other new energy initiatives). According to the Chinese President, in the next ten years these efforts will increase the bilateral trade volume from $240 billion of 2013 to $600 billion. The second mechanism is the China–GCC Strategic Dialogue, initiated in 2010 and targeted at building a strategic partnership. While both sides agreed to accelerate the pace of establishing a free trade area, China asserted its desire to play a more active role in regional affairs.[29]

China is highly dependent upon oil and gas imports, principally from the Persian Gulf and Africa, which are carried mainly by tankers over sea lines of communication (SLOCs) and run through maritime choke points. According to the National Bureau of Statistics (NBS), China's imports of crude oil surged 10.1 percent year on year to 460 million tonnes in 2018; natural gas imports came in at 90.39 million tonnes, rising 31.9 percent year on year.[30] Beijing's dependence on crude oil imports from the Persian Gulf, a leading oil-producing region, has been increasing gradually since 1993 when it became a net importer of oil.[31]

In 2018, the value of crude oil imported into China totaled $239.2 billion (up by 46 percent from 2017 to 2018). Forty-five countries supplied crude petroleum oil to China, but close to half (44.1 percent) of Chinese imported crude oil originates from just nine Middle Eastern nations, and six Persian Gulf states are among the top 15 crude oil suppliers to Beijing.[32] An energy imports cut-off enforced during hostile conditions could trigger a rapid collapse of China's economy and paralyze its military forces, hence the BRI and especially the Gulf Pearl Chain would be a breakthrough to reduce its dependence on SLOCs on one side and increase economic and regional integration as it would connect West Asia with Southeast and East Asia, which would be a win-win situation for all the partners.[33]

Connectivity, as the basis of the Belt and Road Initiative, aims at linking land, sea, air and cyberspace environments of countries along the routes. Through six major economic corridors of China–Mongolia–Russia, New Eurasian Continental Bridge, China Central-West Asia, China–Indochina Peninsula, China–Pakistan and Bangladesh–China–India–Myanmar, China will be closely connected with Europe, Africa and the rest of Asia. While the Gulf states are well funded and in urgent need of infrastructure construction, China's experience and technology accumulated in its development process could offer vital assistance. At present, Chinese enterprises have actively participated in the above projects and other infrastructures such as ports, docks, industrial parks, and oil pipelines.[34]

However, the aims to increase the PRC's access to the Persian Gulf's energy resources and connect Beijing's economy with those of the Middle East, Central Asia, and eventually Europe through massive infrastructure building could be seriously affected by the instability generated in the region's hotspots (e.g., Yemen, Iraq, Syria, and Qatar) or geopolitical rivalry (e.g., Iran and Saudi Arabia). Such regional instability presents a formidable obstacle to the BRI's strategic design, as it undermines connectivity, threatens infrastructure projects, and makes an economic corridor through the volatile Middle East to the markets of developed Europe less viable.[35] For instance, the China–Pakistan Economic Corridor (CPEC) and the China–Central-West Asia Economic Corridor (CCWAEC) have important strategic implications for Persian Gulf stability and offer important illustrations of how these initiatives may run counter to the Gulf countries' interests by creating a more challenging geopolitical environment.

The countries in the Persian Gulf, accordingly, have mixed feelings about China's Belt and Road ambitious project. Though the Persian Gulf is not directly along BRI's trade routes, the GCC states have high economic and geopolitical stakes in China's planned economic corridor. They have much to gain from BRI as the initiative aims to enhance Beijing's diplomatic and economic relations with these countries. However, there are concerns among the Arab countries in the Persian Gulf about the initiative's geopolitical implications because

Iran will likely achieve major gains from it since it plays a key role in the BRI as an integral country in China's Eurasian overland route. The implementation of the BRI will undoubtedly enhance Iran's position in the tumultuous Middle East's unstable geopolitical order. Ultimately, however, despite the challenges and risks that the new Silk Road has to offer to the region, the Gulf states are focused on ways to maximize the benefits they reap from this ambitious initiative. These countries have to balance their increasingly important relationship with China against the ways the BRI concomitantly threatens their relations with major external powers or empowers their rivals.[36]

In the end, China and the Gulf states are at Asia's eastern and western ends respectively, linked by the ancient Silk Road across the Gobi desert. The Belt and Road Initiative has become the main focus of strategic cooperation between the two sides. The Gulf states are natural cooperative partners in the BRI,[37] in an important geographical area difficult to bypass. Although the political and security situation in the Gulf region is complicated and unpredictable, presenting challenges to the implementation of the BRI, there still remains room for China to turn around the situation of West Asia and to seize this opportunity, circumventing possible risks and enhancing pragmatic cooperation under the BRI.

Policy coordination, connectivity, trade and investments, energy cooperation, financial integration, and culture, and tourism are the major areas that are most promising for China–Gulf states joint building of the BRI.[38] As a result, the Beijing New Silk Road strategy will provide new momentum for the Gulf region economic transformation. Despite challenges, risks can be turned into opportunities as long as China faces up to them squarely and responds positively.

China's Partnership Diplomacy

China's policy toward the Gulf states has to be defined in a complex regional context, a context involving plenty of local rivalries and enmeshing serious major power competition.[39] The Chinese policy intends to maintain a balance among several priorities that sometimes may be in conflict or tension. First, maintain the mutual respect between China and each of the Gulf state's territorial integrity and sovereignty, and mutual non-interference in each other's internal affairs. Second, maintain a peaceful and stable international environment for advancing China's modernization drive, promoting development, and improving its people's livelihood.[40]

Third, maintain a peaceful environment in the Persian Gulf, in line with the above, to protect China's regional interests. Fourth, preserve good relations with all countries in the region, and finally, avoid a major confrontation with the US while limiting its regional hegemony and promoting regional as well as global multi-polarity.[41] Based on its Persian Gulf policy, China seeks to strengthen the mutual interdependency with the countries in the region in various sectors such as energy, and investments in construction and infrastructure projects, to leverage its economic capabilities to realize the successful implementation of the BRI.

In recent years, partnership diplomacy has become a primary foreign policy tool for the Chinese government. The concept of 'partnership' emerged within Chinese diplomacy after the end of the Cold War and continues to flourish. Beijing established its first strategic partnership with Brazil in 1993. Since then, building strategic partnerships has become one of the most notable dimensions of Chinese diplomacy.[42] Since then, the number of partnerships has steadily increased, reaching 81 in 2016,[43] and as of today, seven of the eight states in the Persian Gulf have established a strategic partnership with China.

China partnership diplomacy includes a scale of relations, ranging from a friendly cooperative partnership at the bottom to a comprehensive strategic partnership at the high end.[44] Each of the five categories of relations features specific priorities, signaling the level of importance Beijing attaches to that particular state. Relationships can be upgraded depending upon the progress made, as in the case of the United Arab Emirates (UAE), with which China established a strategic partnership in January 2012.[45] During President Xi's state visit in July 2018, the relationship was elevated to a comprehensive strategic partnership.[46]

According to Chinese levels of Strategic Partnerships diplomacy (from highest to lowest): *Comprehensive Strategic Partnership* (全面战略伙伴关系) is the full pursuit of cooperation and development on regional and international affairs. *Strategic Partnership* (战略伙伴关系) coordinates more closely on regional and international affairs, including military. *Comprehensive Cooperative Partnership* (全面合作伙伴关系) maintains the sound momentum of high-level exchanges, enhanced contacts at various levels, and increased mutual understanding on issues of common interest. *Cooperative Partnership* (合作夥伴關係) develops cooperation on bilateral issues, based on mutual respect and benefit. *Friendly Cooperative Partnership* (友好合作关) strengthens cooperation on bilateral issues such as trade.[47]

An analysis of China's practice of strategic partnership diplomacy yields a four-point description, calling them a commitment to: build stable bilateral relationships without targeting a third state; promote deep economic engagement; focus on cooperation in areas of mutual interests while not focusing on domestic affairs of potential disagreement; routinize official visits and military exchanges.[48] Taken together, these provide a useful framework for understanding China's choice to use strategic partnership diplomacy.

The post-Cold War unipolarity has provided China (a rising power) with a unique strategic opportunity to develop power and influence in the Persian Gulf without facing overt challenges from the United States. Balancing against Washington during the unipolar era would not advance Beijing's interests, but at the same time neither would bandwagoning nor neutrality. Dynamic balancing is too risky, and bandwagoning or neutrality is not consistent with Chinese ambitions.[49] Instead, China has taken advantage of the relative stability provided by US dominance to develop strong ties with strategically important states in the Persian Gulf (e.g., Iran, UAE, and Saudi Arabia). These relations have been built mostly on economic foundations, but as they become increasingly multifaceted, there is a corresponding growth of strategic considerations.

In the competitive Persian Gulf dominated by Washington, Beijing has had to build a regional presence that does not alienate the US or any Gulf states while pursuing its interests. Strategic partnership diplomacy has provided the space to methodically build up its economic relations while the US security umbrella provides a low-cost entry into the Persian Gulf. Beginning with trade, economic ties became increasingly multifaceted and sophisticated, incorporating finance and investment. The relationships with the Gulf states have progressed beyond the economic to include political and security objectives, but in a way that has consistently allowed China the flexibility of being everyone's friend in the competitive regional environment.[50]

China's Gulf partnership diplomacy

China's partnership diplomacy in the Persian Gulf began when China and the UAE established a strategic partnership in January 2012. Since then, every state in the Gulf except Bahrain (which has a friendly cooperative partnership status) has signed either a strategic or comprehensive strategic partnership with China (see the table overleaf). A key integral feature of the BRI is the designation of specific countries along the Silk Road routes as strategic partners. Unlike the US, China does not have security alliances, but in lieu thereof does have intimate diplomatic relations with all the Gulf state, which are labeled strategic partnerships. Such partnerships are predicated more on trade and economic relations than on security cooperation.

This growing diplomatic attention to the Gulf can be attributed to several factors. First, the economies of China and the Gulf states are highly complementary. The two sides have deepened cooperation in the fields of energy, trade, project contracting, and investment. According to China Customs Statistics (export–import), China–Gulf states trade volume increased to nearly $227 billion by 2018.[51] Chinese foreign direct investment (FDI) into the GCC is substantial, at nearly $90 billion between 2005 and 2018. This is important for the Gulf monarchies as they are all under pressure to create more diverse economies, and so are embarking upon massive infrastructure and construction projects. Chinese firms are uniquely well-positioned to take advantage of this, with a competitive approach to infrastructure development driving much of its BRI.[52]

China's Partnerships with the Gulf States

State	Level of Partnership	Year Signed
Bahrain	Friendly Cooperative Relations	September 2013
Qatar	Strategic Partnership	November 2014
Iraq	Strategic Partnership	December 2015
Iran	Comprehensive Strategic Partnership	January 2016
Saudi Arabia	Comprehensive Strategic Partnership	January 2016
Oman	Strategic Partnership	May 2018
Kuwait	Strategic Partnership	July 2018
United Arab Emirates	Comprehensive Strategic Partnership	July 2018

Second, oil exports have been the traditional mainstay of China's trade with the Persian Gulf, driven by China's large appetite for crude that accompanied its rapid economic development through the 1990s and 2000s. In 2018, the value of crude oil imported into China totaled $239.2 billion (20.2 percent of total crude oil imports). Forty-five countries supplied crude petroleum oil to China, but close to half (44.1 percent) of Chinese imported crude oil originates from just nine Middle Eastern nations, and six Persian Gulf states are among the top 15 crude oil suppliers to Beijing. This energy relationship is set to continue since the Gulf exporters look to East Asia in general and China in particular as a reliable long-term energy export market, with the International Energy Agency (IEA) expecting Beijing to double its oil imports from the region by 2035.[53]

Third, implementation of the Belt and Road Initiative is the important factor that underscores the increasingly strategic component of Beijing partnership diplomacy with the Gulf states. The $1 trillion BRI, put forward in October 2013 by Chinese President Xi Jinping, seeks to connect Beijing to the global market by linking Asia and Europe via a set of land and maritime trade routes. The concept had been taking shape for several years and has now become a cornerstone of President Xi's foreign policy. This is extending Chinese influence and interests far beyond its traditional East Asia sphere, and with the Persian Gulf's unique geostrategic location connecting several important states and regions in the BRI, Beijing places a premium on region stability, evident in the fact that seven of eight regional states have the two highest levels of partnership diplomacy with China (e.g., four states with strategic partnership and three states with comprehensive strategic partnership).[54]

Finally, in the wake of Arab uprisings, the Gulf monarchies were pressured into boosting economic growth to maintain social stability. These countries are moving toward social and economic development and accelerated industrialization to assuage domestic conflicts and avoid being left behind in the wave of globalization. To this end, they have been actively rolling out plans for long-term development. Thus, comprehensive and upgraded Chinese engagement will provide new impetus for Gulf economic growth. In this way, there is a common interest for China and the Gulf states to integrate and synergize the Belt and Road Initiative with major initiatives of future-oriented reforms for national rejuvenation (e.g., Saudi Arabia's Vision 2030, UAE's Vision 2021, Oman's Vision 2020, Kuwait's Vision 2035, and Qatar's and Bahrain's respective Vision 2030s).[55]

During his first European trip as Chinese premier, Wen Jiabao defined the key features of a comprehensive strategic partnership as follows: "By 'comprehensive', it means that the cooperation should be all-dimensional, wide-ranging and multi-layered. It covers economic, scientific, technological, political and cultural fields, contains both bilateral and multilateral levels, and is conducted by both governments and non-governmental groups. By 'strategic', it means that the cooperation should be long-term and stable, bearing on the larger picture of China–EU relations. It transcends the differences in ideology and social system and is not subjected to the impacts of individual events that occur from time to time. By 'partnership', it means that the cooperation should be equal-footed, mutually beneficial, and win-win. The two sides should base themselves on mutual respect and mutual trust, endeavor to expand converging interests and seek common ground on the major issues while shelving differences on the minor ones."[56]

China's comprehensive strategic partnership, the highest level in its hierarchy of diplomatic relations, with the Gulf states (e.g., Iran, UAE or Saudi Arabia) includes three essential components: high levels of political trust, dense economic ties, and good relations in other sectors such as cultural exchanges. Beyond the structure of the bilateral relationship, the state's stature in global affairs is an important consideration; Beijing only considers this level of partnership with states that play an important role in international economics and politics.[57] It is also commonplace to upgrade the strategic partnership to a comprehensive one a few years after its launch. Usually, a solid record of cooperation can be widely seen as a blessing for further upgrading the partnership or a good omen for initiating similar partnerships.[58]

Given these requirements, it is unlikely that other relationships with Gulf states would be elevated to a comprehensive strategic partnership. For example, China–Qatar relations are quite dense but not at the same level as the UAE or Saudi Arabia, and given Qatar's ongoing dispute with the fellow members of the GCC, it is more likely that Beijing will not allow the relationship to elevate to a comprehensive strategic partnership.[59] Oman's relations with China are also deep, and the Duqm port project indicates a more strategic direction. Economically, however, Oman is less important to China, making it an unlikely candidate. Iraq also does not meet any of the three conditions, and because Bahrain has no existing formal partnership with China and bilateral trade is negligible, there is no chance that it will be considered.[60]

China has three principal comprehensive strategic partnerships in the Middle East: Saudi Arabia, the UAE, and Iran. Saudi Arabia is China's largest trading partner in West Asia, and Beijing is the Kingdom's largest trading partner worldwide. Chinese construction companies have been playing a growing role in developing Saudi infrastructure; meanwhile, the Kingdom has been especially eager to build refineries and petrochemical production facilities in China that are specially tailored to use Saudi grades of crude oil. The Kingdom seems to be developing China as a hedge against a decline in Western oil consumption, and also a hedge against Western discomfort with authoritarianism within Saudi Arabia.[61]

China is also the UAE's largest trading partner, and Dubai Port is a vital global shipping and logistics hub for Chinese goods. More than 200,000 Chinese nationals live in the UAE, which is emerging as an entrepôt for Chinese traders seeking proximity to overseas markets.

The UAE sees a leading role for itself in China's Belt and Road Initiative, building on what is already a robust trading relationship.[62] However, and perhaps most importantly, Iran has a special geographical and communication status in West Asia, in that it is connected to South and Central Asia, the Middle East, and Europe through both land and sea routes. In addition, access points at the Persian Gulf, the Gulf of Oman, and the Caspian Sea combine to make Iran one of the important centerpieces of the Belt and Road. Therefore, Iran is critical to China's ability to realize the BRI network to connect Asia, Europe, and Africa.[63]

In the end, China's partnership diplomacy will continue to be an important instrument in China's foreign policy in the years ahead. At the same time, China's presence in the Persian Gulf will require a more overarching strategic design and more sophisticated diplomatic tactics. China will, therefore, need to be more proactive and creative in mobilizing strategic partnerships as a policy instrument together with other diplomatic tools for successful implementation of its Belt and Road Initiative.

Although various studies have analyzed the political, economic, cultural and military relations between China and the Middle East in recent years,[64] only a few of them relate to the emerging strategic partnerships between China and the Persian Gulf states.[65] The studies that analyzed the relations between China and the Gulf countries preferred to focus mainly on key areas that include energy security, political relations, trade ties, cultural relations, security coordination, and arms sales.[66] Some of these studies preferred to focus on the wave of uprisings that has engulfed the Arab world since 2011;[67] others have chosen to examine the relations between the Gulf monarchies and extra powers,[68] as well as to analyze the evolution of Sino–GCC relations.[69] Few studies have analyzed the mutual effect of China's Belt and Road strategy on all the Gulf states.[70] Therefore, this study will present a comprehensive analysis of the mutual influence of China's Belt and Road strategy on the emerging partnerships in the Persian Gulf.

This book examines China's relationship with the nations of the Persian Gulf based on a two-dimensional approach: the implementation of the new Silk Road strategy and the emerging partnerships between them. China's levels of interdependence with these states under consideration have increased dramatically in recent years, spanning a wide range of interests (e.g., energy security, trade cooperation, and infrastructure construction). Light will be shed on the complexities and challenges of China's Belt and Road Initiative to reveal how the synergy between the new Silk Road strategy, and the local, national development plan, will shape the Persian Gulf in the future. The balance of global politics also will be critically affected by these powerful emerging partnerships and convergence of interests.

China's Gulf partnership diplomacy has provided a platform for deepening and expanding the cooperation between China and the Gulf states under the framework of the Belt and Road Initiative. Since 2013 China has forged special political relations with every state in the Gulf region, except Bahrain, which has signed either a strategic or comprehensive strategic partnership. There is a clear and direct connection between China's emerging partnerships with the Gulf states and the implementation of the New Silk Road strategy. Therefore, the key to understanding China's upgraded involvement in the Persian Gulf must be in the context of the successful implementation of the BRI. The New Silk Road is an important guide for China–Gulf states partnerships diplomacy since the region holds a unique position in the PRC's new policy framework.

The central thesis of this book is that the Persian Gulf region has a significant and unique role in the successful implementation of China's Belt and Road strategy, as well as the emerging partnerships between them (e.g., comprehensive strategic partnerships, friendly cooperative relations, and strategic partnerships). These partnerships help the PRC to achieve effective management and control the flow of its energy, goods or products needs, and to open new markets and trade routes. Beijing has been mostly successful in employing strategic partnerships, a prominent instrument in its limited diplomatic toolkit, in order to guarantee integration between the national development plans of the Gulf monarchies, or economic reconstruction (e.g., Iraq and Iran), and China's Belt and Road vision.

The national development plan of the Gulf states and China's BRI have converged under common economic interests and a development path that complements each other, and their strategic synergy will bring new opportunities for both sides. As a result, the realization of BRI strategy will also provide a new momentum for the economic transformation of the Gulf states. The implementation of the New Silk Road strategy will unleash a regional infrastructure boom by connecting China with Asia, Europe, and Africa by land and sea, and boost renminbi internationalization by encouraging its use in both trade and financial transactions.

1
Saudi Arabia

In the last few years, Saudi Arabia and China have built a new framework for their comprehensive strategic partnership based on shared or mutual complementary economic and commercial interests. This chapter examines the new horizons opened by the growing comprehensive strategic partnership between Riyadh and Beijing, in order to understand the extent of economic engagement and the level of bilateral relationship between the two nations. The strategic synergy between the Belt and Road Initiative and Saudi Vision 2030 has forged a joint economic development path which will bring new opportunities for both sides. Nevertheless, there are several challenges that could complicate the broader bilateral partnership.

Since the establishment of diplomatic relations in 1990, the ties between the PRC and Saudi Arabia have witnessed sustained and rapid development, characterized by enhanced mutual political trust, ties which were elevated to a comprehensive strategic partnership in 2016. This level of partnership means that Beijing has built a deep relationship with the Kingdom and maintains significant cooperation on economic, political, and security issues. As Chinese President Xi Jinping said to Saudi Arabia's crown prince, Mohammed bin Salman al-Saud (MBS), "China regards Saudi Arabia as a good friend and partner" and is ready to "open up a new horizon for bilateral friendship and strategic relationship." The relationship between two nations has "advanced in an all-around way, at multiple levels and in a wide variety of fields".[1]

The Kingdom of Saudi Arabia is situated close to the center of a Belt and Road megaproject that connects Asia, Africa, and Europe, and this strategic location means that Saudi's Vision 2030 could fuse perfectly with the Belt and Road initiative. Accordingly, Riyadh could serve as a natural and essential partner of China in building the Belt and Road Initiative. This chapter examines the new horizon and the growing comprehensive strategic partnership between Riyadh and Beijing, and the synergy between the Belt and Road Initiative and the Saudi Vision 2030 in order to understand the extent of economic engagement and bilateral relationship between the two nations. Chinese President Xi Jinping stated his view that the two countries should speed up the signing of an implementation plan on connecting the Belt and Road Initiative with the Saudi Vision 2030.[2]

The main argument presented is that Beijing's comprehensive strategic partnership framework with Riyadh is based on shared or mutual complementary economic and commercial interests, especially with the integration and implementation of the Belt and Road Initiative and Saudi Vision 2030. This development in relations is emerging at the same time that both countries find themselves the object of widespread international criticism, and both countries seek political allies and economic opportunities. The Saudi Vision 2030 and China's Belt and Road vision have converged on a common economic development path, and their synergetic strategy will bring new opportunities for both sides.

Saudi Vision 2030

In 2016, Saudi authorities unveiled 'Vision 2030', aimed at making the Kingdom a global investment powerhouse and the heart of the Arab and Islamic world while also diversifying the country's economy, now heavily dependent on oil. The Saudi national strategy is designed to reduce its dependence on energy-related exports and increase its service sector in areas such as health care, education, recreation, and tourism.[3] The economic reform program relies on parallel reforms and procedures to be carried out constituting three main axes: a Public Investments Fund Program, a Financial Balancing Program and a National Transformation Program. This combined vision centralizes a vibrant society, diversifies the thriving economy and develops an ambitious, effective government and responsible citizenry.[4]

Saudi Arabia and the Belt and Road Initiative

China's comprehensive strategic partnerships with Riyadh includes six major areas for cooperation within the Belt and Road Initiative. These areas are policy coordination, connectivity, trade and investments, energy cooperation, military ties, tourism and cultural ties. However, each country views the Belt and Road Initiative framework according to its perspective and the consequences for its own national interests and international status. Therefore, the two countries have very different attitudes about how to realize the vision.

Policy coordination

As part of China's comprehensive strategic partnerships with Saudi Arabia, promoting political cooperation between countries, creating mechanisms for dialogue and consensus-building on global and regional issues, developing shared interests, deepening political trust and reaching a new consensus on cooperation are important to integrate the Saudi Vision 2030 into the Belt and Road Initiative framework.[5]

The Beijing–Riyadh comprehensive strategic partnership developed following frequent top-level exchanges and cooperation agreements to promote policy coordination, trade and economic ties. The new round of interaction between the highest leaders of the two countries opened a new era of comprehensive and rapid development of China–Saudi Arabia relations. In January 2016, President Xi Jinping made a historic visit to the Kingdom, and the two countries established a comprehensive strategic partnership and decided to establish a High-Level Joint Committee of China and Saudi Arabia to push bilateral relations into a new stage of rapid development.[6]

In August 2016, Saudi Deputy Prime Minister Crown Prince MBS visited China; he held the first meeting of China–Saudi Arabia High-Level Joint Committee and attended the G20 Hangzhou Summit. During the visit both parties signed bilateral cooperation agreements in politics, energy, finance, investment, real estate, water resource, quality testing, science and technologies, and cultural exchanges.[7] In March 2017, King Salman Bin Abdulaziz al-Saud paid a state visit to China, which further promoted the alignment of development strategies of the two countries and deepened the practical cooperation under the One Belt and One Road Initiative (BRI) framework.[8]

In August 2017, Chinese Vice Premier Zhang Gaoli visited Saudi Arabia and held the second meeting of High-Level Joint Committee with Crown Prince MBS, which brought the practical cooperation in various fields to a new level. During the meeting the two sides signed a list of critical projects for production capacity and investment cooperation, of which 30 projects were identified.[9] In February 2019, Crown Prince Muhammad Bin Salman visited China and held the third meeting of China–Saudi Arabia High-Level Joint Committee with Chinese Vice Premier Han Zheng. The two sides agreed to strengthen the synergy of the Belt and Road Initiative and the Saudi Vision 2030, and enhance pragmatic cooperation on energy, infrastructure construction, and finance.[10]

In this context, it is essential to understand the new horizon and the growing comprehensive strategic partnership between Riyadh and Beijing, and the impact on the implementation of the Belt and Road Initiative, in light of the frequent top-level exchanges and the cooperation agreements signed. The considerable warming in relations between Riyadh and Beijing came at a time when both countries were under increasingly harsh global criticism and thus eager to find political support as well as business opportunities.

For Beijing, the West has been actively demanding that China stop its crackdown on the Muslim minority in Xinjiang. According to reports on Human Rights Practices for 2018, China had significantly intensified its campaign of mass detention of members of Muslim minority groups in Xinjiang. They were reported to have arbitrarily detained from 800,000 to possibly more than two million Uighurs, ethnic Kazakhs and other Muslims in camps with the purpose of erasing religious and ethnic identities.[11] In March 2019, the US State Department said the sort of abuses in China had inflicted on its Muslim minorities had not been seen "since the 1930s", and US Secretary of State Mike Pompeo said China was "in a league of its own when it comes to human rights violations".[12] In May 2019, the US accused China of putting more than a million minority Muslims in "concentration camps".[13]

Riyadh received harsh global criticism over the killing of *Washington Post* journalist Jamal Khashogghi in Saudi Arabia's Consulate General in Istanbul as well as for the country's human rights record,[14] and its role in the conflict in Yemen,[15] thus forcing the Kingdom to turn elsewhere for a new partners and a friendly business environment to secure support for Saudi Vision 2030.[16] For instance, at the G20 summit in Argentina late November 2018, when most leaders shunned MBS in the wake of the Khashoggi murder, Chinese President Xi Jinping was one of the few leaders, along with Vladimir Putin, who publicly offered support to the Saudi prince.[17]

More important, the Saudi Arabia government seeks to diversify its economy, attract more foreign direct investments and increase its global market presence for alternative sources of revenue in the wake of low oil prices. The Belt and Road Initiative represents fresh business opportunities for the Kingdom. Key to this endeavor is establishing a comprehensive strategic partnership between Riyadh and Beijing, namely to link up the two strategic conceptions: China's

BRI and Saudi Arabia's Vision 2030. According to Chinese State Councilor and Foreign Minister Wang Yi, there should be a 'deeper synergy' between the Belt and Road megaproject, and the Saudi Vision 2030 development strategy. Beijing's backing of Saudi Arabia's blueprint for building a thriving economy by exploring cooperation in numerous fields may include infrastructure projects supporting the BRI and Vision 2030. Adel bin Ahmed al-Jubeir, Saudi Arabia's Foreign Minister, has stated that the country's economic diversification and industrial development roadmap was 'highly consistent' with the Asian powerhouse's BRI megaproject. Connecting the two projects would help Beijing and Riyadh strengthen cooperation in industries including energy, mining, economy and trade, investment and tourism.[18]

Connectivity

The facilitation of connectivity is one of the important ways to integrate the Saudi Vision 2030 into the Belt and Road Initiative framework. China has always regarded Saudi Arabia as a priority in its Middle East foreign policy as well as an important cooperation partner in the BRI, for several reasons. First, given its core Islamic values, Saudi Arabia plays a vital role in politics, economy, religion, and security affairs in the Middle East and among Islamic countries.[19] Second, Beijing could utilize the Kingdom's unique location at the nexus of three continents, Asia, Africa, and Europe.[20] Third, the Kingdom has a large and scalable infrastructure that would ease the flow of goods and commodities efficiently among the three continents. Moreover, Saudi Vision 2030 also prioritizes connectivity and economic integration, which is at the heart of the BRI.[21]

Further, integrating Saudi Arabia into the BRI is a significant geopolitical and useful geographic space for the Chinese presence in the Persian Gulf. This is not only because it increases Riyadh's capabilities to respond to Chinese energy needs, but also because it promotes the opening of the MSRI to the Red Sea. The Saudi ports (e.g., Yanbu and Djeddah) improve the access of the Chinese civil fleet to the Red Sea, then to the Suez Canal and thus to the Mediterranean markets of the Middle East, the Near East, the Maghreb, and Southern Europe.[22]

Additionally, the development of transportation networks is vital for the implementation of the BRI, and Saudi Arabia's transportation infrastructure supports sectors like petroleum, petrochemicals, mining, industry and commerce. The Kingdom is now building various performance enhancing systems like electronic systems, active customs procedures, and advanced information systems.[23] Finally, Saudi's Vision 2030 could fuse perfectly and contribute to the construction of the BRI. For example, in March 2017, Beijing–Riyadh signed a series of deals worth about $65 billion involving 35 cooperative projects, with a clear majority of these being directly linked with the Saudi Vision 2030.[24]

The Kingdom's participation in the China–Pakistan Economic Corridor (CPEC) projects is timely as Beijing and Riyadh are moving closer and aligning their goals under BRI and Saudi Vision 2030. The CPEC, the flagship project of China's BRI, is a series of bilateral infrastructure projects designed to connect China's far west region of Xinjiang with Gwadar Port in Pakistan via a network of major highways and railways, higher-capacity ports, power stations, oil pipelines and trading hubs. Located in the southwestern province of Balochistan, Gwadar is the crown jewel of China's $60 billion investment in its BRI projects in Pakistan.[25]

The Kingdom's support of BRI is significant, and the most practical example of the Saudi investment in Pakistan under CPEC is when Saudi Arabia's crown prince MBS signed eight MoUs worth about $20 billion. These included $10 billion in investments for a refinery and petrochemical complex at Gwadar in Pakistan, which lies at the heart of the China–Pakistan Economic Corridor, and the center of the Beijing–Islamabad BRI relationship.[26] Saudi Arabia's agreement to participate in CPEC projects is also a key example of its warming relations with China and hugely beneficial for the success of BRI.

As Chinese Foreign Ministry spokesman Lu Kang told a media briefing, "the CPEC is an important project under the Belt and Road Initiative. The BRI projects followed wide consultations and shared benefits. So such cooperation has always been open and transparent. If any other party would like to contribute positive factors to promote the inter-connectivity and prosperity of the region on the basis of consultation, I think this is a positive factor."[27]

It is important to understand that the Kingdom's participation in CPEC projects would provide China an open window of opportunity to gain access easily to Africa and Eurasia through Oman and Riyadh. China also desires to link with Central Asia via Afghanistan through CPEC. Furthermore, China's active presence in Gwadar and the Persian Gulf would make China a "two-ocean power" at the same time.[28]

Another major project of the Saudi Vision 2030 is the creation of the NEOM ["new future"] megacity in the north-west of the country that could integrate with China's BRI. The project will be built on

26,500 square kilometers of uninhabited land along the Red Sea coast-line near Egypt and Jordan. Riyadh hope it will pull in more than $500 billion of investment and contribute $100 billion to the Saudi Arabian economy by 2030. This large project (the largest of the 2030 Vision) is the most obvious example of the radical transformation that the Kingdom aims to achieve by transforming itself from an oil economy into a diversified industrial and touristic economy. Riyadh also plans to turn NEOM into a new economic zone that operates under separate traditional commercial rules from the rest of the Kingdom.[29]

Once completed in 2025, NEOM is expected to become the largest city entirely managed by artificial intelligence (AI). All transport will be autonomous, and power will come from renewable energies. Accordingly, Chinese companies will surely seek a role in building some of the infrastructures in the megacity, using AI cutting-edge technology focused on sustainable development. In his last visit to China, February 2019, Crown Prince MBS sought to attract Chinese investors for the innovative city project, and to convince Chinese hi-tech leaders to develop projects in NEOM. The participation of Chinese companies is crucial for the development of NEOM. The new city of NEOM could serve as a laboratory for the latest innovations for Chinese high-tech companies and could be an integral part of the BRI.[30]

Energy cooperation

As part of China's comprehensive strategic partnerships with Riyadh, investment in energy infrastructure is considered one of the important areas for cooperation to integrate Saudi Vision 2030 into the BRI framework. Therefore, the new Silk Road can provide a new framework for more extensive Chinese investments in the Kingdom energy industry. Although the Beijing–Riyadh partnership is growing significantly, especially under the BRI-Saudi Vision 2030 program, the relationship remains an energy-economic partnership, based on energy products and benefitting both sides.

Beijing's dependence on crude oil imports from the Persian Gulf, a leading oil-producing region, has been increasing gradually since 1993 when it became a net importer of oil.[31] In 2018, the value of crude oil imported into China totaled $239.2 billion (20.2 percent of total crude oil imports). Forty-five countries supplied crude petroleum oil to China, but close to half (44.1 percent) of Chinese imported crude oil originates from just nine Middle Eastern nations, and six Persian Gulf states are among the top 15 crude oil suppliers to Beijing. In 2018, Saudi Arabia was ranked in the second place (up 44.6 percent) in the top 15 crude oil suppliers to Beijing and in the first place in West Asia, exporting some $29.7 billion (12.4 percent of PRC's total imported crude) worth of oil to China.[32]

The Sino–Saudi energy partnership was solidified in 2009 when Beijing surpassed the US as the top destination of Riyadh oil exports. Although Russia overtook Saudi Arabia as China's number-one supplier of oil in 2016, Beijing's reliance on Saudi oil will remain central to its energy security calculus.[33] According to the OPEC, Saudi Arabia possesses around 18 percent of the world's proven petroleum reserves and ranks as the second-largest crude oil producer and the largest exporter of petroleum. The oil and gas sector accounts for about 50 percent of GDP, and about 70 percent of export earnings.[34]

According to the Saudi Energy Ministry, at the end of 2017 Saudi Arabia's total oil reserves, including those in a zone shared with Kuwait, are up 0.8 percent to 268.5 billion barrels. The total gas reserves, including those in the shared zone, were revised up 5.6 percent to 325.1 trillion standard cubic feet. For almost 30 years, despite rising production, large swings in oil prices, and improved technology, the Kingdom had annually reported the same number for reserves, at around 261 billion barrels. The results indicate that Riyadh's reserves of oil and gas are bigger than reported.[35]

The growing ties between the two countries are fueled by Beijing's quest for the energy resources needed to feed its fast-growing economy and Riyadh's demand for cutting-edge technology, as the Saudi Arabia government tries to shift the Kingdom economy away from relying too much on oil revenue. As Chinese Foreign Minister Wang Yi told his Saudi counterpart, China sees 'enormous potential' in the Kingdom's economy and wants more high-tech cooperation.[36]

In the framework of the BRI, investment in energy infrastructure is considered one of the important cooperation areas between the countries involved. Therefore, this initiative can provide a new framework for more extensive Chinese investments in the Saudi Arabia energy industry. The Kingdom is the world's largest oil exporter, and China is the world's largest oil importer. Hence it is not surprising that the two countries are interested in deepening their cooperation with each other under the Belt and Road strategic outline and the Saudi Vision 2030 program. Saudi Arabia is now seeking to sustain its dominance in the Chinese energy market in the face of intensifying competition, mainly on the part of Iran and Russia. To this end, and to help stabilize the supply, Riyadh is operating in China through investments and the establishment of oil refineries and strategic stockpiling facilities for Saudi oil in China.

Development of refineries and petrochemical complexes

In January 2016, during President Xi Jinping's three-nation tour of the Middle East, China Petroleum and Chemical Corp (Sinopec), Asia's largest refiner, signed a strategic agreement with Saudi Aramco, to further explore business opportunities in Saudi's oil and gas industry. The deal came after construction began on the second phase of a major Red Sea oil refinery, a joint venture between Sinopec and Saudi Aramco, with the first phase becoming fully operational in April 2016. The venture, Yanbu Aramco Sinopec Refining Co (YASREF), estimated to cost nearly $10 billion, covers an area of about 5.2 million square meters. It will process 400,000 barrels of heavy crude oil per day. Aramco will hold a 62.5 percent stake in the plant, while Sinopec holds the rest.[37]

The YASREF refinery, established jointly by Sinopec and Saudi Aramco, is touted as the safest, most advanced and efficient refinery. The project is highlighted as a good example of the energy partnership between China and Saudi Arabia and future bilateral cooperation within the BRI, due to its smooth operation, advanced technologies, and high efficiency. The joint venture has earned profits since it entered production in 2016. It has produced crude oil of 49.97 million tons, and fine gasoline and diesel oil of 39.98 million tons, which were sold to Europe and Asia.[38]

In February 2018, Saudi Aramco agreed to supply China's Huajin, a refinery and chemical complex controlled by Chinese defense conglomerate China North Industries Group Corp (NORINCO), 12 million barrels of crude oil under an annual deal for 2018. Although it is a fraction of Aramco's total supplies to China, the annual deal will help the Saudis boost its market share in the world's largest crude buyer in its race against Russia.[39]

In September 2018, Saudi Basic Industries Corp (SABIC) signed an MoU with China's Fujian provincial government to build a petro-chemical complex, but SABIC did not give any details of the investment or a timeline. The Saudi company is already a partner with Chinese state oil and gas firm Sinopec Corp in an ethylene plant owned by Sinopec's Tianjin Petrochemical Corp. According to SABIC, the MoU is part of SABIC's strategy to diversify its operations, seek new investment opportunities, and strengthen its position in the Chinese market.[40]

In February 2019, during the visit of the Crown Prince MBS to Beijing, Saudi Aramco signed an agreement worth more than $10 billion for a refining and petrochemical complex in China. Saudi

Aramco formed a joint venture with NORINCO Group and PanjinSincenon to develop a fully integrated refining and petrochemical complex in the city of Panjin in Northeast China's Liaoning province. The partners will create a new company, Huajin Aramco Petrochemical Co Ltd.; the Saudi producer will have a 35 percent interest, while China will hold the rest. The project will include a 300,000 barrel per day refinery with a 1.5 million metric tons per annum ethylene cracker and a 1.3 metric tons per annum PX unit. Saudi Aramco will supply up to 70 percent of the crude feedstock for the complex, which is expected to start operations in 2024. The investments could also help Saudi Arabia regain its place as the top oil exporter to China, a position Russia has held for the last three years.[41]

There are additional plans to set up fuel retail businesses, which will further integrate into the value chain. By the end of 2019, a three-party company is expected to be formed between Aramco, North Huajin, and the Liaoning Transportation Construction Investment Group Co. Ltd. to build a large-scale retail network over the next five years in Zhejiang province. Saudi Aramco also signed three MoUs aimed at expanding its downstream presence in Zhejiang province, one of the most developed regions in China. Aramco aims to acquire a 9 percent stake in Zhejiang Petrochemical's 800,000-bpd integrated refinery and petrochemical complex, located in the city of Zhoushan. Aramco's involvement in the project will come with a long-term crude supply agreement, and the ability to utilize Zhejiang Petrochemical's large crude oil storage facility to serve its customers in the Asian region.[42]

The demand stirred up by new Chinese refiners has been pushing Saudi Arabia back to be a top supplier to the world's largest oil buyer. This could increase China's oil imports from the Kingdom between 300,000 barrels per day (bpd) and 700,000 bpd. Saudi Aramco will sign five crude oil supply agreements that will take its 2019 contract totals with Chinese buyers to 1.67 million bpd. With the recent crude oil supply agreements and potential increase of refinery capacity, Saudi's market share in China could jump to nearly 17 percent next year if buyers requested full contractual volumes.[43]

Oil agreements and MoUs

In November 2016, Pan-Asia PET Resin (Guangzhou) Co – one of the biggest polyethylene terephthalate (PET) chip producers – signed an MoU with the National Industrial Clusters Development Program of Saudi Arabia to push forward preparation of the petrochemical and chemical fiber integrated production project. The project was initiated in response to China's BRI and is in line with Saudi Vision 2030.[44] In October 2018, Pan-Asia signed Investment Framework Agreement with Saudi Arabia's Energy Minister Khalid al-Falih, marking two key breakthroughs for its $3.2 billion petrochemical and chemical fiber integrated project in Saudi Arabia.[45]

In March 2017, during the visit of King Salman to China, the partners agreed to increase their cooperation in the oil sector, including Saudi oil exports to Beijing.[46] Saudi Basic Industries Corporation (SABIC) and Sinopec signed a strategic agreement to study opportunities for joint projects in both countries. The agreement supports the efforts of the two countries to integrate the Saudi Vision 2030 and China's BRI. Under the agreement, Riyadh and Chinese petrochemical companies are planning, for the first time, to study a joint venture with Chinese investment in the Kingdom. The agreement also seeks to explore opportunities for further investments in the existing joint venture Sinopec SABIC Tianjin Petrochemical Company (SSTPC) that will contribute to industrial development in the two countries, allowing them to target downstream key markets, such as automotive, electronics, lighting, and building and construction, packaging, and medical equipment.[47]

In June 2017, China's Development Research Center signed an MoU with Saudi Aramco to jointly collaborate on economic development, especially in the downstream energy sector. The focus of the collaboration will be on Saudi Aramco's downstream presence in China, including within oil refining, oil product marketing and retail, and oil storage. The research will also explore opportunities for Chinese companies to partner with Saudi Aramco or other Saudi Arabian entities on investment and partnerships.[48]

In addition, Saudi Arabia's state oil company, Saudi Aramco, is reckoned to be the world's most valuable company with an estimated value of $2 trillion.[49] Aramco plans to boost its refining capacity to between 8 million and 10 million barrels per day, from the current level of about 5 million bpd, and double its petrochemicals production by 2030. Alongside plans to add more value from each barrel of oil produced, the kingdom is undertaking an economic overhaul that includes the initial public offering (to take place by 2021) of Saudi Aramco on the local and a yet open international stock exchange.[50] In October 2017, Chinese state-owned oil companies PetroChina and Sinopec expressed interest in the direct purchase of 5 percent of Saudi Aramco. Chinese investment in Saudi Aramco could be entering a new era of energy strategic partnership with Riyadh and laying the groundwork for a profound economic shift in the Middle East and the world.[51]

In December 2018, state-owned Power Construction Corporation of China (PowerChina) signed a contract for construction of marine facilities for the mega-shipyard King Salman International Complex in Saudi Arabia. The project is located in eastern Saudi Arabia facing the Arabian Gulf and is an essential part of Saudi Vision 2030. The successful signing of the project is also an achievement for PowerChina in carrying out China's BRI. The contract, with a value of over three billion dollars, is the largest cash settlement project PowerChina has ever undertaken. The project will become the world's largest 'super shipyard' and is expected to build four offshore drilling platforms and more than 40 ships every year, including three large crude carriers (VLCC). After completion, it will provide engineering, manufacturing, and repair services for offshore rigs, commercial ships and service vessels.[52]

In January 2019, Pan-Asia PET Resin set out plans to build plants producing 2.5 million metric tons/year (MMt/y) of purified tereph-thalic acid, 1 MMt/y of PET resin, and 200,000 metric tons/year each of polyester engineering plastics, thin film, and polyester fiber. According to the Chinese company, the project is the first wholly foreign-owned petrochemical project in Saudi Arabia. The project is situated in the Jazan City for Primary and Downstream Industries (JCPDI), located at the junction of Europe, Asia, and Africa; the area enjoys transportation advantages from the Red Sea to the Suez Canal, allowing Pan-Asia to better serve the European, North African, and Central Asian markets.[53]

The project is considered a major foreign-funded project in the Kingdom as well as a key project to promote China–Saudi Arabia production capacity cooperation. The project, designed to cover the upstream and downstream of the PET industrial chain, will also help Riyadh reduce its reliance on imported products and optimize its economic structure. The construction of the first phase of the project was expected to start in the first quarter of 2019 and to come on stream in the third quarter of 2020.[54]

Renewable energy cooperation

According to a report by the International Renewable Energy Agency's Global Commission on the Geopolitics of Energy Transformation, Beijing's need to secure oil supplies and other natural resources to sustain its growth has led it to foster new and deeper ties with countries in Asia, Africa, and Latin America, as well as diversify its domestic energy supply with renewables. China has positioned itself as the world's renewable energy superpower. In aggregate, it is now the world's largest producer, exporter, and installer of solar panels, wind turbines, batteries, and electric vehicles, placing it at the forefront of the global energy transition. Thus, Saudi Arabia's growing reliance on a Chinese-built renewable generation points to a wider shift in energy geopolitics.[55]

As part of Riyadh's ambitious Vision 2030, the Kingdom is seeking to position itself as a global trade hub. Saudi Arabia has established a special economic zone (SEZ) near Riyadh's flagship airport (RUH). With the lure of tax incentives, the Integrated Logistics Bonded Zone (ILBZ) could serve as a hub for assembling solar (photovoltaic) components. Chinese solar firms have already sought to deepen their cooperation with their Saudi counterparts.[56] In May 2018, the Chinese solar panel manufacturer LONGi signed an MoU with the Kingdom's major commercial and industrial trading company, El Seif Group, to establish large-scale solar manufacturing infrastructure in Saudi Arabia. The partnership could also lead to further manufacturing opportunities in the Middle East region. Initially, the companies are understood to be undertaking various feasibility studies for collaboration in both the photovoltaic (PV) upstream and downstream sectors.[57]

Saudi Arabia is courting China for help with the next stage of the production of renewable energy, which is forecast to develop 41 gigawatts of solar capacity by 2032.[58] In February 2019, Saudi Arabia's Public Investment Fund (PIF) signed an MoU with China's National Energy Administration (NAE) on renewable energy cooperation. The MoU comes as part of the strengthening of cooperation between the two entities in the field of renewable energy and promoting Saudi Arabia's position as a leading center for the development of renewable energy projects. The MoU will contribute to enabling the PIF to support and develop manufacturing, power generation and emerging technologies in the Kingdom's renewable energy sector over the next ten years.[59]

In January 2019, two Chinese solar giants unveiled Saudi manufacturing plans. The world's fourth-largest PV maker, Longi, is planning a $2 billion Saudi Arabia-based solar panel back sheet production plant in association with the South Korean firm OCI. Meanwhile, the world's largest thin-film PV manufacturer, Hong Kong-listed Hanergy, announced it would be investing more than $1 billion in a fabrication center to meet Saudi solar demand. The investment, which includes an unlikely partnership with local menswear manufacturer Ajlan & Bros, would see Saudi Arabia hosting the only large-scale thin-film manufacturing base in the Middle East. The announcements mean Beijing's interests are well positioned to benefit from renewables growth in Saudi Arabia.[60]

In December 2018, Riyadh announced a 1.5-gigawatt solar procurement round that is expected to be dominated by Chinese companies alongside Middle Eastern renewable heavyweights, such as Acwa Power and Masdar. Beyond the current tender, with capacity split across seven projects, Saudi Arabia is aiming to install more than 27 gigawatts of renewables by 2024. Most of this capacity will be solar PV, a power source where Beijing reigns supreme. Seven of the top ten PV module makers worldwide in 2018 were Chinese companies, including four of the top five and all of the top three. Admittedly, it will be some time before the value of Chinese renewable energy equipment sales in Saudi Arabia comes even close to the price the Asian giant pays for oil from Riyadh.[61]

Nuclear energy

Although the Kingdom's nuclear program is in its infancy, Saudi Arabia declared in 2011 that it planned to spend over $80 billion to construct 16 reactors, and Chinese companies and others want to provide them. Nuclear power is essential to Saudi Arabia to help it meet its growing energy demand for both electricity generation and water desalination, while reducing its reliance on depleting hydrocarbon resources. Nuclear energy would allow the Kingdom to increase its fossil fuel exports. About one-third of the kingdom's daily oil production is consumed domestically at subsidized prices; substituting nuclear energy domestically would free up this petroleum for export at market prices.[62]

Moreover, Saudi Arabia is also the largest producer of desalinated water in the world. According to government-owned Saudi Saline Water Conversion Corp (SWCC), the Kingdom has raised its desalinated water production to five million cubic meters per day (m3/d) at the end of 2017. Ninety percent of its drinking water is desalinated, a process that burns approximately 15 percent of the 9.8 million barrels of oil it produces daily. Nuclear power could meet some of this demand.[63]

In January 2016, during the visit of Chinese President Xi Jinping to Saudi Arabia, the two countries signed an MoU on the construction of a high-temperature gas-cooled reactor (HTR). No details of the size of the high-temperature gas-cooled reactor or the project timeline building were disclosed. China Nuclear Engineering Corporation (CNEC) has been working with Tsinghua University since 2003 on the design, construction, and commercialization of HTR technology. The partners signed a new agreement in March 2014 aimed at furthering cooperation in both international and domestic marketing of the advanced reactor technology.[64]

In August 2017, Saudi Arabia and China agreed to cooperate on nuclear energy projects to support the kingdom's nuclear energy program. CNNC signed an MoU with the Saudi Geological Survey (SGS) to promote further existing cooperation between the two sides to explore and assess uranium and thorium resources. The Saudi Technology Development and Investment Co (Taqnia) signed an MoU with CNEC to develop water desalination projects using gas-cooled nuclear reactors. Chinese nuclear companies could offer complete construction and operation packages with attractive financing options. Civil nuclear cooperation is officially a part of China's BRI, and combating climate change is central to China's pitch.[65]

The China–Saudi Arabia comprehensive strategic partnership is essential to help meet growing energy demand, especially under the Belt and Road strategic outline and the Saudi Vision 2030 program. The energy partnership between the two countries includes expanding cooperation in the fields of development of refineries-petrochemical complex, renewable energies, and nuclear energy.

Trade and investments

Part of China's comprehensive strategic partnerships with Saudi Arabia includes efforts to ease as much as possible the barriers to free trade, investment, industrial cooperation, and technical and engineering services to facilitate the integration of Saudi Vision 2030 within the Belt and Road Initiative framework. Both countries would have to undertake a series of measures, such as expanding free-trade zones, improving trade structures, seeking new potential areas for trade and improving the trade balance, devising new initiatives for the promotion of conventional forms of trade, developing trans-border electronic trade and other advanced models of business, creating a system for supporting trade in services to strengthen and expand conventional trade, increasing customs cooperation, and regularly sharing information in these areas.[66]

Over the past decade, Beijing–Riyadh economic relations have been transformed dramatically. Both countries have achieved fruitful results in trade and investments as they seek greater complementarity between the BRI and the Saudi Vision 2030. According to China Customs Statistics (export–import), China's trade volume with Saudi Arabia grew from $49.9 billion in 2017 to about $63.2 billion in 2018, and Riyadh has become China's most important trade partner in the Middle East.[67] China is Saudi Arabia's largest trade partner, outstripping nearby European nations and a close ally to the US. In 2017, China imported $31.7 billion from Saudi Arabia,[68] and in 2018 the imports reached $46 billion, citing a 33 percent increase in bilateral trade last year.[69]

According to the China Global Investment Tracker, Beijing's investments and construction in Saudi Arabia from 2013 to 2018 reached $14.9 billion.[70] In 2018, according to Sultan Mofti, deputy governor for investment attraction and development at the Saudi Arabian General Investment Authority, 19 Chinese manufacturing companies obtained licenses in Saudi Arabia, 86 licenses in construction, six in information technologies, and eight in services.[71] In 2017, Beijing invested $88.79 million in Saudi Arabia, and the Kingdom invested $150 million in China.[72]

Furthermore, many Chinese companies are operating in the Kingdom market in the fields of infrastructure, construction, and communications, and employ tens of thousands of Chinese workers. By March 2017, around 160 Chinese organizations were operating in several sectors of the Saudi economy and around 175 Chinese projects developed, notably in the telecommunication and construction sectors.[73] The two countries have collaborated on numerous projects in the health, transportation and construction sectors. Saudi Arabia has become an increasingly important market for Chinese consumer goods, including electronics, textiles, and food, which accounted for most Saudi imports.[74]

Meanwhile, Beijing and Riyadh have identified the first batch of key projects on industrial capacity and investment cooperation worth $55 billion. The development of industrial clusters in Jizan is well underway, and groundbreaking was held recently on the $3.2 billion Guangzhou Pan-Asia PET petrochemical project, which was the first investment project in the clusters. Major energy and infrastructure projects, such as the Yanbu Refinery in Saudi Arabia, the Panjin Refinery in China's Liaoning Province, the Rabigh Power Station and the Landbridge Railway, are being advanced steadily or are under close discussion. Cooperation on new and high technology has delivered successful outcomes. A Chinese satellite installed with an optical camera of Saudi Arabia was launched last year, accomplishing the first lunar probe by an Arab country. Two Saudi Arabia-made satellites were successfully brought into orbit by China's Long March launch vehicle.[75]

The frequent high-level exchanges push forward and expand the two-way trade and investment between the two countries. In January 2016 Chinese President Xi Jinping visited in Saudi Arabia, (about which few details were disclosed), and the two countries decided to establish a comprehensive strategic partnership.[76] In September 2016, Saudi Deputy Crown Prince MBS visited the G20 Summit held in Hangzhou, where the two countries signed 15 agreements and MoUs. The agreements range from energy development and oil storage to cooperation promises on housing development and water resource issues. In addition, Huawei, a leading global ICT solutions provider, received an investment license from Saudi Arabia.[77]

In March 2017, during Saudi King Salman's visit to Beijing, China and Saudi Arabia signed trade and investment packages worth $65 billion that included a wide range of areas on investment, space research and more than 20 agreements on oil investment and energy. Among the agreements was an MoU between Saudi Aramco and China North Industries Group Corporation to build two refineries, one in the Chinese Fujian province, and one in Yanbu in Saudi Arabia.[78]

In August 2017, during Chinese Vice Premier Zhang Gaoli's visit to Saudi Arabia, both countries signed 60 various agreements and MoUs worth nearly $70 billion. The agreements and MoUs covered investment, trade, energy, postal service, communications, and media.[79] China and Saudi Arabia also announced the intention to establish and operate a $20 billion investment fund jointly.[80] In February 2019, China and Saudi Arabia signed 35 MoU economic cooperation agreements worth a total of $28 billion at a joint investment forum during a visit by Saudi Crown Prince MBS to Beijing. The agreements cover some key sectors, including energy and water, industry and manufacturing, petrochemicals, mining and minerals, housing, transport, logistics, and e-commerce.[81]

The agreements include an MoU between Saudi Arabia's Ministry of Energy, Industry & Mineral Resources and Pan-Asia Resin in the petrochemicals sector with a total planned investment of $1.5 billion. An MoU between the Saudi Authority for Industrial Cities & Technology Zones (Modon) and Teda Investment Holding Company is for a total investment of $1 billion. An MoU between Jabal Omar Development Company and China State Construction Engineering Corporation in the infrastructure sector detailed a total planned investment of $533 million. An MoU between Sagia and Goldwind International Holdings for cooperation in establishing a wind-turbine manufacturing hub in the Kingdom set out a total investment of $18 million.[82]

In the end, the two sides reaffirmed their commitment to strengthen and expand two-way trade and investment in various fields under the BRI framework, and to align the Belt and Road initiative with Saudi's Vision 2030. As Saudi Arabia's Minister of Energy, Industry, and Mineral Resources, Khalid bin Abdulaziz Al-Falih, said in an interview with Xinhua, that Saudi investment in China was 'just starting'.[83]

Military ties

As part of China's comprehensive strategic partnerships with Riyadh, defense cooperation has become an increasingly significant part of integrating Saudi Vision 2030 into the BRI framework. Traditionally, the US was a major defense partner with the Kingdom, but Saudi Arabia wants diversification in meeting its defense needs. The Beijing–Riyadh security relations have focused primarily on weapons sales from China to Saudi Arabia, particularly systems that other suppliers (e.g., US and the West) refused to sell to the Kingdom, among other things, due to the restrictions of non-proliferation regimes and pressure from Israel.

Nevertheless, overall, Chinese security exports to Riyadh constitute merely a niche, since over the years the Kingdom acquired most weapons from the West (mainly from the US and the UK), while imports from Beijing were only marginal in volume, though qualitative strategically. Riyadh's dependence on US military equipment restricts its ability to purchase large quantities of Chinese arms.[84]

Nonetheless, Beijing is neither capable nor interested in supplanting Washington as the strategic security guarantor of Riyadh's safety and Persian Gulf regional stability, and shouldering the burden this entails. The scope of the US military presence and its ability to project power, coupled with the quality of its weapons systems, the depth of its military and political relations, and its interoperability with allied militaries, are beyond the PRC's competitive capabilities, at least in the near and medium future.[85]

Historically, the security dimension in Beijing–Riyadh relations has been limited. The extent of the security relations is generally attributed to Riyadh's acquisition of 36 China's DF-3 (CSS-2 by NATO) nuclear-capable intermediate-range ballistic missiles (IRBMs) and nine launchers in the late 1980s,[86] and subsequently DF-5 (CSS-5) intercontinental ballistic missiles from Beijing. Riyadh is also reported to have procured the more advanced DF-21 missile system in 2007, allegedly with Washington's approval. Nevertheless, Saudi Arabia has demonstrated at least a passing interest in purchasing additional Chinese defense systems, including the jointly produced Chinese-Pakistani JF-17 fighter, but no such contract has been signed.[87]

Though Saudi Arabia is one of the biggest buyers of US weapons, the country cannot buy ballistic missiles from the US because of the 1987 Missile Technology Control Regime, an informal multi-country pact that seeks to limit the sale of rockets carrying weapons of mass destruction. According to US intelligence, Saudi Arabia escalated its ballistic missile program with the help of China. This could be another step in the Saudi push forward its attempt to obtain nuclear weapons, and will impair the decade-long effort to limit the amassing of missiles in the Middle East.[88]

In the past several years the potential for Sino–Saudi military cooperation has increased, especially as Washington's appetite to play a role in the Middle East is diminishing while that of China is growing. The Kingdom has increased its interest in purchasing Chinese military technology, as Beijing is willing to sell arms to Riyadh without the geopolitical strings that frequently accompany US arms sales. In particular, Saudi Arabia views China as a potentially important supplier of highly sophisticated missile and offensive weapons technologies. Both countries may enhance cooperation in the defense sector to satisfy each other's interests.[89]

In 2014, after Saudi Arabia became frustrated at restrictions on the export to the Kingdom of Western-origin UCAVs such as the GA-ASI Predator and Reaper, Saudi Crown Prince MBS met Chinese General Wang Guanzhong in China to reach a deal to supply Wing Loong IIs. The Wing Loong (Pterodactyl) series is produced by the Chengdu Aircraft Industry Group (CAIG) that had previously exported the Wing Loong, a medium-altitude, long-endurance UAV, which can also be fitted with missiles to Saudi Arabia. According to the Chinese state news agency Xinhua, Saudi Arabia will acquire 300 Chinese Wing Loong IIs worth approximately $10 billion. Riyadh is the first Arab country to obtain this type of drone. However, the drone has not performed well in the Arabian Desert.[90]

In March 2017, during Saudi King Salman's visit to China, the two countries signed deals worth as much as $65 billion and a partnership agreement to construct a new facility to produce uncrewed aerial vehicles, in an agreement signed by China Aerospace Long-March International (ALIT) and manufacturers in Saudi Arabia. The new facility can operate as a hub for manufacturing and services for other CH-4 operators in the Middle East, including Egypt, Iraq, and Jordan. According to IHS Janes Defence Industry news, the King Abdulaziz

City for Science and Technology signed a partnership with the state-owned China Aerospace Science and Technology Corporation (CASC) to establish a manufacturing plant in Saudi Arabia for the CH series of UCAVs. Riyadh already operates the turboprop-powered CH-4 UCAV series, but it was not made clear whether this new agreement covers only that type, or also the jet-powered CH-5.[91]

Another area of military cooperation between the two countries is in the field of observation satellites. In December 2018, two Saudi Arabian Earth observation satellites and ten small secondary payloads rode a Long March 2D rocket from the Jiuquan space base in China's northwestern Inner Mongolia region. The main payloads aboard the Long March 2D rocket were the SaudiSat 5A and 5B, two Earth-imaging satellites each weighing nearly a half-ton. The SaudiSat 5A and 5B satellites were built by the King Abdulaziz City for Science and Technology in Riyadh. The new spacecraft is the largest satellite manufactured in Saudi Arabia, capable of providing the country's government with high-resolution imagery of sites across the globe.[92]

In January 2016, President Xi Jinping's visit to Saudi Arabia yielded a commitment from both sides to increase bilateral security cooperation, especially in the counterterrorism arena.[93] In November 2016 in Riyadh, Saudi King Salman met with Meng Jianzhu, a special envoy of Chinese President Xi Jinping to discuss a range of security issues.[94] Both sides announced a commitment to forge a five-year plan to increase bilateral security cooperation. This plan would include joint counter-terrorism exercises, and Chinese navy vessels have visited the Saudi port of Jeddah, cementing Saudi Arabia's status as a vital Chinese ally in the Middle East.

In October 2016, China and Saudi Arabia staged their first joint anti-terrorism exercise 'Exploration 2016' held over fifteen days in China's southwestern city of Chongqing. The exercise featured Special Forces units attached to the Royal Saudi Land Forces and their People's Liberation Army (PLA) counterparts. The exercises were designed to improve the respective capacities of both countries to conduct counterterrorism, hostage rescue, and other complex operations.[95]

In the end, the deepening security relations, the joint anti-terrorism exercises, and the acquisition of sensitive military technology, are the expression of the Beijing–Riyadh comprehensive strategic partnership which has developed in recent years, reflecting Riyadh's desire to reduce its security dependence on Washington and to erode Iran's international and regional influence. More important, Washington's scathing criticisms of Saudi Arabia's sponsorship of terrorism and open calls for a re-evaluation of US military assistance to Saudi Arabia could cause the latter to form a full-fledged defense partnership with Beijing in the years to come. However, in light of historical experience, Riyadh hopes mostly that expanded security links with China will give it fast access to sophisticated missile systems and convince Washington to outbid Beijing by exporting some of its most prized military assets to Saudi Arabia.

Tourism and Cultural Ties

Part of China's comprehensive strategic partnerships with the Kingdom includes enabling the people of the two countries to bond along the Silk Road, vital to integrating the Saudi Vision 2030 within the Belt and Road Initiative framework. The promotion of extensive cultural and academic exchanges aim to win public support for deepening bilateral and multilateral cooperation, as well as providing scholarships, holding annual cultural events, increasing cooperation in science and technology, and establishing joint laboratory or research centers and international technology transfer centers.[96]

Linguistic, cultural, and tourism cooperation is another important aspect of the Sino–Saudi comprehensive strategic partnership, and both nations have outlined their intention to expand the collaboration in these areas in the coming years. There have been dynamic cultural exchanges between the two countries. The exhibition of 'Roads to Arabia: Archaeological Treasures of Saudi Arabia', the "Exhibition of Chinese Cultural Relics" in the Kingdom, the joint archaeological excavation which unearthed relics indicating the maritime Silk Road at the port of Al-Serrian, and the performance by the Chinese symphony orchestra and musicians at the World Heritage Site of Al-Ula, are all vivid examples of exchanges and mutual learning between different civilizations.[97]

In September 2018 the exhibition 'Treasures of China' was held in the Kingdom. This exhibition marks the first major China cultural relic exhibition hosted by the National Museum in Riyadh. The display includes 264 items provided by 13 museums and cultural institutions, such as the Palace Museum, among which are 173 Chinese cultural relics. It also showcased objects from China–Saudi Arabia joint archaeological excavations. Close to half the items are on display overseas for the first time. The exhibition consists of five sections in chronological order: 'Beginning of Civilization, Establishments of Etiquette', 'Unification, Consolidation and Development', 'Prosperities and Diversified Communication', 'Start-up of Business and Marine

Trade', as well as 'Palace and Royal Art'. These cultural exchanges are important in illustrating how both nations see the future of bilateral relations.[98]

In February 2019, the Crown Prince MBS signed an agreement during his visit to China to include the Chinese language in curricula across the Kingdom. The Saudi plan is to include the Chinese language as a curriculum at all stages of education in schools and universities across the Kingdom. This will enhance the cultural diversity of students in the Kingdom and contribute to the achievement of the future national goals in the field of education in line with the Saudi Vision 2030. Introducing the Chinese language into the Saudi curricula is an important step toward opening new academic horizons for students at the various educational levels in the Kingdom. Learning the Chinese language will also serve as a bridge between the peoples of the two countries that will contribute to promoting trade and cultural ties.[99]

The proposal to include the Chinese language as a curriculum aims to strengthen friendship and cooperation between the Kingdom and China, and to deepen the comprehensive strategic partnership at all levels. Currently, there are hundreds of Saudi students in Chinese universities (about 700 students have finished their studies and returned to Saudi Arabia), and the Kingdom has opened a branch of the King Abdul Aziz Public Library in Beijing to encourage exchanges between scholars, researchers, and students in both countries.[100] The country's cultural mission has signed 18 education and science cooperative agreements with 18 Chinese universities.[101]

In an interview to Chinese state news agency Xinhua, Saudi Arabia's Minister of Energy, Industry and Mineral Resources, Khalid bin Abdulaziz Al-Falih, said "Our culture is very compatible with the Chinese culture. We have sent hundreds of our students to study in China, and when they came back speaking Chinese, it makes thousands of Saudi people understand how great China is and how wonderful the Chinese people are. We need more of that; there will be great prosperity for both countries."[102]

In recent years, China's links with the GCC countries have strengthened due to the introduction of additional and direct airline routes, the strong growth of the Chinese economy and Chinese tourists' increasing disposable income. According to data from Colliers International published ahead of Arabian Travel Market (ATM) 2019, the number of Chinese tourists traveling to the GCC is expected to increase 81 percent from 1.6 million in 2018 to 2.9 million in 2022. The GCC countries currently attract just one percent of China's total outbound market, but positive trends are expected over the coming years for as many as 400 million. The Colliers data shows that Saudi Arabia will experience the highest proportionate increase in arrivals from China, with a projected compound annual growth rate (CAGR) of 33 percent between 2018 and 2022. Both Saudi Arabia and China's cultural and educational exchanges have been cited as one of the key elements driving this influx.[103]

According to China's Ambassador to Saudi Arabia, Li Huaxin, Saudi Arabia is set to be a major world tourist destination given its cultural, heritage, humanitarian, and civilization potential. He also affirmed that if tourist visas are introduced for foreign delegations in the Kingdom, the number of Chinese tourists will increase considerably. The Chinese Ambassador also stressed that Sino–Saudi relations have developed, especially in the area of culture, tourism, and archaeological exploration.[104]

In summary, according to the World Travel & Tourism Council's (WTTC) annual review, the travel and tourism sector contributed 9 percent ($65.2 billion) of the economy of the Kingdom in 2018.[105] Since the Saudi Vision 2030 aims to increase the revenue generated from tourism to 18 percent in the next 14 years, the development of Saudi Arabia's tourism sector is a vital part of its economic transformation.[106] Thus, the growing number of Chinese tourists traveling to the Kingdom can contribute to achieving this goal. According to data from the China Tourism Academy (CTA), 140 million Chinese visited various tourist destinations, up 13.5 percent from the previous year's 129 million, and they spent more than $120 billion.[107]

Summary

In recent years, Saudi Arabia and China have expanded and transformed the nature of their relationship to a comprehensive strategic partnership. This study examines the new horizons and the growing comprehensive strategic partnership between Riyadh and Beijing, and the synergies between the Belt and Road Initiative and the Saudi Vision 2030 in order to understand the extent of economic engagement and bilateral relationship between the two nations.

The chapter has demonstrated that Beijing's comprehensive strategic partnership framework with Riyadh is based on shared or mutual complementary economic and commercial interests, especially with the integration and implementation of the Belt and Road Initiative and Saudi Vision 2030. The significant warming in their relations comes at a time when both countries are under increasingly harsh global criticism and thus are eager to find political support as well as business opportunities. This creates a substantially increasing convergence of interests that are building a new horizon framework for cooperation, strengthening and expanding the comprehensive strategic partnership between the countries.

Policy coordination, connectivity, trade and investments, energy cooperation, military ties, tourism and cultural ties are the significant areas that are most promising for the Riyadh and Beijing comprehensive strategic partnership framework and the joint building of the Belt and Road Initiative. Saudi's Vision 2030 and China's BRI have converged on a joint economic development path, and their strategic synergy will bring new opportunities for both sides. As a result, the realization of the Belt and Road Initiative that intertwines with Saudi's Vision 2030 will provide new momentum for Riyadh's economic transformation.

Both countries have much to gain from the new horizon and the growing comprehensive strategic partnership. China needs Saudi energy reserves and investments to secure oil supplies and other natural resources to sustain its growth, as well as to utilize the Kingdom's unique location at the nexus of three continents and its vital role in politics, economy, religion and security affairs in the Middle East and among Islamic countries. The Saudi Vision 2030 could fuse perfectly and contribute to the construction of the BRI. Saudi Arabia, on the other hand, can benefit from diversifying its relationships and expanding its diplomatic and economic ties with the world's fastest-growing major economy; Beijing can help it to diversify its economy, attract more foreign direct investments and increase its global market presence for alternate sources of revenue.

Nevertheless, there are several challenges to the growing comprehensive strategic partnership. First, Riyadh relies on Washington for security and geopolitical assistance, while China–US relations have become increasingly tense. There is growing concern in the US about the implications of Chinese investments along the route of the New Silk Road that position Beijing in direct competition with Washington for economic influence in key countries around the world. In the short run at least, the Kingdom will continue to look to Washington for military and political support and the partnership with Beijing will remain primarily economic.

Second, China has a long-standing economic and defense partnership with Iran (the 'mortal enemy' of Saudi Arabia), particularly over the past decade and especially in the context of intensified Saudi–Iranian regional rivalry and the dispute over the Iranian nuclear program. In addition, there are disagreements over Bashar al-Assad's future in Syria and long-standing Chinese disdain for Saudi Arabia's sponsorship of Islamist networks as well as suspicions about China's intentions in Yemen's civil war, given the diplomatic efforts to end the conflict. Third, the Kingdom's interests in Asia are not concentrated only on Beijing, but also Japan and India, which are viewed by Chinese as competitors in East Asia and Southeast Asia.

Moreover, the implementation of the BRI would be seriously affected by the instability generated by Riyadh and Tehran in hotspots such as Yemen, Iraq, Syria, and Qatar. Such regional instability presents a formidable obstacle to the BRI's strategic design, as it undermines connectivity, threatens infrastructure projects, and makes an economic corridor through the volatile Middle East to the markets of developed Europe less viable. Finally, Saudi Arabia has struggled to look beyond state-manipulated economies as part of large-scale reform efforts. Part of this trend has been an emphasis on privatizing historically state-owned enterprises while boosting foreign investment outside the oil and gas sectors. Initiatives exist to privatize state assets, but this process has proceeded slowly. In sum, all these factors could complicate the broader bilateral partnership.

2
Iran

This chapter seeks to examine the new dynamic of the growing comprehensive strategic partnership between Iran and China in order to understand the impact and the extent of the re-imposition of US secondary sanctions on Iran's engagement and integration in the implementation of the Belt and Road Initiative. Tehran has a special geographical and communication status in West Asia which makes it one of the important centerpieces of the new Silk Road trade route. However, Washington's decision to withdraw from the Irani nuclear agreement and to re-impose sanctions has created barriers in the new dynamic in Sino–Iranian trade and obstacles to integrating Iran into the realization of the Belt and Road Initiative.

In recent years, the PRC and the Islamic Republic of Iran established a comprehensive strategic partnership,[1] by complementing each other in various aspects such as trade, energy, and production capacity cooperation. The successful cooperation between the two nations arises from the historical ties tracing back to the ancient Silk Road as well as mutually complementary economic and political interests that facilitate these interactions. As Iranian Foreign Minister Mohammad Javad Zarif said, "Our relationship with China is very valuable to us. We consider the comprehensive strategic partnership between Iran and China as one of our most important relations."[2]

The $1 trillion One Belt, One Road initiative (BRI), put forward in October 2013 by Chinese President Xi Jinping, seeks to connect Beijing to the global market by linking Asia and Europe via a set of land and maritime trade routes. The concept took shape over a period of several years and has now become a cornerstone of President Xi's foreign policy. The Islamic Republic was a significant gateway to the ancient Silk Roads, and thanks to its central position between the Arabian Peninsula, Central Asia, and South Asia, Iran continues to be an important crossroads in the new Silk Road.[3] Given Iran's geographic and logistical location, engaging it within the BRI framework is essential to the realization of the new Silk Road trade route. Tehran's geopolitical position enables the PRC to exploit existing trade route connecting Central Asian states with the Persian Gulf region and to create new transport corridors, with particular reference to the so-called Southern Corridor of the BRI, which is to cross Central Asia, Iran, Turkey, and the Balkans. Hence, the ultimate success of the Belt and Road Initiative depends to a large extent on Iranian participation and support, especially as far as geopolitical and logistical issues are concerned.[4] For this reason, the BRI framework provides Beijing and Tehran with an opportunity to strengthen and deepen their comprehensive strategic partnership.

In May 2018, President Trump announced that the United States was withdrawing from the Joint Comprehensive Plan of Action (JCPOA), setting in motion the re-imposition of secondary sanctions on Iran, which returned in full in November of that year.[5] Washington's decision to withdraw from the JCPOA and to re-imposition of sanctions created barriers in the new dynamic in Sino–Iranian trade and obstacles to integrate Iran as part of the realization of the Belt and Road Initiative.

In this context, it is essential to understand the new dynamic and the growing comprehensive strategic partnership between the two countries and Washington's decision to withdraw from the nuclear agreement and to re-impose sanctions on the implementation of the Belt and Road Initiative. This chapter examines the new dynamic and the growing comprehensive strategic partnership between Iran and China in order to understand the impact and the extent of the re-imposition of US secondary sanctions on Iran engagement and integration in the implementation of the Belt and Road Initiative.

The main argument presented is that Beijing's comprehensive strategic partnership framework with Tehran is based on shared or mutual complementary economic and political interests, especially to integrate Iran within the Belt and Road Initiative framework. Nonetheless, the re-imposition of US secondary sanctions on Iran could hurt the new dynamic in Sino–Iranian comprehensive strategic partnership and have a long-term effect on China's ability to integrate Iran with the BRI and thereby significantly to impair the ability to realize the project.

Officially, China said it will maintain normal economic and trade exchanges with Tehran despite Trump's decision to withdraw from the nuclear agreement and re-impose sanctions on Iran. As Chinese President Xi Jinping declared, "No matter how the international and regional situation changes, China's resolve to develop a comprehensive strategic partnership with Iran will remain unchanged." However, according to data from the General Customs Administration of the People's Republic of China, the trade between the two countries has fallen dramatically in the two months following the re-imposition of US secondary sanctions.[6]

Iran and the Belt and Road Initiative

The PRC comprehensive strategic partnership with the Islamic Republic includes seven areas for cooperation within the Belt and Road Initiative. These areas are policy coordination, connectivity, trade and investments, energy cooperation, financial integration, military ties and culture and tourism. However, each country views the BRI framework and reacts to it according to its own perspective and the consequences for its national interests and international status. Therefore, there are very different attitudes among the countries that are part of the BRI framework regarding how to realize the vision.[7]

Policy coordination

According to China's comprehensive strategic partnership with Iran, the highest level in Beijing hierarchy of diplomatic relations, the aim is to promote political cooperation between countries, to create mechanisms for dialogue and consensus-building on global and regional issues, to develop shared interests, deepen political trust, and reach a new consensus on cooperation are important in order to integrate Iran into the BRI framework.[8]

In January 2016, shortly after the JCPOA was implemented, President Xi Jinping made a successful visit to Iran during which the two heads of state agreed to establish a comprehensive strategic partnership. President Xi stressed the fact that both countries were natural partners as far as the implementation of the Belt and Road Initiative was concerned. Furthermore, seventeen cooperation documents centered on the new Silk Road were signed in the areas of science, technology, communications, transportation, energy, and many other fields. The two sides also agreed to develop a roadmap for the strategic partnership during the next 25 years and to increase trade to $600 billion over the next ten years. Nevertheless, the programs discussed in these documents are yet to be fully operational.[9]

In February 2019, ahead of the visit to Beijing by Saudi Arabia's crown prince, Chinese President Xi Jinping welcomed a delegation that included Iran's Foreign Minister, Oil Minister and Parliament Speaker and called for stronger cooperation to boost ties. President Xi spoke to the Iranian Parliament Speaker Ali Larijani of the enduring friendship between the two countries and said that the PRC's determination to develop its comprehensive strategic partnership with Iran will stay unchanged despite changes in the global and regional areas. The Chinese President called on both sides to deepen mutual trust and advance communication and coordination, increase cooperation on security and anti-terrorism, and improve cultural and people-to-people exchanges.[10]

Connectivity

According to China's comprehensive strategic partnership with Iran, facilitation of connectivity is one of the important ways to integrate Tehran into the BRI framework. It was recommended that the Islamic Republic optimize its infrastructural connections and also adapt its technical systems to those of the other countries in the BRI framework. This would lead Bejing and Tehran to jointly contribute to the development of international transport routes and the creation of an infrastructural network that could gradually connect all the regions in Asia and specific points in Asia, Africa, and Europe. Also, they agreed that there should be serious attempts to create low-carbon and green infrastructure.[11]

Iran has a special geographical and communication status in West Asia, in that it is connected to South and Central Asia, the Middle East and Europe through land and sea routes. In addition, access points at the Persian Gulf, the Gulf of Oman and the Caspian Sea combine to make Iran one of the important centerpieces of the Belt and Road. Therefore, the development of Iran's transport infrastructure is necessary for the realization of infrastructural connections in an important part of the BRI network to connect Asia, Europe, and Africa.[12]

According to Iranian Minister of Transport Abbas Akhodi, his country is focusing on expanding its railway network so that it can better align with the PRC's Central Asian logistics strategy. The main goal for Iran's Department of Transportation would be to improve connections of the national rail network to neighboring railway networks. The Iranian development of international transport routes are seen as crucial to Chinese trade priorities, to expand commerce with Turkey and widen access for its goods to Iranian ports near the Strait of Hormuz. Beijing hopes to see trains running between the western Chinese region of Kashgar and Istanbul as soon as 2020. Iranian railways figure to serve as key links in routes through both Central Asia and the Caucasus.[13]

In February 2016, the first noticeable event in the framework of the BRI took place when the first direct freight train from China arrived in Iran. The train, carrying 32 containers, arrived in Tehran after a 14-day, 10,399 kilometers (6,462 miles) journey from Yiwu city in east China. The cargo train's journey was 30 days shorter than the time usually taken by ships to sail from Shanghai to Iran's Bandar Abbas port. In September 2016, the second freight train service connected Chinese city Yinchuan with Iran. According to Iran's Transport Minister, one freight train could now travel from China to Iran every month. These trains would eventually be bound for Europe, helping Tehran develop into a transit center between the two continents.[14]

Iran has a relatively good regular railway network, but the capability to link routes from Turkey through to Pakistan and India is of immense strategic importance to the framework of the BRI. The Iranian government plans are for three high-speed lines, from Tehran–Mashad near the border with Turkmenistan, Tehran–Tabriz, close to the borders with both Azerbaijan and Turkey and from Tehran to Isfahan.[15] China is the leading investor in Iranian transportation projects, especially railway development. The Tehran–Qom–Isfahan high-speed rail project and the electrification of Tehran-Mashhad Railway, at an estimated cost of about $4.2 billion, are the most important railway development projects in Iran, in both of which the PRC government and Chinese companies play important roles.[16]

The most important project agreed on by the two countries is the Tehran–Qom-Isfahan high-speed railway. State-owned China Railway Engineering Corp is building the Qom–Isfahan two-lane high-speed railway, with a length of 410 km, connecting Tehran to Qom and then to Isfahan in just 1.5 hours, with trains traveling at 300 km/h. Over the next two decades, approximately 12.5 million passengers will be carried by this railway each year. According to Iran's Minister of Roads and Urban Construction, Abbas Akhondi, the first phase of this project would be carried out at a cost of $22 billion. The Chinese contracting company would provide finance and carry out 40 percent of the construction.[17]

The second important project in the area of rail communications between the two countries is the electrification of the Tehran-Mashhad railway. According to the agreement, the task of reforming and constructing the current Tehran-Mashhad railway for trains to travel at speeds of 200 km/h, building an electric railway for trains to travel at speeds of 250 km/h and procuring 70 electric locomotives, was assigned to the consortium. The electrification of the Tehran-Mashhad line will reduce commute time between the two cities from 12 hours to about 6 hours, linking Tehran with Iran's second-largest city, Mashhad, in the east near its border with Turkmenistan and completing just under a third of the proposed BRI line required to link Tehran to western China.[18]

A consortium comprising Mapna Group Company, several Iranian companies, and the Chinese side is collaborating on this project. The total value of the contract stands at $1.7 billion; China's Exim Bank (the Export–Import Bank of China) will finance $1.5 billion of the project, and $200 million will be provided by Iran.[19] The development and speeding-up of this railway could be regarded as an important step in the implementation of a key part of the Silk Road's rail route, because the track would enter Iran from the north-eastern part of the country and then continue to the north-west through Tehran and finally reach Turkey.[20] Chinese extensive engagement in Iran's railway projects suggests that Iran is seen as the southern route to Europe which effectively bypasses Russia.

Both these railway lines form a part of one of the six corridors in the new Silk Road. Six corridors have been defined along the route of the BRI framework. One of them is the China–Central Asia–Western Asia Corridor, a part of which passes through Iran, using the two aforementioned railway lines. This corridor enters Iran from Turkmenistan and follows two routes: an east–west route to Turkey and a north–south route to the Persian Gulf.[21] According to an article in *Foreign Affairs*, Beijing considers Central Asia its "exposed underbelly that needs to be closely integrated into China's economic and political sphere".[22]

Moreover, Iran's railway network can connect with the Baku–Tbilisi–Kars (BTK), a regional rail link project to directly connect Azerbaijan, Georgia, and Turkey, that became operational in October 2017. The BTK railway ferryies cargo across the Caspian Sea from Central Asia to Azerbaijan and is an essential step in reviving the historical Silk Road.[23]An Iranian rail link would provide a more contiguous and cost-effective route. Connecting with Iran's north–south rail links would provide a mostly vertical axis connecting China's central east-west corridor to the Middle East and the Arabian Sea.[24]

During 2012–2016, Chinese companies became the largest investors in and constructors of transport infrastructure in Iranian neighbor states, particularly those in Central Asia. Therefore, Iran's increasing need in the area of transport infrastructure and the growing capabilities of Chinese companies created more opportunities for sharing interests for the two countries. In November 2015, China

Railway proposed a high-speed rail link that will carry both passengers and cargo between China and Iran. The most recently proposed route would begin in Urumqi, the capital of PRC's western Xinjiang province, and end in Tehran some 3,200 km (2,000 miles) away, where it would eventually continue northwest through Turkey into Europe. Along the way, it would stop in Kazakhstan, Kyrgyzstan, Uzbekistan, and Turkmenistan. Beijing plans to build a rail line that would cut down the time needed to transport goods and increase the route's competitiveness against ocean freight alternatives. The trains themselves would run at speeds of up to 300 km/h for passenger trains and 120 km/h for freight trains.[25]

In May 2018, within two days after the US announced its withdrawal from the nuclear agreement, China inaugurated a new railroad connecting Bayannur, in Inner Mongolia, to Tehran. The train, carrying 1,150 tonnes of sunflower seeds, traveling 8,352 kilometers through Kazakhstan and Turkmenistan, arrived in Tehran in 15 days. The new train route will shorten transportation time by at least 20 days compared with ocean shipping. The railroad was planned and its construction began several years before the US announcement, but the timing of the inauguration was not coincidental; rather, it was meant to convey a message of partnership to Iran.[26]

Nevertheless, the US withdrawal from the JCPOA and the re-imposition of the sanctions has increased the difficulties for Iran to participate in the realization of the new Silk Roads. More important, this will cause new, essential challenges for Tehran-Beijing cooperation to the development of international transport routes and the creation of an infrastructural network that could gradually connect all the regions in Asia and also specific points in Asia, Africa, and Europe. The Belt and Road Initiative is a multilateral project, and its success will depend on its ability to attract as many countries as possible. Iran has been a major gateway to the ancient Silk Roads, and thanks to its central position between the Arabian Peninsula, Central Asia and South Asia, it continues to be a critical crossroads. However, the re-imposition of the US sanctions could slow down the construction of infrastructure through Iran, and divert foreign investors from this economic corridor linking Europe to China. According to the official statistics published by the Iranian Government, Tehran needs $14.5 billion investment per year over the next decade to improve its current transport infrastructure and to build new facilities.[27]

Trade and investments

The PRC's comprehensive strategic partnership with Iran is aimed at mitigating as much as possible the barriers to free trade, investment, industrial cooperation, and technical and engineering services in order to facilitate the integration of Iran within the BRI framework. Both countries must take a series of additional measures, such as expanding free-trade zones, improving trade structures, seeking new potential areas for trade and improving the trade balance, devising new initiatives for the promotion of conventional forms of trade, developing trans-border electronic trade and other advanced models of business, and regularly share information in these areas, in order to create a system for supporting trade in services to strengthen and expand conventional trade and increase customs cooperation.[28]

The trade and ties between China and Iran date back over 2,000 years to the ancient Silk Road caravan routes that brought the textile to Europe. China has traditionally been Iran's leading trading partner. During the past eight years, China has always been the most important economic partner of Iran, and approximately 30 percent of the total Iranian foreign trade has been done with Beijing.[29] During President Xi Jinping's visit to Tehran, the customs administrations of the two countries reached an agreement on customs information sharing. According to a joint plan of action in customs cooperation, Beijing would transport a proportion of its exported commodities to Iranian ports and then transport them further to Europe.[30]

According to the latest data released by the Chinese Customs Administration, the trade turnover between the two countries was $51 billion in 2014, 31 percent more compared to the preceding year. In 2015 the figure stood at $34 billion, indicating a 34 percent plunge. In 2016, the trade turnover between Iran and China stood at $31.2 billion, down 7.7 percent from 2015. In 2017, the trade turnover between the two countries stood at $37.18 billion.[31] According to China Customs Statistics (export–import), China's trade volume with Iran stood at $35 billion in 2018, and Tehran was China's third partner in the Middle East.[32]

Beijing has also been one of the major foreign investors in the Islamic Republic over the past decade.[33] Its investments have taken place in various sectors from energy to transportation. China has invested in various energy projects in Iran including the South Pars Gas Field and the Abadan Refinery.[34] Beijing's investments totaled $48.6 billion in the 2005–2018 period. Of this $27 billion, $11.83 billion was investment in energy, $6.3 billion in transport, $2 billion in utilities and

$5 billion in metals, and another $21.6 billion in construction contracts relating to energy, transportation, chemicals, and metals.[35] Meanwhile, based on the official statistics published by the Iranian government, over the next decade Tehran needs to attract $500 billion in investment for various sectors of its economy, a large part of which must be provided from abroad.[36] China is one of the most critical countries Tehran hopes to make these investments, and the BRI can provide a framework for increased Chinese investments in Iran.

The Islamic Republic is an important emerging economy with rich energy resources and a market of 80 million people that is larger than the whole Central Asian market with its 66 million people. In the post-JCPOA era, the prospect of Iran's potential economic growth is encouraging, which, in turn, could lead to a considerable increase in its economic interactions with China.[37] Overall, the two states have set the ambitious goal of increasing bilateral trade tenfold, to $600 billion, by 2026. However, such a high increase in the bilateral trade turnover looks unrealistic, at least for the time being, and many obstacles need to be removed in order to achieve such an ambitious economic goal.[38]

Following the 2015 nuclear agreement, Tehran has received most of its foreign finance from Beijing. Based on an agreement between Iran's Central Bank and the CITIC Trust Group, the Group has provided Iran with a $10 billion credit line to finance medium- and long-term Iranian projects (e.g., energy and transport projects). This is the most extensive credit line extended to Iran in recent decades.[39] In addition to the credit line, the China Development Bank signed preliminary deals with Iran worth $15 billion for other infrastructure and production projects. Moreover, the PRC has also opened two credit lines worth $4.2 billion to build high-speed railway lines linking Tehran–Mashhad–Isfahan.[40] More broadly, following the US with-drawal from the JCPOA, many major European companies have ceased their activities in Iran and ended their cooperation with the country.[41] This makes China the only major foreign investor in the country, and in the future Tehran is expected to focus more on Beijing to attract foreign investment.

Nevertheless, Washington's decision to re-impose the economic sanctions could negatively impact Beijing's investments and trade with Tehran, although officially, Chinese Foreign Ministry spokesman Geng Shuang said that China would maintain "normal economic and trade exchanges" with Iran, despite Trump's decision to re-impose sanctions on Tehran.[42] However, given the potential risk of being targeted by the American sanctions, only those small- and medium-sized Chinese companies with no presence in the Western markets and fewer ties with the global financial system are expected to become active in this sphere.

According to trade data from the General Customs Administration of the People's Republic of China, the Beijing–Tehran trade fell dramatically in the two months following the re-imposition of US secondary sanctions. Chinese exports to Iran, mainly crucial machinery and parts for Iran's manufacturing sector, fell from $1.2 billion in October 2018 to just $428 million in February 2019.[43] Exports had averaged $1.6 billion a month in the period from 2014 until the beginning of 2018. Imports from Iran, mainly crude oil, which had fallen to $1 billion in October, rose after November when the Trump administration granted China a waiver to permit continued oil purchases. The imports hit $1.3 billion in February, of which $866 million is attributed to oil imports.[44]

The trade data demonstrate a new negative dynamic in China–Iran trade under sanctions, and it is not yet conclusive as to whether these restrictions primarily reflect the decision to limit commerce to humanitarian trade. In the end, if the PRC remains unwilling or unable to sustain its investments and trade ties with Tehran in the face of US sanctions, the consequences will prove significant to Iran's economy rehabilitation.

More importantly, in the post-JCPOA era the prospects for Iran's contribution to the BRI has become further complicated. The re-imposition of sanctions on Iran has not only increased the risks of economic interactions with Iran, especially in the fields of investment and infrastructural projects, but also posed severe challenges to the country's economic stability. Indeed, the Chinese government is still committed to the JCPOA and the continuation of regular trade ties with Iran. However, Chinese companies which have considerable benefits in the US and are afraid of being punished by Washington are having increasing difficulties in cooperating with Iran to promote the BRI-related projects. For instance, two major Chinese telecommunication companies, ZTE and Huawei, have faced severe penalties from the US over their trade ties with Iran.[45] The US sanctions have created new complexities in Iran–China interactions in general and their cooperation within the context of the BRI in particular.

Energy cooperation

According to China's comprehensive strategic partnership with Tehran, investment in energy infrastructure is considered one of the important cooperation areas to integrate Iran into the BRI framework.

Therefore, the new Silk Road can provide a new framework for more extensive Chinese investments in the Iranian energy industry. Beijing offers Tehran a market for its energy exports and investment in energy infrastructure; Iran enables China to diversify its energy sources, so as not to be overly reliant on, for instance, Saudi Arabia or Russia.

According to the Energy Information Administration (EIA), Iran contains some of the world's largest proven deposits of oil and natural gas. Tehran deposits contain an estimated 157 billion barrels of crude oil and a further 1,193 trillion cubic feet of natural gas deposits, making those the fourth and second-largest deposits in the world, respectively. The abundance of energy reserves, Iran's relatively proximate geographic location to China and its geopolitical situation in the Middle East, make Tehran an attractive country with which to develop a relationship for the PRC's energy security.[46] Hence, the Islamic Republic is one of the key countries involved in the BRI framework, with considerable potential to attract Chinese investment and technology for the development of its energy infrastructure.

Tehran is one of the world's most important oil producers, and Beijing is the largest energy consumer in the world, and hence, one of the most important options to attract global resources required for promoting Iran's energy infrastructure development. The PRC is the most important buyer of Tehran oil and receives about one-third of Iranian oil exports. China's enormous demand for energy resources has led to its long-standing commercial and political ties with Iran.[47]

Furthermore, the Islamic Republic's geographical status enables it to connect the energy infrastructure of West Asia countries involved in the BRI. Tehran is the only country in the Middle East with the potential to meet part of Beijing's oil and gas needs through both land and sea. Currently, all Iranian oil exports to China are conducted by sea, but Central Asia and Pakistan are two potential land routes that could connect Iran's energy resources to the Chinese market. Tehran has also already connected parts of its energy infrastructure to some of the other important Silk Road countries; namely, Turkmenistan, Turkey, and Pakistan. Development of the ties between Tehran and these countries in the form of separate trilateral cooperation initiatives with the participation and investment of Chinese companies could be regarded as another source of potential in this area.[48]

Since Beijing is predicted to become the world's largest energy consumer by 2030, it is wasting no time in availing itself of Iran's energy resources. The PRC's demand for oil imports is expected to grow from 6 million barrels per day to 13 million by 2035, and Iran, ranked fourth in the world with proven oil reserves and second with reserves of natural gas, is considered a reliable supplier.[49] Conversely, Tehran will need massive investments in its energy sector in the future and considers China an important source of investment. In the next five years, Iran needs to attract $134 billion investment in the upstream oil sector and an additional $52 billion in its petrochemical industry. The National Iranian Oil Company currently has 515 projects as well as 88 mega-projects and 2000 sub-projects on its agenda.[50]

In the JCPOA era, and, as a result of the lifting of most of the international sanctions against Iran, the situation had gradually improved for energy cooperation between the two countries. In the year since the finalization of the nuclear deal, there was an increase in the activities of Chinese oil and gas companies in Iran. In February 2017, the two countries signed a $3 billion contract to upgrade the Abadan oil refinery capacity, the largest refinery in Iran. Sinopec Company provided the initial $1.2 billion in finance for the first phase of the project. The deal called for improving the quality of oil byproducts by upgrading the refinery's production process, and expected to be completed in four years.[51]

In December 2018, Sinopec offered a $3 billion deal to further develop the Yadavaran oil field in south-west Iran, replacing the British-Dutch oil giant, Royal Dutch Shell, which concluded that operations in Iran were too risky and to avoid repercussions in its US market activities. The Yadavaran is one of the world's biggest undeveloped oilfields with reserves of 31 billion barrels of light and heavy crude oil. The deal would double production at the field to 180,000 barrels a day within six months. Sinopec believes that the offer would not violate a US ban on signing new development deals with Iran, as its proposal for further development of Yadavaran is part of an existing contract to operate the field.[52]

In November 2016, China National Petroleum Corporation (CNPC) brought online the first phase of North Azadegan with 75,000 barrels per day (bpd) of output. The field on the border with Iraq is estimated to contain 5.7 billion barrels of crude reserves. In March 2017, former managing director of the National Iranian Oil Company (NIOC), Ali Kardor, said the second phase of North Azadegan was being considered for development under a new contract model, and CNPC was interested.[53]

In the post-JCPOA era, the most important Chinese investment in the Iranian energy sector was made, when a $4.879 billion contract was signed between the National Iranian Oil Company, and a consortium consisted of Total (a French multinational integrated oil and gas company), CNPC, and Iran's Petropars, for the development of phase 11 of South Pars Gas Field, the world's largest gas field. The project will have a production capacity of 400,000 bpd. The contract provisioned a 50.1 percent and a 30 percent share for Total and CNPC, respectively, with Petropars enjoying the remaining 19 percent.[54] However, shortly after the US withdrawal from the JCPOA, Total announced its continuing in the project would depend on whether it could secure a sanctions waiver from Washington. As a result, the Iranian oil ministry announced that Total's share in the contract would be handed over to CNPC.[55]

President Trump's decision to withdraw from the JCPOA and to reimpose sanctions includes measures meant to punish any international company that does business with Iran's oil sector. The idea, according to Secretary of State Mike Pompeo, is to eventually reduce Iranian oil exports to zero. Just a few days before the re-imposition of secondary sanctions in November, the PRC was among eight countries that received a Significant Reduction Exemption (SRE) from the US government which permitted the continued importation of Iranian oil, if the proceeds of Tehran's sales were exclusively used for the purchase of humanitarian goods, such as foodstuffs and medicine.[56]

The Chinese response to the new round of unilateral sanctions has been tepid and, to some extent, unsatisfactory. Beijing partially filled the vacuum left by European companies forced to abandon Iran, but suspended investments in the South Pars gas field and delayed many infrastructure projects. At the time the US sanctions were re-imposed, China was buying 650,000 barrels a day of Iran's crude, or 6.3 percent of total Chinese imports, which would put their worth at $ 15 billion. According to data, China's crude oil imports from Iran is 27.9 percent lower in the period January–March 2019 than in the same period a year ago.[57]

CNPC convinced the US administration that it needed to continue investing in the North Azadegan and Masjid-i-Suleiman (MIS) oilfields to recoup the billions of dollars spent under buy-back contracts signed years ago. In December 2018, however, CNPC decided to suspend its investment in Iran's South Pars natural gas project in response to US pressure and to minimize tensions amid trade negotiations between Beijing and Washington. South Pars is the world's largest gas field, and CNPC's investment freeze is a blow to Tehran's efforts to maintain financing for energy projects. Iran had 120 days to review CNPC's role in South Pars and decide whether to keep the Chinese firm as a dormant investor or cancel the deal, but so far, no decision has been made.[58]

According to Reuters, some 20 million barrels of Iranian oil sitting on China's shores in the northeast port of Dalian for the past six months now appears stranded as Washington hardens its stance on importing crude from Tehran. The Islamic Republic sent the oil to Dalian ahead of the reintroduction of US sanctions last November 2018, as it looked for alternative storage for a backlog of crude at home. The oil is being held in bonded storage tanks at the port, which means it has yet to clear Chinese customs. Despite a six-month waiver to the start of May that allowed China to continue some Iranian imports, shipping data shows little of this oil has been moved because the uncertainty over the terms of the waiver and independent refiners has made China unable to secure payment or insurance channels, while state refiners struggled to find vessels. The future of the crude, worth well over $1 billion at current prices, has become unclear.[59]

Chinese officials have publicly stated that they have no intention of following Washington's demands to stop importing Iranian oil completely, but also agreed to refrain from increasing its oil purchases from Iran. Chinese oil companies (e.g., Sinopec) have made arrangements to keep Iranian oil flowing after US sanctions come into force.[60] For example, they have switched to using Iranian tankers to deliver the oil, to sidestep sanctions and reduce their own risk.[61] Meanwhile, the re-imposition of US sanctions helped the PRC to secure deep discounts on Iranian oil, while selling Chinese goods to Tehran at inflated prices paid from the restricted Iranian oil funds sitting in escrow accounts at Chinese banks.[62]

China was a signatory to the 2015 deal, and expressed opposition to any unilateral sanctions against Iran. Nonetheless, the Chinese oil companies faced mounting pressure from Washington to comply with the new energy sanctions, or face sanctions themselves if they had not obtained US waivers by November 2018.[63] Chinese oil giants Sinopec and CNPC stopped loading Iranian oil in November 2018.[64] However, they resumed again after obtaining the US waiver which allows them to buy 360,000 barrels per day for 180 days. In any case, this is only half of what the Chinese were importing at the time the sanctions were announced.[65]

In the previous sanctions period from 2008 to 2016, Chinese businesses and companies significantly expanded their commercial presence in Iran, stepping in as Western companies exited the market.[66] In the face of US secondary sanctions, Iran's government had hopes that China would continue to purchase crude oil in high volumes and invest in energy development projects. However, the Bank of Kunlun, the state-owned bank at the key Chinese conduit for transactions with

Iran, decided in October 2018 to suspend most financial transactions with Iran. Even before the sanctions came into effect, the Bank of Kunlun had stopped handling euro-dominated payments from Teheran. The bank, a subsidiary of the CNPC, is the main channel for money flows between the two countries; in 2012 it had faced US sanctions for doing business with Iran and for transferring money to an Islamic Revolutionary Guard Corps (IRGC) linked group.[67]

Although the Bank of Kunlun resumed trade in January 2019, the bank announced a new policy that it would only service trade which was exempt from US secondary sanctions. This means to trade in food, medicine, and consumer goods, for which China is not Iran's leading source of imports. The Bank of Kunlun's move is consistent with the terms of the oil waiver, which requires Iran's earnings be paid into an escrow account and to be used exclusively for non-sanctioned bilateral trade.[68] Beijing will hold Iran's money, which can be used only to buy non-sanctioned goods inside China, another financial benefit for Chinese companies.

More important, while Europe has made extraordinary efforts to both assert its economic sovereignty and preserve the nuclear deal, even going so far as to establish a new state-owned trade financial intermediary, China has taken no commensurate effort to shield its trade from the long arm of American law. To be sure, it remains a mystery how the new circumstances in the aftermath of the US re-imposition of sanctions will impact China's role in Iran's petroleum sector. Nevertheless, it is possible that Chinese-Iranian oil trade could recover to a new steady state in 2019, and that Beijing could designate a new bank to facilitate non-oil exports. However, when the waivers come up for renewal in early May 2019, the Trump administration could make such a waiver contingent on China continuing to downsize its non-oil trade with Iran.

After the waivers ended in May 2019, the Trump administration demanded that the five nations that used the waivers would need to stop all imports of Iranian oil. In July 2019, the administration imposed economic sanctions on the Chinese state-owned Zhuhai Zhenrong oil trading company and its chief executive, Li Youmin, for buying Iranian oil in violation of an American ban. Zhuhai Zhenrong and Sinopec are the two main Chinese companies that import Iranian oil. This was the first time the Trump administration penalized a Chinese company and its executives for defying recent US sanctions on Iranian oil exports.[69]

However, since Iran is more important for China as an energy supplier than as an export market, China will likely sacrifice its exports to sustain oil imports. Seventy weeks after the US imposed sanctions on

Zhuhai Zhenrong oil trading company, China is still importing oil from Iran. According to official customs data, China imported 855,638 tons in June 2019, the equivalent of about 209,000 barrels a day. While that is less than in May and the lowest since mid-2010, the data adds to speculation that Beijing may risk running foul of US sanctions in order to secure crude supplies from Iran.[70]

While European oil companies have explored ways to circumvent US sanctions or seek waivers, the threat of sanctions is likely to scare away many foreign companies from doing business in Iran. This will leave a void that Chinese oil companies are likely to fill and gain a near monopoly on the Iranian energy sector. This can also cause Tehran to become more amenable to Chinese global initiatives, such as the Belt and the Road Initiative. However, while these moves follow the common pattern of Chinese foreign policy, most notably Beijing's willingness to take more significant risks and conduct business in shunned nations, they have wider implications for its relations with the US. Eventually, in the midst of the trade war with Washington, Beijing seems to lack the political will to contrast the effects of US sanctions by increasing the quantity and quality of its presence in the Iranian energy sector.[71]

Financial integration

Under China's comprehensive strategic partnership with Tehran, the formation and promotion of financial integration between the two countries is considered one of the essential cooperation areas to integrate Iran into the BRI framework. There are a number of measures for the realization of financial integration between the two countries: including deepening financial cooperation and building a stable currency system, establishing an investment and financing system and a credit information system in Asia, expanding the scope and scale of bilateral currency swaps between the two countries, and developing the bond market in Asia.[72]

China and Iran need to make joint efforts with others to establish the Asian Infrastructure Investment Bank (AIIB), and to conduct negotiations with parties to the Shanghai Cooperation Organization (SCO) financing institution, and financial institutions with good credit ratings. China and Iran also need to issue RMB-denominated bonds in China, and encourage qualified Chinese financial institutions and companies to issue bonds in both RMB and foreign currencies outside China, thereby encouraging use of funds collected in countries along the BRI.

Sino–Iranian financial cooperation is still at the initial stage. In June 2015, Iran signed the documents with China to join the AIIB, which were ratified only in January 2017 after a long delay.[73] The AIIB was planned to play a key role in financing the Iranian projects related to the BRI and facilitate foreign investment in the country.[74] However, Iran is still an observer state in the SCO and, thus, is not able to contribute to the creation of its financial institution. Beijing's refusal to swiftly incorporate Iran in the SCO can be explained by its concerns that Iranian membership would give the SCO an unambiguously anti-Western character.[75]

The CITIC investment group, a Chinese state-owned investment firm, has provided a $10 billion credit line for Iranian banks to finance water, energy, and transport projects. In addition to the credit line, the China Development Bank signed preliminary deals with Iran worth $15 billion for other infrastructure and production projects. The credit line will use euros and yuan to help bypass US sanctions that have continued despite the JCPOA. Since the lifting of sanctions at that time, Beijing opened two credit lines worth $4.2 billion to build high-speed railway lines linking Tehran with Mashhad and Isfahan.[76]

Another area of financial cooperation between the two countries is strengthening the internationalization of the RMB. Since 2012, Iran has accepted the Chinese currency for its crude oil exports to Beijing.[77] In the post-JCPOA era, this phenomenon could be amplified. Tehran may seek to diversify its currency reserves and reduce its reliance on US dollars. In August 2018, Tehran replaced the US dollar with China's yuan in its official currency rate reporting platform to reduce the country's vulnerability to US economic sanctions as well as the depreciation of the rial.[78]

Military ties

Under China's comprehensive strategic partnership with Iran, defense cooperation, including arms and technology trade and joint military drills, has become an increasingly significant part of integrating Tehran into the BRI framework. As the Chinese Defense Minister Wei Fenghe said, in September 2018, relations between the armed forces of China and Iran are developing positively. Beijing is ready to strengthen the strategic communication with Tehran, expand the spheres of cooperation, achieve new fruitful results of cooperation between the two armies, and thereby contribute to the development of a comprehensive strategic partnership of the two states.[79]

Military relations between the two countries date back to the early

1980s, but they went through a period of reduced cooperation as a result of international nuclear sanctions on Tehran. In the 1980s and early 1990s, Beijing provided Iran with arms, tactical ballistic missiles and anti-ship cruise missiles in its fight against Iraq. China has facilitated Iran's military modernization, even being suspected of transferring technology and equipment to Tehran via North Korea. Both countries developed significant arms sector cooperation, with Beijing supplying Iran with advanced fighter aircraft, tanks, radars, cruise missiles, fast-attack patrol craft, and other weapons. The US has sanctioned several Chinese entities for allegedly assisting Iran's missile, nuclear, and conventional weapons program.[80]

Chinese military cooperation with Tehran declined in the 2000s, coinciding with international concern over Iran's evolving nuclear program and the imposition of UN sanctions. Resolutions adopted in the United Nations Security Council (UNSC) – with Beijing's support – prohibited cooperation with Iran's nuclear and ballistic missile industries and were expanded in 2010 with a resolution imposing an embargo on exports of major conventional weapons to Iran. These included tanks, large-caliber artillery systems, combat aircraft, certain naval ships, and missiles with a maximum range of at least 25 kilometers.[81]

In the post-JCPOA era, the PRC was once again poised to resume its arms exports to Iran according to UN Security Council procedures. The JCPOA retained the UN arms and missiles embargoes for five and eight years respectively, although China could attempt to secure waivers as a permanent member of the Security Council.[82] In November 2016, Chinese defense minister Chang Wanquan concluded a three-day trip to Tehran, the latest in a series of high-ranking bilateral military exchanges over the past two years, and called the latest meetings a "turning point" in the strategic partnership. Both sides signed an agreement pledging closer military cooperation in a number of areas including military training and counterterrorism operations, and they pledged to hold joint military exercises in the near future.[83]

According to UN Security Council approval, Beijing could provide Iran's navy with a wide range of naval equipment, including frigates, submarines, and missiles. For instance, China could transfer advanced cruise missiles or technical expertise that could enable Iran to improve its domestic production of anti-ship or land-attack cruise missiles.[84] The PRC could also enhance its cooperation with Tehran in areas such as unmanned aircraft systems, space, or counter-space systems, missile defense components, or electronic warfare capabilities. In October

2015, Iranian electronic defense firm SaIran signed an agreement with Chinese firms to begin using their BeiDou-2 satellite navigation system for military purposes. The system's military-grade signals are more accurate than commercially available GPS services, so they could significantly improve Iran's use of satellite navigation in its missiles, UAVs, and other hardware. In land warfare, Beijing could allow Tehran to examine, purchase, or even assemble modern Chinese tank designs or armored personnel carriers.[85]

The military ties between the two countries also include joint naval drills. In September 2014, Beijing conducted joint naval exercises with Tehran when two Chinese warships docked at Iran's Bandar Abbas port to take part in joint naval exercises in the Persian Gulf and an Iranian admiral was given tours of a Chinese submarine and warships.[86] Since 2014, Chinese military cooperation with Iran has deepened, including a joint naval exercise in the Strait of Hormuz in June 2017. According to a Tehran news agency, Iran's navy conducted a joint exercise with a Chinese fleet near the strategic Strait of Hormuz in the Persian Gulf. The drill included an Iranian warship as well as two Chinese warships, a logistics ship, and a Chinese helicopter.[87]

Beijing is one of Iran's main suppliers of advanced weaponry, with some $316 million worth of weaponry exported to Tehran between 2007 and 2016. Some of the naval equipment China has sold includes tactical ballistic and anti-ship cruise missiles, advanced anti-ship mines, and Houdong fast-attack boats.[88] According to Commander of the Iranian Navy Rear Admiral Hossein Khanzadi, there are very good capacities for military cooperation between the navies of the two countries, and Iran wants to promote exchanges with the Chinese navy in various areas, including the development of military cooperation at sea, educational ties and joint technical activities.[89]

Another possible collaboration between the two countries can exist in the civil nuclear industry. After the nuclear deal, China saw Iran as a major market for cooperation on peaceful nuclear energy in the Middle East. Under the JCPOA, China is allowed to help Iran develop its civil nuclear program for peaceful purposes. Ever since the Iranian nuclear deal was secured, China vied to grab an opportunity for its own civil nuclear sectors in the Iranian nuclear energy market. The China–Iran cooperation in the nuclear field on its peaceful use is likely to grow from strength to strength. China views the Iran civil nuclear industry as a great scope for an investment opportunity.[90]

From the mid-1980s to the late 1990s, Beijing played a part in Iran's nuclear program. According to a RAND study, China has assisted in the development of Tehran's nuclear program by training Iranian nuclear engineers and providing various types of critical nuclear technology and machinery. It also assisted in uranium exploration and mining, and helped Tehran master the uses of lasers for uranium enrichment. It is not clear whether Chinese aid was provided with the specific aim of helping Iran to develop a nuclear weapons capability, but the effect has been to assist Iran's acquisition of such capabilities.[91] By the time the controversy over Iran's undeclared facilities broke out in 2002, however, Beijing had distanced itself from the program.

In April 2017, after several rounds of talks over the past year, China National Nuclear Corporation (CNNC) and Iran had signed the first commercial contract for the reconstruction of Iran's Arak heavy water reactor. The core of the reactor was removed as part of an international agreement limiting Iran's nuclear program in return for the lifting of economic sanctions. The contract is mainly related to the design concept of the transformation of the Arak reactor and some preliminary design-related consulting services. Under the contract, the Chinese company was to complete the design concept for the renovation of the Arak reactor within the next eight months.[92] Nevertheless, if Washington refuses to extend or provide a new waiver and applies new sanctions, then Chinese cooperation with Iran on civil nuclear projects and the Arak heavy water reactor agreement will be in jeopardy. China government and state-owned enterprises fear possible US sanctions if they continue their cooperation with Iran, and therefore have reduced the speed of civil nuclear cooperation despite their commitment.[93]

Culture and Tourism

China's comprehensive strategic partnership with Iran, enabling the people of the two countries to bond along the Silk Road, is vital to integrate Tehran into the BRI framework. The promotion of extensive cultural and academic exchanges win public support for deepening bilateral and multilateral cooperation, as well as providing scholarships, holding annual cultural events, increasing cooperation in science and technology, and establishing joint laboratory or research centers and international technology transfer centers.[94]

Although the two countries have many common cultural and historical features, the number of people-to-people interactions between them is still minimal. One example is the Confucius Institute as the symbol of China's cultural interactions with other countries. Currently, there are 548 Confucius Institutes around the world, 1,193 primary and high-school Confucius Classrooms and 5,665 teaching sites established in 154 countries and regions. More broadly, in 54 countries involved in the Belt and Road Initiative, there are 153 Confucius Institutes and 149 primary and high-school Confucius Classrooms, but although one of these branches has been established in the University of Tehran, it still does not offer any cultural or educational activities.[95]

Moreover, there are no reliable statistics on the number of fellowships granted by the Chinese Government to Iranian students or the exact number of Chinese students in Iran. Furthermore, the two countries still do not have any plans to hold regular celebrations for each other's cultural years. In the field of science and technology, during President Xi Jinping's visit to Tehran in early 2016, the two sides reached an MoU on establishing technology parks, but the plan is yet to be realized.[96] Both sides also signed several agreements in many areas such as cultural exchange and tourism.

In the tourism sector, the relationship between the two countries is still in its infancy. Iran with four seasons, four thousand years of civilization and numerous historical and cultural monuments, could be a unique destination for Chinese tourists. There are only seven flights per week between Iran and China. In 2017, of the 130 million Chinese tourists who traveled around the world, only 95,000 chose Iran as their destination.[97] Tehran is aiming to increase the number of Chinese tourists to at least 2.5 million visitors, by improving its tourism infrastructures and services. This would include opening more Chinese restaurants, providing translation services, and facilitating visa applications. Meanwhile, the number of direct flights between China and Iran will also be increased.[98]

To this end, China's Belt and Road Initiative could afford both nations an opportunity to enhance the tourism industry. The new Silk Road could also be a tourism route linking Iranian and Chinese nations. According to data Wu Yi obtained from the airlines and the embassy, before 2015 the number of Chinese tourists to Iran was less than 50,000 every year. However, with the lifting of the sanctions on Iran in 2016, the number of Chinese tourists to Iran doubled itself, of which 60 to 70 percent were business tourists.[99] Thus, in this sphere also there is considerable potential for cooperation and interaction between the two countries, but in reality there is still a long way to go. Although Iran has managed to become a safe destination for the Chinese since 2011, it has not caused it be among China's top 20 destinations.[100]

Summary

Iran–China relations are wide-ranging and trace back to the ancient Silk Road. They were inextricably interwoven in the economic, political and cultural spheres. China's interest in Iran goes beyond its energy resources. It has a keen interest in Iran's geostrategic location, bordering both the Caspian Sea and the Persian Gulf. The location enables China to carry out the realization of the new Silk Road trade route. Hence, the Islamic Republic is expected to be one of the main beneficiaries of China's Belt and Road Initiative.

Beijing's energy dependence and Belt and Road Initiative have made Tehran an increasingly attractive partner. Beijing remains involved in building up Iran's infrastructure, including electricity, dams, cement plants, steel mills, shipbuilding, motorways, and airports. Defense cooperation, including arms and technology trade and joint military drills, has become an increasingly significant part of Iran's relationship with China in the Persian Gulf. Despite China and Iran having established a formal comprehensive strategic partnership, the PRC's economic, political, and strategic interests are too complex and self-contradictory to permit a close alignment with Iran.

In the post-JCPOA era, Beijing seemed likely to remain Iran's top economic partner in the coming years. However, overestimating the Sino–Iranian partnership risks disappointment. The US anti-Iranian policy and the sanctions that accompany it, and the geopolitical rivalry between Iran and Saudi Arabia, could prevent the emergence of a more solid partnership. For these reasons, the potential of Iran to fully integrate within the BRI framework is not high. Nevertheless, the new Silk Road trade route will be the key factor shaping Tehran-Beijing relations in the coming years. In the short to medium term, the Islamic Republic still finds in China an irreplaceable source of economic and political aid.

The future Sino–Iranian comprehensive strategic partnership and their cooperation to realization of the Belt and Road Initiative will likely be influenced by two predominant factors. The first, Tehran's tense relations with the Gulf countries especially Iranian-Saudi competition and, more broadly, Sunni-Shi'i rivalry. The PRC's balancing act between Iran and Saudi Arabia will be much more difficult to sustain in the future. This situation would likely slow down BRI's progress, create tensions with the Gulf countries, and face Beijing with difficult choices about how to navigate Saudi–Iran competition.

The second factor is linked to tensions in the Iran–US relations in a post-JCPOA era and the possibility of confrontation with Washington.

The United States is likely to perceive the PRC's deepening engagement with Iran as a major challenge to its sanctions on Tehran and a factor enabling the Islamic Republic to feel more secure and, consequently, pursue a more expansionist policy in the Middle East. As a result, Tehran would likely reemerge as an important strategic issue in US–Beijing relations, constraining China's freedom of action in West Asia and further increasing the strategic mistrust between the two global powers. Against this backdrop, Washington is likely to put pressure on Saudi Arabia and its other regional allies to limit their engagement with China, creating obstacles to BRI's development and to China–Saudi relations.

3
United Arab Emirates

China–UAE relations are one of the most important bilateral axes in the Persian Gulf region. Over the past years, a new era of closer political and economic ties has begun to develop between the two countries. This chapter examines what lies behind the China–UAE comprehensive strategic partnership and the synergy between the Belt and Road Initiative and UAE Vision 2021 in order to understand the extent of economic engagement and bilateral relationship between the two nations. The ties range from broadening trade, through energy investments, building and acquisitions activities in infrastructure and logistics, financial services, military ties, tourism and cultural cooperation to realizing the Belt and Road Initiative. The mutually beneficial arrangement enables China to expand its Middle East footprint while providing opportunities for UAE to profit from partnerships.

The PRC enjoys highly fruitful cooperation with the United Arab Emirates (UAE), of all the Middle East countries, and in July 2018 bilateral relations were elevated to a comprehensive strategic partnership, Beijing's highest level in its hierarchy of diplomatic relations. According to China–UAE comprehensive strategic partnership, they will strengthen their in-depth bilateral cooperation in various fields, and promote the continuous development of bilateral ties on higher levels, in broader areas and at greater depths.[1] Given China's rise as an economic and political power in the Middle East, the ties with the UAE are expected to become stronger and flourish in the years to come.

The BRI was put forward in October 2013 by Chinese President Xi Jinping. The $1 trillion project seeks to connect Beijing to the global market by linking Asia and Europe via a set of land and maritime trade routes. The concept took form over several years and has now become a cornerstone of President Xi's foreign policy. The UAE is in a unique strategic geographic location, as the gateway between East and West, and its natural resources make the country an ideal regional hub of trade, finance, energy, logistics, and a tourist destination as well as a commercial partner for leading Chinese enterprises to access some of the fastest-growing markets in Central, South, and Southeast Asia; Europe; the Middle East; Africa and beyond. More importantly, the Emirates can play a pivotal role in helping China realize its BRI.

This chapter examines what lies behind the China–UAE comprehensive strategic partnership and the synergy between the Belt and Road Initiative and UAE Vision 2021 in order to understand the extent of economic engagement and bilateral relationship between the two nations. As Sheikh Mohammed bin Rashid Al Maktoum, ruler of Dubai, said in a tweet, "We have many areas of political and economic agreement and a solid base of projects in the energy, technology and infrastructure sectors. More importantly, we have a strong political will to start a greater phase of cooperation and integration."[2]

The main argument to be presented is that Beijing's comprehensive strategic partnership framework with the UAE is based on shared or mutual complementary economic interests. The Emirates' strategic geographic location makes the country a marketplace of great potential and influence in the entire MENA region that is essential for realization of the BRI. The mutually beneficial arrangement of China's investments and UAE's unique strategic geographic location on global trade routes enables China to expand its Middle East footprint while providing opportunities for the UAE to profit from the partnership and promote its vision 2021.

UAE Vision 2021

In 2010, Sheikh Mohammed bin Rashid Al Maktoum, Vice President and Prime Minister of the UAE and Ruler of Dubai, launched the 'UAE Vision 2021'. The Vision aims to make the UAE one of the best countries in the world by the year 2021 when the nation celebrates the Golden Jubilee of its formation as a federation. In order to translate the ruler's vision into reality, its pillars have been mapped into six national priorities, which represent the key focus sectors of government action in the coming years. First, united in responsibility, an ambitious and confident nation grounded in its heritage. Second, united in destiny, a strong union bonded by a common destiny. Third, united in knowledge, a competitive economy driven by knowledgeable and innovative Emiratis. Fourth, united in prosperity, a nurturing and sustainable environment for quality living. Fifth, well-rounded lifestyles, the UAE will nurture a high quality of life built on world-class public infrastructure, government services, and a rich recreational environment. Final, a well-preserved natural environment: As a leader of the green revolution, the UAE is conscious of its responsibility to safeguard nature and mitigate the effects of climate change on its habitat and ecosystems in order to ensure that future generations inherit an environmentally sustainable world.[3]

UAE and the Belt and Road Initiative

The PRC's comprehensive strategic partnership with the Emirates includes seven major areas for cooperation within the Belt and Road Initiative. These areas are policy coordination, connectivity, trade and investments, energy cooperation, financial integration, military ties, and culture and tourism. However, each country views the Belt and Road Initiative framework and reacts to it according to its perspective and the consequences for its own national interests and international status. Therefore, the two countries have very different attitudes regarding how to realize the vision.[4]

The UAE Vision 2021 and China's Belt and Road vision have converged on a common economic development path, and their synergetic strategy will bring new opportunities for both sides. As Chinese President Xi said in his visit in Abu Dhabi, the two countries need to translate the China–UAE comprehensive strategic partnership into concrete achievements, cement political mutual trust, continue to take care of each other's core interests and major concerns, and support each other's pursuit of the development path that suits themselves.[5]

Policy coordination

As part of China's comprehensive strategic partnership with UAE, promoting political cooperation between countries, creating mechanisms for dialogue and consensus-building on global and regional issues, developing shared interests, deepening political trust and reaching a new consensus on cooperation are important to integrate the UAE Vision 2021 into the Belt and Road Initiative framework.[6]

In 1984, China and the UAE first established diplomatic ties, and in 2012, the Emirates was the first Gulf country to forge a strategic partnership with PRC.[7] Over the past 34 years, UAE has enjoyed prosperous financial cooperation with China, and the bilateral economic and commerce relations between the two countries is expected to create further opportunities for cooperation. As Chinese ambassador to the UAE, Ni Jian, said, "UAE enjoys the most fruitful cooperation with China among all Middle East countries and the two nations are keen to take these ties to a new level. At present, the China–UAE relationship is at its best. It is an exemplary model of mutual respect, friendship, and win-win cooperation."[8]

In July 2018 during his first, historic state visit to UAE, the Chinese President Xi Jinping said that the establishment of a comprehensive strategic partnership would be conducive to deepening strategic mutual trust and raising the level of mutually beneficial cooperation. China and the UAE are natural partners for jointly building the Belt and Road. China regards the UAE as a key pivot in implementing the Belt and Road Initiative. The two sides need to create stronger links between their development strategies, strengthen communications on industrial policies and plan and manage well the flagship projects within the framework of the Belt and Road Initiative, to boost the economic development of the Middle East region and the Gulf region.[9]

In April 2019, Sheikh Mohammed bin Rashid Al Maktoum, Vice President and Prime Minister of the UAE and Ruler of Dubai, met Chinese President Xi Jinping in Beijing. The meeting was held on the sidelines of the Second Belt and Road Conference for International Cooperation. According to Sheikh Mohammed, collaboration with China serves the future strategic vision of the UAE and supports the objectives of both countries to accelerate development. He stated that the partnership supports the development efforts of both countries and creates new growth opportunities. As noted in the media, the strong mutual will to expand collaboration provides a strong basis for the realization of our future joint strategic objectives.[10]

Connectivity

Under China's comprehensive strategic partnership with the Emirates, facilitation of connectivity is one of the crucial ways to integrate the UAE Vision 2021 into the Belt and Road Initiative framework. The UAE should attempt to optimize its infrastructural connections and also to adapt its technical systems to those of the other countries in the Belt and Road Initiative framework. This would lead Beijing–UAE to jointly contribute to the development of international transport maritime and overland routes, and the creation of an infrastructural network that could gradually connect all the regions in Asia and also specific points in Asia, Africa, and Europe. In addition, there should be serious attempts to create low-carbon and green infrastructure.[11]

Generally, the Gulf countries, the UAE in particular, are essential for Beijing's Belt and Road initiative in order to create a network of manufacturing and logistics centers in Central Asia and Europe.[12] The Persian Gulf region occupies a key position in PRC's BRI. Given that the Persian Gulf is at the crossroads of Europe, Africa, and Asia, Chinese state-owned shipping and logistics companies have already started ramping up infrastructure investments in Gulf ports.[13]

Given its unique geographic location, as the gateway between East and West, the UAE can play a pivotal role in helping realize the Belt and Road vision. The Emirates can provide many facilities in land, air, and sea logistical support throughout the Middle East for the Chinese venture, which will link both sea and land to markets in Asia and Europe, thus taking bilateral and regional cooperation to new heights. China–UAE connectivity cooperation extends to many areas ranging from an industrial and trade zone, container terminals/ports, and logistics centers as part of the cooperation to realize the Belt and Road vision. As the third largest re-export hub in the world after Singapore and Hong Kong, Dubai, with Jebel Ali Free Zone (JAFZA), the world's largest free zone, and Jebel Ali port for re-export, is the site of approximately 60 percent of China's pass-through trade.[14]

Accordingly, the Dubai International Financial Centre (DIFC) has signed an MoU with China Everbright Group to collaborate in BRI-related opportunities. Abu Dhabi Global Market (ADGM) approved the Industrial Capacity Co-operation Financial Group Limited (ICCFG), the first Chinese state-owned financial services firm to be established in the financial center to provide strategic investment and financial support to Chinese enterprises as part of the BRI project. DP World also signed an agreement with the Zhejiang China Commodities City Group (ZCCCG) to jointly construct a new traders market at JAFZA in Dubai to provide further impetus to China's BRI.[15]

Trade zones

In July 2018, the UAE's state-owned DP World, which operates in 40 countries, announced an agreement with ZCCCG to jointly construct a new traders market at its flagship JAFZA. The new facility will cover three square kilometers at the Jebel Ali site, which is the Middle East's largest trade zone.[16] The new traders market in Dubai will host a vast range of goods from food and cosmetics to building materials and technology. However, DP World did not announce the value of the deal or provide a timeframe for its construction. The new traders market will be composed of clusters of traders from all over the world (divided by sector) and will enable Chinese manufacturers to benefit from Dubai's geostrategic location by enabling trade with other places in the GCC, the Middle East, and Indian Subcontinent.[17]

The ICCFG, which is owned by East China's Jiangsu provincial government, will be set up in the Abu-Dhabi's financial hub to offer lending facilities (investment and financial support) to Chinese enterprises operating in the Emirates' industrial zone. This will be the first Chinese financial services firm in the UAE bank free zone ADGM. According to Wang Bin, chairman of China Jiangsu International, about $2 billion of investment will be managed by this financial services platform to support the Chinese companies in the demonstration park.[18]

In September 2017, Dubai Multi Commodities Centre (DMCC), the biggest free trade zone in UAE, signed an MoU with Xi'an International Trade & Logistics Park in central China's Shaanxi Province at the Xi'an Dubai Free Trade Zone Economic Cooperation Conference. The purpose of the MoU is to open doors for investors in both nations and to expand into new markets as well as organizing joint trade missions and economic delegations.[19] In April 2018, Abu Dhabi Ports and the Jiangsu Provincial Overseas Cooperation and Investment Company Limited (JOCIC) announced that 15 Chinese companies had signed agreements to invest in Khalifa Port Free Trade Zone (KPFTZ), the largest free zone in the Middle East, totaling $1 billion in value. Under the terms of the investment cooperation agreement, China–UAE Industrial Capacity Cooperation (Jiangsu) Construction Management Co. would occupy and develop approximately 2.2 sq km of the free trade zone for companies from the Chinese province of Jiangsu. The China–UAE Industrial Capacity Cooperation Industrial Park is part of the KPFTZ and is expandable to reach 12.2 sq km.[20]

In July 2018, DMCC signed an MoU with China Council for the Promotion of International Trade (CCPIT) to strengthen the strong and longstanding economic ties between Dubai and China. The MoU highlights Dubai's geostrategic position as a global gateway and the ideal partner for leading Chinese companies to access some of the fastest-growing markets in Central, South and Southeast Asia, Europe, the Middle East, Africa, and beyond. The MoU with DMCC will promote significant commercial opportunities available to Chinese enterprises in Dubai.[21]

Logistic centers and container terminals

In June 2018, the Emirates Airline SkyCargo, Dubai's flagship carrier, signed an MoU with Cainiao Smart Logistics Network, the logistics arm of Alibaba, to jointly facilitate the delivery of cross-border parcels. Under the MoU, Cainiao and SkyCargo will work closely to manage e-commerce shipments in the Middle East and neighboring regions via Dubai, the biggest trade and logistics hub in the region. The SkyCargo's network spread, the frequent flights from China and the state-of-the-art hub facilities as well as Dubai's geostrategic location, will contribute significantly to Cainiao's operations in the Middle East and beyond.[22]

In September 2016, COSCO Shipping won a 35-year concession with a five- year option to build and operate a new container terminal at Khalifa Industrial Zone Abu Dhabi (KIZAD). This investment is valued at $738 million and will double the container-handling capacity of Khalifa port. COSCO's Khalifa Port Container Terminal 2 (KPCT 2) will span approximately 70 hectares with three berths and will add 2.4 million TEUs (twenty-foot equivalent units) a year to Khalifa Port's existing capacity of 2.5 million TEUs once the first two phases of the development are completed. The first 800 meters of the quay and the corresponding yard were earmarked to be operational in the first half of 2018 with the additional 400 meters to come on stream in 2020. In July 2017, a consortium of five Chinese companies from Jiangsu province invested $300 million in building diverse industries in KIZAD. This investment is for a 50-year lease on a 2.2 sq km property in the KIZAD.[23]

Ports

The UAE is home to the world's busiest port outside of Asia and a key connection point for PRC's Maritime Silk Road Initiative (MSRI), which is vital as investment flows from China through the Emirates to the rest of the world. UAE's position as a gateway to Africa, the Middle East, and Europe, with its financing capabilities and professional services, along with multi-national and local companies that are capable of running large infrastructure projects, makes this a huge opportunity for Chinese companies.

The PRC seeks to integrate the UAE ports into China's MSRI to boost investment and create a new platform for multilateral economic cooperation as part of the comprehensive strategic partnership between both nations. The Middle East, in general, and the Emirates, in particular, play an essential and crucial part of China's MSRI. Chinese companies are increasingly seizing opportunities in the Gulf as Beijing seeks to expand overseas with their ambitious Belt and Road initiative.[24]

Chinese companies chose Khalifa Port, the flagship of Abu Dhabi Ports, as the next stop on China's 21st Century Maritime Silk Road. This investment in the Khalifa Free Trade Zone and Khalifa Port is all part of the MSRI execution, which seeks to establish an enhanced and interconnected network of Chinese-run ports and manufacturing zones along the route from the east coast of China to Europe. The Chinese companies operating in the Emirates are different from other foreign shipping companies that operate in the UAE's ports since often they do not only come in and open a new port but also invest in an adjoining free trade/special economic zone and other development initiatives. Moreover, Chinese investments in the Emirates can serve as catalysts for other projects to grow up around them (i.e., factories need local suppliers, workers, etc.).

In July 2017, a consortium of five Chinese companies from Jiangsu province signed a $300 million deal with the UAE's Abu Dhabi Ports to develop a manufacturing operation in the free trade zone of Khalifa Port (KIZAD).[25] In December 2018, COSCO Shipping Ports (CSP), a subsidiary of China COSCO Shipping, and Abu Dhabi Ports inaugurated the CSP Abu Dhabi Container Terminal at Khalifa Port (the deep-water, semi-automated container terminal includes the largest container freight station in the Middle East, covering 275,000 meters), positioning Abu Dhabi as the regional hub for COSCO's global network of 36 ports and further connecting the Emirate to the major trade hubs along the BRI. The new terminal in Khalifa Port is the first international green-field subsidiary of CSP that invested $299 million in capital expenditure on construction and machinery at the terminal. CSP and Abu Dhabi Terminals (ADT) also signed an MoU to increase collaboration between the two facilities.[26]

Hence, Beijing's efforts to establish a comprehensive strategic partnership with the UAE must be seen within the wider context of its ambitious Belt and Road initiative, which focuses on connectivity and cooperation stretching from China across Eurasia. As President Xi Jinping said during his successful visit to the UAE, China and the UAE are natural partners for jointly building the Belt and Road. Beijing regards the UAE as a key pivot in implementing the Belt and Road Initiative.[27]

Trade and investments

According to PRC's comprehensive strategic partnership with the Emirates, the aim is to mitigate as much as possible the barriers to free trade, investment, industrial cooperation, and technical and engineering services in order to facilitate the integration of UAE Vision 2021 within the Belt and Road Initiative framework. Both countries should take a series of measures, such as expanding free-trade zones, improving trade structures, seeking new potential areas for trade and improving the trade balance, devising new initiatives for the promotion of conventional forms of trade, developing trans-border electronic trade and other advanced models of business, creating a system for supporting trade in services to strengthen and expand conventional trade, increasing customs cooperation, and regularly sharing information in these areas.[28]

Both countries are working to increase the bilateral trade volume as a part of their comprehensive strategic partnership. Since formal diplomatic relations between China and the UAE were established in 1984, bilateral trade between the two countries has grown from $63 million to $52.6 billion in 2017 (more than 800-fold), compared to $46.3 billion in the previous year.[29] According to China Customs Statistics (export–import), China's trade volume with UAE stood at $45.8 billion in 2018, and the Emirates has become China's second largest trade partner in the Middle East.[30] According to the UAE International Investors Council, the annual trade volume between China and the Emirates is forecast to grow to $70 billion by 2020 as the Asian country tops a list of targets for UAE investors.[31]

In April 2019, China signed $3.4 billion worth of new deals as part of China's Belt and Road Initiative. The latest agreement is expected to boost an existing $53 billion worth of bilateral trade to $70 billion next year. As part of the new deals, the two countries launched several new investments including the development of a 60 million square feet station at the new Silk Road in Dubai for Expo 2020. The first agreement was signed with the Chinese company Yiwu, which will invest $2.4 billion in the project while the second agreement was signed with the China–Arab Investment Fund, which will invest $1 billion to implement a 'vegetable basket' project in Dubai. These agreements will position Dubai well in the One Belt, One Road project where the emirate will be a major supply link to the global initiative and play an important role in international trade by further developing its logistics and shipping sectors.[32]

Beijing is the UAE's second largest trading partner and largest source of imports in the Arab region. According to Ali Obaid Al Dhaheri, the UAE Ambassador to the People's Republic of China, about 60 percent of the Chinese trade is re-exported through the UAE's ports to the MENA as well as the broader African continent. China deems the Emirates the first transit gateway to the MENA region due to its international stature and the facilities provided to investors in all fields,[33] with Dubai's Jebel Ali Free Zone being China's trade strategic gateway to the Middle East and Africa.[34]

The UAE's trade with the PRC accounted for nearly 30 percent of total Chinese exports to Arab countries and about 22 percent of total Arab-China trade, which amounted to $200 billion in 2018.[35] The Emirates has more than 4,000 registered Chinese companies operating in various sectors, including wholesale, financial, insurance, and real estate. There are more than 300 trade agencies, 817 Chinese investors, 5,000 trademarks, and 15 corporations, while between 200,000 and 300,000 Chinese residents are active on the Abu Dhabi and Dubai stock markets.[36] This figure places the UAE at the top of the list of Arab countries in terms of ties with China in addition to the fact that a significant proportion of Beijing's trade with the Arab world is passing through the country's ports as re-exports.

Exchange visits also strengthen a unique trade relationship, as manifested in Chinese President Xi Jinping's state visit to the UAE in July 2018, when the two countries signed 13 agreements and MoUs to strengthen strategic partnerships and bilateral cooperation across various sectors. The Agreements include approval for the Industrial Capacity Co-Operation Financial Group (ICCGC), the first Chinese state-owned financial services firm, to set up a financial center in Abu Dhabi Global Market, while the Abu Dhabi National Oil Company and the China National Petroleum Corporation (CNPC) agreed to explore joint business opportunities.[37]

The trade between China and the UAE is forecast to grow in the coming years. Beijing sees the Emirates as a gateway to access untapped consumer markets and lucrative investment opportunities in the Gulf region. As Chinese President Xi Jinping said, "The UAE is a friendly country and shares our dream, and so the Emirates has become a vital bridge between China and the Arab states."[38] In parallel, the UAE has been active in the PRC's economy, and hundreds of its companies are currently operating in China across various sectors including trade and industry, renewable energy, health, and financial services.[39] UAE enterprises and businesses have some 650 projects in China, such as UAE Stock Exchange and Dubai Pearl Project that are working hard to increase their foothold in China and to attract investors.[40]

In May 2019, Chinese manufacturing major East Hope Group said it is working with KIZAD on the feasibility of setting up development projects worth over $10 billion at Abu Dhabi's industrial hub. Under this agreement, both entities will look into a possible 15-year, three-phase plan to develop 7.6 sq km of land at KIZAD. In the first phase, East Hope would develop an alumina facility, while the second phase would include a red mud research center and recycling project. The final phase of the project would see large-scale upstream and down-stream non-ferrous metal processing facilities, it stated. As part of the agreement, KIZAD would support East Hope Group across all areas as it investigates setting up in Abu Dhabi, including ensuring the best utility prices, acquiring the land, creating a masterplan and handling the import of raw materials through Khalifa Port, and storage. The agreement also includes exploring options for the sustainable genera-tion of energy and a sustainability program to preserve the environment, including a research center.[41]

Moreover, several major Chinese companies outside the financial sector have also begun to get access to untapped consumer markets and lucrative investment opportunities in the UAE. Between 2011 and 2017 about 35 mutual trade cooperation agreements were signed during 120 visits exchanged by officials from the two countries.[42] For example, Chinese companies, including Foton, Cherry, Dongfeng, and GAC Motors, entered the UAE's automobile sector. Chinese car sales are predicted to increase 100 percent each year in the Emirates, and their market share is expected to reach double digits by 2020.[43]

In December 2017, Dubai Food Park (DFP) signed a $367 million investment agreement with Ningxia Forward Fund Management Company to build a China–UAE Food Industrial cluster in Dubai. The project will comprise six major components: meal processing, pack-aged food processing, cold chain storage, production of food packages, e-commerce and commodities exhibition, and bio-safety disposal of wastewater and wastes. The partnership marks a step forward to strengthen bilateral relations at various levels, particularly trade and economic relations between the UAE and China. The project is expected to consolidate China's stake in the Middle East food industry and further expand bilateral relations.[44]

In April 2019, on the sidelines of Annual Investment Meeting (AIM) in Dubai, the Undersecretary for Foreign Trade of the UAE Ministry of Economy Abdulla Al Saleh said that the UAE is set to play a big role in China's Belt and Road Initiative. Both countries have a strategic partnership to promote scientific research and renewable energy and water, and this cooperation is set to expand the mutual trade between the UAE and China.[45]

Financial integration

Under China's comprehensive strategic partnership with the Emirates, the formation and promotion of financial integration between the two countries is considered one of the essential cooperation areas to integrate UAE Vision 2021 into the BRI framework. There are a number of measures for the realization of financial integration between the two countries: including deepening financial cooperation and building a stable currency system, establishing an investment and financing system and a credit information system in Asia, expanding the scope and scale of bilateral currency swaps between the two countries, developing the bond market in Asia. In addition, making joint efforts to establish the Asian Infrastructure Investment Bank (AIIB), and financial institutions with good credit ratings to issue RMB-denominated bonds in China, thereby encouraging qualified Chinese financial institutions and companies to issue bonds in both RMB and foreign currencies outside China and to use the funds thus collected in countries along the BRI.[46]

In June 2015, the UAE signed the Articles of Agreement (AoA) for establishing the AIIB. The UAE joins 57 other nations that have already become founding members and now holds a 2.21 percent share. According to Sultan Ahmad Al Jaber, UAE Minister of State, establishing the AIIB articulates the vision of our wise leadership and the importance they attach to supporting infrastructure development projects. This agreement is crucial in paving the way for accelerating economic development across Asia. In addition to enhancing the country's role within the global economy, the UAE's affiliation to the institution as a founding member will support the country's growing interests in Asia.[47]

Several Chinese banks have made their way into the UAE's banking sector. The Industrial and Commercial Bank of China (ICBC), China's largest lender, the China Construction Bank (CCB), the Agricultural Bank of China (ABC), and the Bank of China (BOC) have all established branches in the UAE to provide financial support to Chinese investments and local enterprises. Other banks, including China Development Bank, also plan to open branches in the UAE. The ABC established its Chinese Renminbi Clearing Center (RMB) for currency exchange in the UAE while the ICBC has become the largest bond issuer in Nasdaq Dubai.[48] At the same time, the UAE has been active and has established many branches and offices in China's banking sector. Union National Bank was the very first Emirati lender to enter China in 2007 and then set up an office in Shanghai; UNB was followed in 2012 by National Bank of Abu Dhabi and Emirates NBD. The Dubai Gold and Commodities Exchange is the first foreign market to use the new yuan-based gold fix, the Shanghai Gold Benchmark Price, to develop derivative products.[49]

The importance of the UAE–China relationship has been further enhanced by the establishment of the Joint Investment Fund, a $10 billion strategic co-investment fund, which was launched in December 2015 to focus on diversified commercial investments in a range of growth sectors. The fund, which reflects the growing partnership between the two countries, will be administered and managed by the Abu Dhabi state fund, Mubadala, and a subsidiary of the China Development Bank. The goal behind the initiative, with both parties providing equal financing, is to build a balanced fund that incorporates diversified commercial investments and covers a spectrum of growing sectors.[50] In 2018, the fund finalized its plans for investment in 12 projects valued at $1.07 billion.[51]

Energy cooperation

In China's comprehensive strategic partnership with the UAE, energy cooperation is considered one of the critical areas of cooperation to integrate UAE Vision 2021 into the Belt and Road Initiative framework. Therefore, the new Silk Road can provide a new framework for more extensive Chinese investments in the Emirates energy industry. The UAE's geostrategic location, strong ties, energy cooperation, and expressed support for the BRI make the Emirates an attractive place for energy security and a key pivot to Silk Road trade routes.

Beijing's dependence on crude oil imports from the Persian Gulf, a leading oil-producing region, has been increasing gradually since 1993 when it became a net importer of oil.[52] In 2018, the value of crude oil imported into China totaled $239.2 billion (up by 46 percent from 2017 to 2018). Forty-five countries supplied crude petroleum oil to China, but close to half (44.1 percent) of Chinese imported crude oil originates from just nine Middle Eastern nations, and six Persian Gulf states are among the top 15 crude oil suppliers to Beijing. In 2018, Baghdad was ranked in 11th place (up 60.8 percent), exporting some $6.7 billion (2.8 percent) worth of oil to China. The UAE's sixth oil supplier of China in the Persian Gulf.[53]

According to the EIA, the Emirates is among the world's ten largest oil producers and is a member of the OPEC and the Gas Exporting Countries Forum (GECF). The UAE holds the seventh-largest proved reserves of oil and natural gas in the world at 97.8 billion barrel, with most of the reserves located in Abu Dhabi (approximately 96 percent). The other six Emirates account for just 4 percent of the UAE's crude oil reserves, led by Dubai with approximately two billion barrels. The UAE holds approximately 6 percent of the world's proved oil reserves.[54] Given its geostrategic location between East and West, the UAE (particularly Dubai) has emerged as the strategic gateway to Energy trade in the Middle East, the major trade network connecting Asia with the Mediterranean and North Africa.[55]

Beijing's Middle East policy has in recent decades been driven mainly by energy and economic interests: besides the large quantities of oil China imports from the region,[56] Beijing now also sees as it an investment destination to expand its footprint across trade routes stretching through central Asia into the Middle East and Africa.[57] In line with this strategic priority, China aspires to implement the BRI, an ambitious plan to revive the ancient Silk Road trading routes with a global network of ports, roads, and railways.[58]

The UAE–China energy partnership, though not as extensive as the Qatari and Saudi Arabian partnerships so far, does not come as a surprise. The Emirates has emerged as a trusted partner of Chinese energy security after landmark agreements in 2017 and 2018 that awarded China National Petroleum Corporation (CNPC) shares in Abu Dhabi's 40-year onshore and offshore concessions, the first time that a Chinese oil company could acquire stakes in upstream cooperation in an oil-producing country in the Middle East. Under the agreements, PetroChina, which is majority-owned by CNPC, has been granted a 10 percent stake in the Umm Shaif and Nasr concession, and a 10 percent stake in the Lower Zakum concession. Both concessions will be operated by state-owned Abu Dhabi National Oil Company (ADNOC Offshore), which produces 4.5 percent of the world's total crude output, on behalf of all concession partners.[59]

In an agreement negotiated during the state visit of President Xi Jinping to Abu Dhabi and afterwards confirmed by the UAE leadership, ADNOC awarded two contracts worth $1.6 billion to BGP Inc., a subsidiary of CNPC, to conduct one of the world's largest 3D onshore and offshore seismic surveys. The survey will search for oil and gas in onshore and offshore sites covering an area of 53,000 sq km. The state-run CNPC already has two concession rights contracts with ADNOC worth around $3 billion. Since ADNOC's plan to expand its refining and petrochemical operations attracted global investors, the company signed a wide-ranging agreement with CNPC to explore energy partnership opportunities in the UAE. CNPC will examine potential investments in downstream projects including an aromatics plant, a mixed feed cracker for petrochemical production, and a new refinery in the Emirates.[60] Moreover, China Petroleum Engineering and Construction Corporation (CPECC), which is affiliated with CNPC, has been involved in other projects in the UAE, including building oil gathering stations, pipelines, power transmission lines, as well as sewage systems.[61]

In addition to supplying China with an important part of its energy security, the UAE can also contribute to China's aim to establish the largest petrochemical complex.[62] This is modeled after an MoU that ADNOC signed with Saudi Aramco to jointly develop and build an integrated refinery and petrochemicals complex on India's west coast, at a total cost of $44 billion. The project will be the single largest overseas investment in the Indian refining sector and joint partnership (50:50) between the consortium from India and Saudi Aramco and ADNOC.[63]

Solar energy

Solar energy investments was another component in the UAE–China energy partnership. UAE is a global leader in renewable solutions, environment conservation, and climate change mitigation, while Beijing is the driving force for a global surge in solar energy investments. According to the Global Trends in Renewable Energy Investment 2018 report, China saw some 53 gigawatts of solar capacity added (more than half the global total), and $86.5 billion invested, up 58 percent in 2017.[64] China–UAE have investments in the region's largest renewable energy projects that use concentrated solar power (CSP) and photovoltaic panels in Abu Dhabi and Dubai, with a total generation capacity of 1,800 megawatts.[65]

Moreover, China's Silk Road Fund will invest $3.9 billion in a concentrated solar power (CSP) project in Dubai, the first Middle East project financed by the fund. The CSP project will be the world's largest and most advanced solar thermal power plant and the second ACWA Power project in Dubai that the Silk Road Fund is investing in.[66] Beijing is also providing financing (Chinese banks are providing two thirds of the $3. billion) and construction for the 2,400MW Hassyan Clean Coal project, the first Chinese power station in the Mideast, which is developing in partnership with China's Harbin Electric, Dubai Electricity and Water Authority (DEWA), and Saudi Arabia's ACWA Power (a developer, investor/operator of a portfolio of power generation and desalinated water production plants).[67]

Military ties

Under China's comprehensive strategic partnership with UAE, defense cooperation, including arms and technology trade and high-level exchange of visits, has become an increasingly significant part of integrating UAE Vision 2021 into the BRI framework. According to a UAE–China joint statement on strategic partnership in July 2018, the two countries are keen to enhance practical cooperation between the two armies. This aim is represented in high-level exchange visits and communication, joint weapons training and the training of military personnel. The two sides are also keen on cooperating in the science, technology, and defense industry development of mutual interest through preparing a joint working plan. The two countries are keen on enhancing cooperation and exchange of information on maritime security. The two sides agree on rallying efforts on counter-terrorism issues, exchanging of expertise and information on combating terrorism, and strengthening individual training and capacity-building in that regard.[68]

In March 2019, Minister of National Defense Wei Fenghe said, China attaches great importance to the development of its relations with the UAE and regards the Middle Eastern country as a natural partner for joint construction of the Belt and Road Initiative proposed by China. In recent years, military ties between the two countries have witnessed rapid and in-depth development, demonstrated by frequent mutual visits by top military officials and the fruitful cooperation in related areas. China is willing to work with the UAE to promote bilateral military ties to a higher level and implement the important consensus reached by the leaders of the two countries.[69]

In February 2019, according to China's State Administration for Science, Technology, and Industry for National Defense (SASTIND), China Shipbuilding Industry Corporation (CSIC) established a representative office in Dubai. CSIC's new office will be used as a base to expand sales across the Gulf region and will be focused on pursuing both military and civilian business opportunities. The CSIC's presence in Dubai is in line with China's 'One Belt, One Road' initiative to deepen economic ties with countries in the Middle East.[70]

According to the Stockholm International Peace Research Institute, the Middle East is one of the world's biggest arms markets, and the region accounted for 32 percent of global weapons imports in the 2013–17 period. The Middle East's arms imports grew by 103 percent from the 2008–12 period to 2013–17 because most states were directly involved in violent conflict. Meanwhile, Beijing's arms exports to the region jumped 38 percent in the 2013–17 period from the previous five years, and it is now the fifth-largest arms exporter in the world, supplying weapons to 48 countries.[71]

China, according to the Royal United Services Institute, was a significant supplier of military drones to Middle East countries, especially those that are barred from importing them from the US. The UAE has had Chinese Wing Loong I drones since 2016 and started receiving its purchases of the upgraded and deadlier Wing Loong II in early 2018. The UAVs, intended for surveillance and reconnaissance, can carry a range of weapons including missiles and laser-guided bombs to blow up targets on land or in the air.[72]

Tourism and Cultural Ties

As part of China's comprehensive strategic partnership with the Emirates, enabling the people of the two countries to bond along the Silk Road is vital to integrate the UAE Vision 2021 within the Belt and Road Initiative framework. The promotion of extensive cultural and academic exchanges are aimed to win public support for deepening bilateral and multilateral cooperation, as well as providing scholarships, holding yearly cultural events, increasing cooperation in science and technology, and establishing joint laboratory or research centers and international technology transfer centers.[73]

Linguistic, cultural, and tourism cooperation is another important aspect of the China–UAE comprehensive strategic partnership, and both nations have outlined their intention to expand the collaboration in these areas in the coming years. China and the Emirates have come to recognize the importance of overcoming linguistic-cultural barriers; thus they are working in cooperation to increase the number of Emirati and Chinese professionals who are acquainted with each other's societal norms and customs, methods of performing business, and national and institutional interests.[74]

The two governments are pursuing this goal in a variety of ways, perhaps most importantly in the sphere of education. For some time, Chinese and Emirates universities have offered a wide range of Chinese and Arabic language courses, and also promoted Chinese cultural events, including an annual celebration of the Spring Festival. The academic cooperation between the two countries is part of the effort to promote cultural understanding between the nations.[75] In December 2015, China and the UAE signed an agreement for collaboration in scientific education, the granting of university scholarships, and the exchange of faculty members.[76]

In May 2019, China's Sun Yat-Sen University (one of China's elite research institutions), the United Arab Emirates, and Gulf Medical University (GMU) signed an MoU for educational, training, research collaboration as well as joint research and academic and student exchanges to forge stronger ties between China and the Middle East. The collaboration includes several research, academic, staff, and student exchanges. The alliance will include the joint delivery of the Executive Master's in Healthcare Management and Economics (EMHME), offered by GMU's College of Healthcare Management and Economics.[77]

Meanwhile, according to the Hanban website, the Chinese government established Confucius institutes for providing Chinese language and culture teaching resources worldwide. By the end of 2018, 548 Confucius Institutes and 1,193 Confucius Classrooms and 5,665 teaching sites established in 154 countries and regions, receiving more than nine million students. In 54 countries involved in the Belt and Road Initiative, there are 153 Confucius Institutes and 149 primary and high-school Confucius Classrooms.[78] In the Middle East, there are fifteen Confucius Institutes and two of them are in the UAE.[79] The first Confucius institutes in the Persian Gulf region opened in 2011 at the University of Dubai and the second was officially inaugurated in 2012 at the Zayed University. Both institutes offer students the opportunity to learn the Chinese language as well as courses related to Chinese culture.[80] At the same time, the UAE became the first Arab country to establish an institution for Islamic studies in China.[81]

China's cooperation with the Emirates has increased the number of Chinese students learning the Arabic language, and at least 40 institutions (universities and schools) around the country now offer Arabic classes.[82] In the UAE, 20 Chinese teachers in eleven schools already started teaching Chinese language, and the country is planning in 2019 to teach the Chinese language in 100 schools.[83] To strengthen their relationship, China and the Emirates have also initiated study abroad programs and educational exchanges,[84] including professors and administrative staff.[85]

The two governments also encouraged cultural diplomacy and dialogue, which will contribute to further deepening the comprehensive strategic partnership in the future. For instance, cultural activities such as the Chinese New Year celebrations 2018 were held in seven places in the Emirates and attracted an extraordinary number of Chinese tourists and locals.[86] In July 2018, the UAE–China Week – including Chinese Film Week and the Chinese Book Exhibition Week – was held for the first time, celebrated in both to highlight local heritage. The same venue also hosted daily events featuring traditional Chinese plays and musical performances along with showcasing traditional Emirati culture.[87] Noura Al Kaabi, Minister of Culture and Knowledge Development, said: "UAE–China Week facilitated cultural intermingling and has become a platform to allow thought leaders and artists to meet, exchange views, and learn about each other's cultures and traditions."[88] Furthermore, the Chinese president on his visit to the Emirates announced the opening of a Chinese cultural center in Abu Dhabi, and PRC support and participation for Expo 2020 in Dubai, which will be the first expo held in the Middle East.[89]

China's links with the GCC states have strengthened due to the introduction of additional and direct airline routes, the steady growth of the Chinese economy, and Chinese tourists' increasing disposable income. According to data from Colliers International published ahead of Arabian Travel Market (ATM) 2019, the number of Chinese tourists traveling to the GCC is expected to increase 81 percent from 1.6 million in 2018 to 2.9 million in 2022, and the UAE will steadily increase their Chinese visitor arrivals with a growth of 13 percent. The GCC countries currently attract just one percent of China's total outbound market, but positive trends are expected over the coming years, to as many as 400 million tourists.[90]

According to the Chinese Ministry of Culture and Tourism, 149.72 million outbound trips were made by Chinese tourists in 2018, up 14.7 percent from the previous year.[91] The UAE is now the most favored first stop for Chinese tourists traveling to Arab destinations in the Middle East. In 2017, the number of Chinese tourist arrivals in the Emirates exceeded one million for the first time in history, and about 3.5 million Chinese tourists transited through the UAE. To facilitate and encourage the people-to-people exchange, Beijing granted visa-free status to citizens of the UAE in 2017, making it the first Middle Eastern state to enjoy such an arrangement in China.[92]

Dubai has become one of the favorite tourist destinations for Chinese tourists to the UAE (30 flights a week). According to the Dubai tourism office, the number of Chinese tourists to Dubai rose by 12 percent in 2018 than in 2017. The number of visitors to Dubai in 2018 hit 15.95 million, up 0.8 percent than 2017, and China ranked the fourth year-on-year growth with 875,000 visitors.[93] China's expanding tourism relationship with the Emirates will help to strengthen the comprehensive strategic partnership between both nations.

Summary

The Emirates' strategic geographic location makes the country a marketplace of great potential and influence in the entire MENA region. This chapter examined various aspects behind the China–UAE comprehensive strategic partnership and the synergy between the Belt and Road Initiative and UAE Vision 2021 in order to understand the extent of economic engagement and bilateral relationship between the two nations. The findings showed that the Chinese comprehensive strategic partnership with UAE is one of the most critical developments in the Persian Gulf region and a key pivot in implementing the Belt and Road Initiative.

The success and the rapid growth of China's ties with the Emirates stem from the UAE's pivot role as a regional re-export hub, with infrastructure, financial services, energy, transport, and communication, as well as a business-friendly environment. This provides a regional base of operations that gives Chinese companies a greater presence throughout the Arabian Peninsula and Middle East – circumstances essential for the realization of the BRI. Both states have become important partners to each other, especially because of the Emirates' attempts to diversify their economy away from oil-reliance (UAE Vision 2021). The mutually beneficial arrangement of China's investments and the UAE's unique strategic geographic location on global trade routes enables China to expand its Middle East footprint while providing opportunities for UAE to profit from the partnership.

4
Iraq

In April 2017, China made a policy decision to take an active role in the economic reconstruction of Iraq in the post-Islamic State era. Chinese Foreign Minister Wang Yi proposed that Iraq could become a component of the Belt and Road Initiative. This chapter examines the deepening China–Iraq strategic partnership, and the synergy between the Belt and Road Initiative (BRI) within the rebuilding of Iraq in order to understand the extent of the bilateral engagement and Iraq's integration within the implementation process of the BRI. Beijing's strategic partnership framework with Baghdad is based on shared or mutual complementary economic interests, primarily a comprehensive strategic partnership on energy cooperation within the context of the Belt and Road Initiative. However, in the post-Islamic State era, violence, terrorism, political instability, and social divisions are expected to continue to pose significant threats to Chinese investments in Iraq.

The relations between the PRC and Iraq have developed significantly in the past years, ever since the two countries established a strategic partnership in 2015. Upgrading their relationship to a strategic partnership has opened up a new chapter in China–Iraq friendship, which has brought new opportunities for mutually beneficial cooperation in various fields. As Chinese President Xi Jinping said in a meeting with Iraqi Prime Minister Haider al-Abadi, the new strategic partnership would provide "a solid foundation" for future advances in the relationship, and Chinese assistance in "energy, electricity, communication and infrastructure" projects in Iraq, tied to China's Belt and Road Initiative, will assist in Iraq's economic reconstruction.[1]

The One Belt, One Road Initiative, put forward in October 2013 by Chinese President Xi Jinping, is a $1 trillion project designed to connect Beijing to the global market by linking Asia and Europe via a set of land and maritime trade routes. The concept took form over several years and has now become a cornerstone of President Xi's foreign policy. Iraq stands at an ideal position, being neighbored by three participants in the BRI in the form of Turkey, Iran, and Saudi Arabia. The Iraqi government would stand to benefit more from engaging in bilateral projects with these countries to connect its infrastructure to theirs in order to gain access to the Belt and Road. Although Baghdad is not an official part of the BRI framework, it is surrounded by countries that are, and can, therefore, serve as a natural extension of the initiative.[2]

In this context, it is essential to understand the new phase in the rebuilding and reconstruction of Iraq , a process of deepening China–Iraq strategic partnership, and the impact on the implementation of the BRI. This chapter examines the developing China–Iraq strategic partnership, and the synergy between the Belt and Road Initiative and the rebuilding process of Iraq, in order to understand the extent of the bilateral engagement and Iraq's integration within the implementation of the BRI.

The main argument presented is that Beijing's strategic partnership framework with Baghdad is based on shared or mutual complementary economic interests, and the main foundation of this comprehensive strategic partnership is energy cooperation within the context of the Belt and Road Initiative. Chinese investment in the construction of power stations, cement factories, oilfields, and other projects, as part of their contribution to reconstruction in Iraq under the BRI framework, generates mutually beneficial cooperation and more economic benefits to the two nations.

Iraq and the Belt and Road Initiative

The PRC's strategic partnership with Iraq includes six major areas for cooperation within the Belt and Road Initiative. These areas are policy coordination, connectivity, trade and investments, energy cooperation, financial integration, and military ties. Nevertheless, each country views the Belt and Road Initiative framework and reacts to it according to its perspective and the consequences for its national interests and international status. Consequently, the two countries have very different attitudes about how to realize the vision. Despite the development of closer ties, the China–Iraq relationship remains largely centered on Iraqi oil and gas.

Policy coordination

As part of China's strategic partnership with Iraq, promoting political cooperation between countries, creating mechanisms for dialogue and consensus-building on global and regional issues, developing shared interests, deepening political trust and reaching a new consensus on cooperation are important elements of the potential to integrate the rebuilding of Iraq within the Belt and Road Initiative framework.[3]

In December 2015, during the visit of Iraqi Prime Minister Haider al-Abadi to China, the two countries decided to upgrade their relationship to a strategic partnership. According to Chinese President Xi Jinping, the new strategic partnership would provide "a solid foundation" for future advances in the relationship. The Chinese President also said that the PRC was ready to strengthen the integration of the two countries' development strategies within the framework of the Belt and Road Initiative and assist Iraq's reconstruction in energy, electricity, communication, and infrastructure. Beijing pledged to encourage and support Chinese companies to participate in the construction of large projects in Iraq.[4]

China and Iraq signed five agreements and MoUs on economic, technological, military, diplomatic, and oil and energy cooperation. The first MoU included participation in building the economic belt of the Silk Road and the Maritime Silk Road for the twenty-first century. The second MoU related to economic and technological cooperation between the two countries. The third was a framework agreement on cooperation in the field of energy. The fourth was in the field of military cooperation between the two countries, and the fifth was an agreement on the mutual visa exemption for diplomatic passports.[5]

In August 2018, using the occasion of the 60th anniversary of the establishment of diplomatic relations between China and Iraq, Chinese President Xi Jinping said he was willing to work with the Iraqi president to deepen the bilateral strategic partnership, adding that both countries would carry out mutually beneficial cooperation. In his congratulatory message, the Chinese president pointed out that, since the establishment of diplomatic relations 60 years ago, bilateral relations have maintained a good momentum of development, and cooperation in various fields has steadily advanced due to the joint efforts of both sides. The establishment of the strategic partnership in 2015 opened up a new chapter in China–Iraq friendship, which has brought new opportunities for bilateral ties. Beijing attaches great importance to the development of China–Iraq relations, adding that the two sides should synergize development strategies under the framework of jointly building the Belt and Road, and carrying out mutually beneficial cooperation to bring more benefit to the two peoples.[6]

According to China's Ambassador to Iraq, Chen Weiqing, the Silk Road reduced the distance between the Chinese and Iraqi people, strengthened their friendship by starting friendly exchanges between the two cradles of past civilization and the joint development of the two countries in the present. In the post-Islamic State era, Iraq has entered into a new phase of building and reconstruction, and this provides new opportunities for further developing China–Iraq relations.[7]

In April 2019, a senior Chinese delegation led by Deputy Minister of Foreign Relations of the CPC Central Committee, Lee Joon, visited Iraq and expressed their country's readiness to contribute to the rebuilding of areas destroyed during the war with the Islamic State. According to a statement by the Iraqi Foreign Ministry, "Iraq attaches great importance to the strengthening of relations with the Republic of China and the expansion of . . . ties in all its political, economic and security forms." Iraq called for "increasing China's support for Iraq in the reconstruction of infrastructure through the expansion of investments between the two countries, as well as coordination in the area of security".[8]

China's new ambassador to Iraq, Zhang Tao, stated that Beijing is willing to work together with Baghdad to further deepen political mutual trust, strengthen pragmatic cooperation in various fields under the framework of the Belt and Road Initiative, and deepen the China–Iraq strategic partnership. Iraqi President Barham Salih confirmed his country's willingness to extend relations with China and declared that he regards China as an important strategic partner and that Baghdad is willing to actively participate in the construction of the BRI to continuously further bilateral political, economic, and cultural cooperation.[9]

Energy cooperation

As part of China's strategic partnership with Iraq, investment in energy infrastructure is considered one of the areas of cooperation critical to integrate Baghdad into the BRI framework. The central theme of the strategic partnership between the two nations is energy cooperation. Therefore, the new Silk Road can fuel a long-term and comprehensive strategic partnership on energy cooperation for more large-scale Chinese investment in the Iraqi energy industry. Beijing is considered the foremost trading partner of Baghdad, and Iraq, in turn, is the second biggest oil supplier to China in West Asia, and the fourth biggest trading partner of China in the Middle East. Beijing imports about $20 billion worth of crude oil from Baghdad a year, while Iraqi imports from China now reach $7.9 billion annually.[10]

In 2013, China became the world's largest net importer of total petroleum and other liquid fuels, and by 2017 had surpassed the US in annual gross crude oil imports by importing 8.4 million barrels per day (b/d) compared with 7.9 million b/d of US crude oil imports. In that year, an average of 56 percent of China's crude oil imports came from countries within the Organization of the Petroleum Exporting Countries (OPEC). New refinery capacity and strategic inventory stockpiling, combined with declining domestic production, were the significant factors contributing to its increase in imports.[11]

Beijing's dependence on crude oil imports from the Persian Gulf, a leading oil-producing region, has been increasing gradually since 1993 when it became a net importer of oil.[12] In 2018, the value of crude oil imported into China totaled $239.2 billion (up by 46 percent from 2017 to 2018). Forty-five countries supplied crude petroleum oil to China, but close to half (44.1 percent) of Chinese imported crude oil originates from just nine Middle Eastern nations, and six Persian Gulf states are among the top 15 crude oil suppliers to Beijing. In 2018 Baghdad was ranked in fourth place (up 62.3 percent), exporting some $22.4 billion (9.4 percent) worth of oil to China.[13]

According to the U.S. Energy Information Administration (EIA), Iraq is the second-largest crude oil producer in OPEC, after Saudi Arabia. It holds the world's fifth-largest proved crude oil reserves, nearly 149 billion barrels (representing 18 percent of proved reserves in the Middle East and almost 9 percent of global reserves). Most of Iraq's major known fields – all of which are located onshore – are either producing or are in development. Iraq's crude oil production grew by an average of about 300,000 barrels per day (b/d) from 2013 through 2017 (including oil produced in the Iraqi Kurdistan Region), and it averaged 4.5 million b/d in the first half of 2018.[14] According to the International Monetary Fund (IMF), Iraq's economy is heavily dependent on crude oil export revenues. In 2017, crude oil export revenue accounted for an estimated 89 percent of Iraq's total government revenues.[15]

Energy security and infrastructure development are areas in which the two countries have great potential to cooperate within the context of the BRI. Baghdad is one of the world's most important oil producers, and Beijing is the largest energy consumer in the world. Under current conditions, and up to the foreseeable future, China is one of the most important options to attract global resources required for promoting

Iraq's energy infrastructure development. They are, obviously, linked together by their common interests in that their energy industries supplement and complement each other. On the one hand, China will look to direct investment in infrastructure assets associated with Baghdad's oil industry, which has emerged as an increasingly important export partner over the past decade. On the other, Beijing will aim to garner geopolitical influence by participating in broader reconstruction efforts in a country lying along a key artery of its Belt and Road Initiative.[16]

In December 2015, China and Iraq pledged to establish a long-term, stable energy partnership. As part of the MoU, Beijing expressed its willingness to increase energy cooperation with Iraq, including oilfield projects and refinery construction in the country. Both countries agreed on a long-term and comprehensive strategic partnership on energy cooperation, especially in the oil and gas sector. More investment was to be channeled to the energy sector, and governments and enterprises were encouraged to cooperate in the areas of crude oil trade, oil-gas exploration and development, oilfield engineering service technology, construction of storage and transportation facilities, chemical refining engineering, and energy equipment. The two countries also reached a consensus on using China-made equipment to support oil-gas exploitation in Iraq.[17]

Oil

In the past decade, Chinese energy companies, such as CNPC, Sinopec, CNOOC, Sinochem and Norinco, have become involved in investment and oil extraction in several major Iraqi oil fields, including al-Ahdab, ar-Rumaylah, al-Halfaya, and Misan. The close energy cooperation between Beijing and Baghdad brought about an increase in Iraqi oil exports to China from zero in 2007 to 270 million barrels annually by 2017, so that Iraq became China's second largest oil supplier in West Asia, next only to Saudi Arabia.[18]

Today, the Chinese oil state-owned enterprises have a visible presence in the development of Iraq's major oil fields. The three major Chinese oil companies – China Nationa Petroleum Corporation (CNPC), China National Offshore Oil Corporation (CNOOC), and Sinopec – all operate in Iraq. CNPC and CNOOC operate in Iraq's south, and Sinopec operates in the Kurdistan Region, areas responsible for more than 90 percent of Iraq's oil production. However, because of the different types of contracts under which the Chinese oil operate, the high risks do not automatically generate high profits.[19] Other oil companies such as China Petroleum Pipeline Engineering Corporation (CPPE), a subsidiary of the CNPC, Zhenhua, and private-sector oil companies Geo-Jade Petroleum and United Energy Group Oil Corporation, were also involved in purchasing Iraqi oil and investing in its fields.

In December 2017, the Iraqi oil ministry signed a deal with China's state-run Zhenhua Oil, a subsidiary of China's defense conglomerate Norinco, to develop the southern portion of the East Baghdad oilfield, where investment needed to develop the oilfield could reach $3 billion. Iraq has made significant changes to the new service contract with the Chinese company that links global oil prices and the cost of development. The new contract will allow Zhenhua to receive a $3.5 fee for each barrel of crude produced from the oilfield and will serve as a model for all upcoming contracts with international companies. Baghdad plans to utilize 20 million cubic feet of gas produced as a by-product of oil production from the East Baghdad oilfield to supply a nearby power station.[20] Moreover, CNPC expressed that it was interested in developing the Majnoon Oil Field in southern Iraq. The field was under the management of Royal Dutch Shell, but the company had been looking for a way out, handing over its operations to Basra Oil Corporation.[21]

As of November 2018, stated-owned Zhenhua Oil was set to sign a letter of intent with Iraq's state oil marketer SOMO for the establishment of a joint venture, to be based in the northern Chinese port city of Tianjin. The joint venture, under negotiation for months, was intended to offer China another crude supply option as the country is under pressure to cut oil purchases from Iran, after Washington re-imposed sanctions on Tehran.[22]

Iraq is OPEC's second-largest oil producer, after Saudi Arabia. Its refining capacity was curtailed when ISIS overran its largest oil processing plant in Baiji, north of Baghdad, in 2014. In April 2018, Baghdad signed a contract with two Chinese companies, PowerChina, and Norinco International, to build an oil refinery at the port of Fao on the Gulf, and is seeking investors to build three more.[23] The refinery in Fao will have a 300,000 barrel-per-day capacity and include a petro-chemical plant. Two additional refineries, each with a 150,000-bpd capacity, are planned in Nasiriya, southern Iraq, and in the western Anbar province. The third, with a 100,000-bpd capacity, is planned in Qayara, near Mosul, the northern Iraqi city.[24]

Chinese oil companies are the biggest investors in Iraq's energy sector, especially in the modernization and development of its oil infrastructure.[25] According to China's state-run Xinhua news agency, three

Chinese companies are set to begin developing oil fields in Iraq, seeking to ensure supplies as their country faces a growing demand for energy. Private-sector oil companies Geo-Jade Petroleum and United Energy Group, as well as state-owned China Zhenhua Oil, have won tenders for the development of oil fields in Iraq. Geo-Jade will develop the blocks of Naft Khana in the eastern province of Diyala and Huwieza in the southeastern province of Maysan. Hong Kong-listed United Energy signed an exploration and development contract to develop the al-Sindibad block in the southern province of Basra. Zhenhua Oil will develop an eastern Baghdad oil field, with production expected to start in 2019. It aims for 40,000 barrels a day within five years.[26]

According to the head of the state-run Oil Marketing Co, Iraq aims to supply China with about 60 percent more crude. Baghdad is ready to ship about 1.45 MMbpd to Beijing in 2019. The director general of SOMO said, on the sidelines of the China International Import Expo, that this compares to current sales of 900,000 bbl to long-term buyers, among them state traders Chinaoil and Unipec. SOMO's push into China includes a deal to start an oil trading venture with Zhenhua Oil, which will be based in Tianjin. The venture tentatively plans annual sales of about 8 million metric tons or about 160,000 bpd to smaller, independent refiners known as teapots as well as large petrochemical plants.[27]

Moreover, the Iraqi oil ministry held an auction for international energy companies, with eleven blocks on offer near the borders with Iran and Kuwait and in offshore Gulf waters. In January 2019, Baghdad signed a contract with China's CNOOC to conduct a seismic survey for two oil exploration blocks. The offshore survey was to be the first in Iraq's territorial waters in the Gulf and the onshore block near the border with Iran. The oil ministry held an auction for international energy companies, with eleven blocks on offer near the borders with Iran and Kuwait and in offshore Gulf waters.[28]

Gas

According to the Oil & Gas Journal (OGJ), Iraq's proved natural gas reserves were the 12th largest in the world (nearly 135 trillion cubic feet (Tcf) at the end of 2017. About three-quarters of Iraq's natural gas reserves are associated with oil, most of which lie in the supergiant fields in the south of the country. In 2017, Iraqi dry natural gas production was 357 billion cubic feet (Bcf), with an additional 18 Bcf reinjected during the year. Iraq also flared 629 Bcf of natural gas, ranking as the second-largest source country of flared gas in the world behind Russia.[29] Hence, Baghdad is one of the key countries involved in the BRI framework, with considerable potential to attract Chinese investment and technology for the development of its energy infrastructure

In February 2019, China's Petroleum Engineering and Construction Corporation (CPECC) and Iraq's Basra Gas Company (BGC) signed a contract for constructing a natural gas liquids (NGL) plant in Iraq's southern province of Basra. The BGC will increase current gas production capacity by 40 percent in the Basra facility. The new project will also reduce gas flaring and increase dry gas supply and NGL export capabilities. The Basra NGL facility will be built in Ar-Ratawi area in the west of Basra and is scheduled for completion at the end of 2020.[30]

Connectivity

As part of China's strategic partnership with Iraq, facilitation of connectivity is one of the important ways to integrate the rebuilding of Iraq within the Belt and Road Initiative framework. Baghdad must optimize its infrastructure reconstruction projects to connect them to its neighboring countries in order to gain access to the BRI framework. Iraq lies along a key route of the BRI, which seeks to foster growing East-West overland trade by promoting greater logistical connectivity. Beijing and Baghdad can thus jointly contribute to the development of international transport overland routes and the creation of an infrastructural network that could gradually connect all the regions in Asia and also specific points in Asia, Africa, and Europe.

The Belt and Road Initiative is important for Iraq because it is located on the Al-Hareer Road, a 12,000 km-long land and sea road linking Asia, the Middle East and Europe hundreds of years ago with commercial, cultural, religious, and philosophical links. This road enabled the exchange of goods and products, such as silk, perfumes, incense, and spices as well as the cultural and scientific exchanges.[31]

At present, Iraq has not been listed as an active participant in the Belt and Road Initiative.[32] However, given that Baghdad's southern (Saudi Arabia), northern (Turkey) and eastern (Iran) neighbors are all slated to be participants of the BRI, it is in an ideal position. The Iraqi Government would stand to benefit greatly by engaging in bilateral projects with these countries to connect its infrastructure to theirs in order to gain access to the Belt and Road without being an official part of the initiative. More broadly, since Iraq is surrounded by countries that are part of the BRI, it can, therefore, serve as a natural extension of the Silk Road, as well as serving as a support base for the pursuance of several Chinese interests in the region, such as Syrian reconstruction. Hence, there is great potential for regional synergy in which Iraq can play a bridging role.[33]

Financial integration

As part of China's strategic partnership with Iraq, the formation and promotion of financial integration between the two countries is considered one of the cooperation areas to integrate Iraq's rebuilding process within the Belt and Road Initiative framework. There are several measures needed for the realization of financial integration between the two countries, including: deepening financial cooperation and building a currency stability system, establishing an investment and financing system and a credit information system in Asia, expanding the scope and scale of bilateral currency swaps between the two countries, developing the bond market in Asia, making joint efforts to establish the Asian Infrastructure Investment Bank (AIIB) and financial institutions with good credit ratings to issue RMB-denominated bonds in China, and encouraging qualified Chinese financial institutions and companies to issue bonds in both RMB and foreign currencies outside China and to use the funds thus collected in countries along the BRI.[34]

The Sino–Iraqi economic cooperation is still in the initial stage, and Baghdad has the potential to become a new AIIB member. In March 2019, the Iraqi Ministry of Transportation, Abdullah Luaibi, discussed the possibility of speeding up procedures of Iraq's accession to the AIIB. According to a statement by the ministry's media office, the Transportation Minister held an extensive meeting to discuss "drawing a road map in cooperation with the Chinese side to activate the role of Iraq in the Belt and Road Initiative". The AIIB could play a key role in financing investment opportunities in Iraq's infrastructure related to the BRI and facilitate foreign investment in the country.[35]

In March 2019, Iraq and China were set to finalize a significant bilateral agreement that would give investors access to roughly $10 billion in credit for companies to invest, super-charging China's involvement in the Iraqi economy. The deal was designed to accelerate the pace and widen the breadth of Beijing's involvement in the Iraqi economy, including the energy sector, and provide money needed for reconstruction and infrastructure projects that cannot be funded by the Iraqi budget alone.[36]

Trade and investments

Part of the PRC's strategic partnership with Iraq includes attempting to mitigate as much as possible the barriers to free trade, investment, industrial cooperation, and technical and engineering services in order to facilitate integration of the rebuilding process of Iraq's war-depleted country within the Belt and Road Initiative framework. Both countries must take steps in that direction, such as expanding free-trade zones, improving trade structures, seeking new potential areas for trade and improving the trade balance, devising new initiatives for the promotion of conventional forms of trade, developing trans-border electronic trade and other advanced models of business, creating a system for supporting trade in services to strengthen and expand conventional trade, increasing customs cooperation, and regularly sharing information in these areas.[37]

Although Beijing's rapidly increasing energy demand, especially for petroleum and other liquid fuels, has made Iraq an important business partner, the cooperation goes well beyond oil and gas. Chinese companies are also investing in rebuilding infrastructure and reconstruction projects under the framework of the BRI that will become a crucial theme of their bilateral relations and could create new opportunities for partnerships in promising sectors between the Chinese companies and Baghdad.

According to China Customs Statistics (export–import), China–Iraq trade volume increased to nearly $30.3 billion by 2018;[38] increased cooperation between the two countries is expected in various fields. The volume of trade exchange between the two countries is increasing every year by 10 percent. Beijing is considered the biggest trading partner of Baghdad, and Iraq is the second biggest oil supplier to China, and the fourth biggest trading partner of China in the Middle East.[39]

Beijing plays a meaningful role in Iraq's reconstruction in all areas. The Chinese government attaches great importance to participating in reconstruction, and Chinese companies are paying serious attention to training and qualifying Iraqi cadres. A significant number of Chinese companies are investing in Iraq, given Iraq's geographical significance in BRI. Chinese investments in Iraq are concentrated in oil explorations and infrastructure such as power plants, cement factories, and water treatment stations. As Iraqi Ambassador to Beijing Ahmad Berwari has said, "Chinese companies in Iraq produce about 60 percent of the electricity in the Iraqi capital, Baghdad."[40]

Since China and Iraq upgraded bilateral ties to a strategic partnership, the cooperation has generally been expanding significantly in various fields. This is best reflected through the growth of bilateral trade between the two countries, which grew from $2.6 billion in 2008 to $30 billion in 2018. More than half of the electricity in Baghdad city, the capital of Iraq, is produced by Chinese companies. In February 2018, China and other international states pledged $30 billion, mostly in credit facilities and investment, for reconstruction efforts in Iraq.[41]

According to Wang Di, Chinese Ambassador to Kuwait and envoy to the Kuwait international conference for the reconstruction of Iraq, China will continue to provide assistance within its capacity to Iraq through bilateral ways and participate in the economic reconstruction of the war-torn country. In recent years, the practical cooperation between the two counties is steadily moving forward, and China is willing to further cooperate with Iraq in all areas under the framework of the Belt and Road Initiative.[42] The Chinese approach brings together Iraq's reconstruction process and its integration within the implementation of the BRI framework. As Chinese Foreign Minister Wang Yi said to his Iraqi counterpart Ibrahim al-Jaafari on the sidelines of the Ancient Civilization Forum, "China will continue its active participation in the economic reconstruction of Iraq and do everything it can to help the country, and he thanked Iraq for its support of the BRI."[43]

In February 2019, Chinese company Tianjin Electric Power Construction Co., Ltd. (TEPC) won the bidding for an 800MW combined cycle power plant project in Maysan, Iraq. The project involves building an 800MW 9F class gas-steam combined cycle unit, which is expected to be completed in 33 months. The project marked the first oversea project TEPC won in 2019 as well as another breakthrough TEPC made in exploring the Iraqi market.[44]

The governor of Iraq's northern province of Kirkuk called for Chinese investment and expertise in the reconstruction of towns and villages in the province that were destroyed in battles against the Islamic State. "We in Kirkuk need Chinese expertise and support in the light of official and legal frames. Chinese companies can cooperate with the Kirkuk's provincial Chamber of Commerce and the Investment Board. We in Kirkuk are facing a severe shortage of services, especially in the field of electricity and the municipality, and we have some 130 destroyed towns and villages." For his part, Chinese Ambassador to Iraq Chen Weiqing confirmed his keenness to cooperate with the Kirkuk province in the field of transport, communications, electricity, industry, and agriculture.[45]

Military ties

As part of the PRC's strategic partnership with Iraq, security cooperation including arms and technology trade has become an increasing part of integrating Baghdad into the BRI framework. In December 2015, during a visit to China, Iraqi Prime Minister Haider al-Abadi signed five agreements and MoUs on economic, technological, military, diplomatic, and oil and energy cooperation with Chinese Premier Li Keqiang.[46] According to the Chinese President, "China is keen to expand its military and defense cooperation, training and building of the Iraqi military capabilities and the exchange of information and military industries, and we are ready to respond to support Iraq in these areas."[47]

In the past, the two countries have also engaged in military trade, though it has often paled compared to Iraq's other military trade partners. During the Iran–Iraq War, Baghdad was a major recipient of Chinese tanks and armored vehicles, which China also sold to Iran during the same period.[48] Shortly after the agreement for Bilateral Military Cooperation 2015, the Iraqi Security Forces (ISF) revealed that it was now capable of conducting drone warfare after having purchased Chinese-made CH-4B armed unmanned aerial vehicles in 2014. The CH-4, built by Chinese Aerospace and Technology Corporation, is a medium-altitude, long-endurance UAV with a payload of 350kg. The CH-4B that Iraq ordered from China can carry a payload of 761 pounds, compared to the CH-4A with its 254-pound payload. Weapons can include two AR-1/HJ-10 anti-tank guided missiles, Chinese equivalents of the Lockheed Martin AGM 114 Hellfire, and two FT-9 GPS-guided bombs.[49]

In February 2018, according to the Iraqi Ministry of Defense, the Chinese-made CH-4B drones executed most of their attack and reconnaissance missions in northwest Iraq. Since their entry into operational service, they performed no fewer than 260 air strikes against Islamic State targets, with a success rate close to 100 percent. This development suggests there is a market in Iraq for Chinese arms and technology trade, specialized military equipment that is either too heavily regulated in the US markets or prohibitively expensive.[50]

According to the Iraqi news agency, the government of Iraq acquired the Chinese FD-2000 air defense system, the export version of the HQ-9, an anti-aircraft system that successfully shot down a ballistic missile in 2010. It has gained a reputation of being a cheap substitute for the American Patriot or Russian S-300. The HQ-9, manufactured by the China Precision Machinery Import-Export

Corporation (CPMIEC), is ideal for defending bases and critical infrastructure from air attack. In sum, Baghdad is a perfect customer for Beijing's arms industry in genuine war-fighting products, including new tanks, APCs, missiles, and UAVs.[51]

Summary

China and Iraq enjoy a traditional friendly relationship. Baghdad is considered China's important cooperative partner in West Asia. In recent years, the practical cooperation between the two counties has been steadily progressing, and Beijing is willing to further cooperate with Iraq in all areas under the framework of the Belt and Road Initiative. Iraq certainly stands to benefit from the integration and participation in the Chinese Silk Road, especially from investments in reconstruction and infrastructure projects. Nevertheless, such benefits are not guaranteed but are highly conditional on the Iraqi Government both knowing what to expect from Beijing and taking a strong, consistent and realistic negotiating position on the matter. In particular, Baghdad needs to be aware of Beijing's risk-averse behavior, its strategic, political and diplomatic limitations, and its economic self-interest.

This chapter has examined the deepening China–Iraq strategic partnership, and the synergy between the Belt and Road Initiative within the rebuilding of Iraq in order to understand the extent of the bilateral engagement and Iraq's integration within the implementation of the BRI. The main finding is that the Beijing–Baghdad strategic partnership is based on shared or mutual complementary economic interests, primarily on energy cooperation within the context of the BRI.

Although oil is key to understanding China's upgraded involvement in the rebuilding process of Iraq, Beijing's relationship with Baghdad is much deeper and broader. China is embarking on a strategic approach to the Persian Gulf in the context of the Belt and Road Initiative, which has evolved into a top national strategy in China. The BRI strategy has become China's most important tactic for engaging with West Asia. This strategy encourages Chinese companies to go abroad in search of new markets or investment opportunities, in the context of China's BRI.

5
Kuwait

In July 2018, the Kuwaiti emir made a state visit to China of great signif-icance, as both countries agreed to establish a strategic partnership to create new opportunities for Kuwait which aspires to diversify its economy and seek investment opportunities. This chapter examines the various aspects behind the establishment of this partnership and explains the synergy between the Belt and Road Initiative (BRI) and the Kuwait Vision 2035 in order to understand the extent of economic engagement and bilateral relationship between the two nations. Beijing's strategic partnership framework with Kuwait is based on shared or mutual complementary economic and commer-cial interests, especially with the integration and implementation of the BRI and the Kuwait Vision 2035. However, despite the considerable increase in Chinese trade and investments in Kuwait, some significant internal obsta-cles and external challenges remain to the successful implementation of the synergy between the Belt and Road Initiative and the Kuwait Vision 2035.

The past two decades have seen substantial changes in the global economy and geopolitical trends, with the rise of the PRC on the global and regional stage. These developments are creating new opportunities for the Middle East (West Asia) countries as they look to diversify their economies, increase trade, and seek investment opportunities in emerging markets; this includes schemes such as forging strategic part-nerships with China to promote the Belt and Road Initiative and to incorporate it into their national development plan. All of this reflects a growing tendency among the GCC states, which seek to benefit from the favorable business conditions in China, as well as China's expertise and experience in its rapid path to economic development.

Kuwait, a tiny country with an area of about 18,000 square kilome-ters, is no exception to this burgeoning trend. This tiny emirate is nestled atop the strategic Arabian Peninsula located in the north-western corner of the Persian Gulf, sharing 462 km of land boundaries with Iraq and Saudi Arabia, and commanding a coastline of 499 km.[1]

Kuwait was one of the first Gulf countries to establish diplomatic relations with China, 47 years ago, on March 22, 1971.[2] The relations between China and Kuwait have been developing smoothly and growing steadily since the establishment of diplomatic relations. The two countries enjoy cordial and friendly bilateral relations, share identical or similar views on many major international and regional issues, and are constantly tendering sympathy and support to each other. They have also been working in coordination to broaden and deepen cooperation in the political, economic, and social fields.

The relative decline of US hegemony and power in the Middle East and the emergence of a rapidly rising China, which seeks to assume significant roles in the region, were seen to have the potential to impact on the stability of the balance of power.[3] With this in view, Kuwait has started to seek ways to invest in stronger ties with China, as well as with other powers, to strengthen its position in this increasingly vulnerable geopolitical balance of power. Kuwait, like the other GCC countries, is determined to preserve its strategic alliance with the US but is also seeking to hedge itself against the threats that emanate from regional crises or power competition to guarantee its security in the future.[4]

The $1 trillion One Belt, One Road initiative, put forward in October 2013 by Chinese President Xi Jinping, seeks to connect Beijing to the global market by linking Asia and Europe via a set of land and maritime trade routes. The concept took form over several years and has now become a cornerstone of President Xi's foreign policy. The Belt and Road Initiative has become a key theme of bilateral relations, and could also create opportunities for partnerships in the many promising emerging markets between China and the countries in the Persian Gulf region. Although the Gulf region is not directly along Belt and Road Initiative's trade routes, the Gulf countries have high economic and geopolitical stakes in Beijing's planned multicontinental trade corridor.

More important, the PRC's goal of securing oil and natural gas reserves from as many diverse sources as possible has brought it close to the Persian Gulf states, which are China's top energy suppliers.[5] A stable Gulf region is vital for Beijing's sustainable growth, and with the completion of the Gulf Pearl Chain, China can achieve effective management and control the flow of its energy needs. Consequently, it can open new markets and trade routes for the Gulf Countries, as the Silk Road would connect Gulf economies with the Southeast and East Asian economies to enhance economic integration and cooperation.[6]

This chpater investigates some of the aspects behind the establishment of the China–Kuwait strategic partnership and examines the synergies between the Belt and Road Initiative and the Kuwait Vision 2035 in order to understand the extent of economic engagement and bilateral relationship between the two nations. Since Chinese President Xi Jinping first unveiled the Belt and Road Initiative in September 2013, Kuwait was among the first Arab countries to sign a cooperation agreement with China under the Belt and Road Initiative framework, as well as one of the founding members of the China-initiated Asian Infrastructure Investment Bank (AIIB).[7]

The chapter's main argument is that the Beijing strategic partnership framework with Kuwait is based on shared or mutual complementary economic and commercial interests, especially with the integration and implementation of the Belt and Road Initiative and the Kuwait Vision 2035. The strategic partnership between Kuwait and China contributes to the development of trade relations that have become diversified beyond the energy industry, and the two sides have economic interests that are increasingly complementary. Policy coordination, connectivity, trade and investments, energy cooperation, and tourism and cultural ties are all areas where commercial relations have strengthened in recent years. The Belt and Road Initiative complements Kuwait's Vision 2035 and could help the Kuwait government achieve its national development strategy.

Kuwait Vision 2035

The Kuwait Vision 2035 was launched in January 2017 by the government of Kuwait, and its name reflects the national plan for development, also known as "New Kuwait", which is designed to make Kuwait a regional leader by 2035. This plan includes "initiatives that will transform our economy, create jobs, attract foreign direct investments and facilitate knowledge transfer in the fields of renewable energy, information technology, and the services sector", as the Minister of State for Cabinet Affairs stated in his opening remarks.[8]

The 'Kuwait Vision for 2035', a long-term national development plan, is a new grand economic plan aimed at transforming the country into a financial, cultural and commercial hub in the northern Persian Gulf with tactics to extend its activities to Asia and Europe via 164 strategic development projects. It also aims to increase foreign direct investment by 300 percent. The vision of the Amir Sheikh Sabah Al-Ahmad Al-Jaber Al-Sabah is to transform Kuwait into a financial, commercial, and service hub at local and international levels, through mega projects and leading economic roles by the private sector.[9]

Kuwait's economy is heavily dependent on petroleum export revenues, which account for 88 percent of the government's budget revenues, 85 percent of exports and 40 percent of GDP.[10] As a result, the Kuwaiti government hopes to push ahead with reforms to diversify the national economy in order to reduce its dependence on oil revenues and to transform the country so that it will provide financial and commercial services worldwide. By 2035 the Kuwaiti government will have made investments of more than $100 billion in key economic and social sectors including oil and gas, North Zone Development, electricity and water, urban development and housing, health, education, transport and communications, tourism and media, and the environment.[11]

The past two decades have seen substantial changes in the global economy and geopolitical trends, with the rise of China on the global stage. These developments are creating new opportunities for the GCC countries as they look to diversify their economies, increase trade, and seek investment opportunities in emerging markets; this includes schemes such as forging strategic partnerships with China to promote the Belt and Road Initiative and to incorporate it into their national development plan. This reflects a growing tendency among the GCC states, which seek to benefit from the favorable business conditions in China, as well as from Beijing's expertise and experience in its rapid path to economic development.[12] The Gulf countries have strongly embraced and, in turn, benefitted from, a network of cooperation lines in various investment and infrastructure projects and other economic fields with China.

Kuwait and the Belt and Road Initiative

The PRC's strategic partnership with Kuwait includes five major areas for cooperation within the Belt and Road Initiative. These areas are policy coordination, connectivity, trade and investments, energy cooperation and tourism and cultural ties. However, each country views the Belt and Road Initiative framework and reacts to it according to its perspective and the consequences for its own national interests and international status. Therefore, the two countries have very different attitudes regarding how to realize the vision.[13] The Kuwait Vision 2035 and China's Belt and Road vision have converged on a common economic development path, and their synergetic strategy will bring new opportunities for both sides. As a result, the realization of the Belt and Road Initiative will provide a new momentum for Kuwait's economic transformation.

Connectivity

According to China's strategic partnership with Kuwait, facilitation of connectivity is one of the important ways to integrate the Kuwait Vision 2035 into the Belt and Road Initiative framework. Kuwait should attempt to optimize its infrastructural connections and also to adapt its technical systems to those of the other countries in the Belt and Road Initiative framework. This would lead Beijing–Kuwait to jointly contribute to the development of international transport maritime and overland routes and the creation of an infrastructural network that could gradually connect all the regions in Asia and also specific points in Asia, Africa, and Europe. In addition, there should be serious attempts to create low-carbon and green infrastructure.[14]

As a small state situated on the Persian Gulf, Kuwait's geographic location has been a significant factor in the development of the strategic partnership with the PRC. Kuwait's natural harbors are easier to access than those of other GCC states, which has led the country to become part of a major trade route. Given its unique geographic location, as a solid gateway for China to increase its ties to the GCC states and the Arabian Gulf countries, Kuwait is poised to play a pivotal role in helping realize the Belt and Road vision. For instance, an overland trade route running through Kuwait and continuing through Saudi territory could provide a safer and shorter route to the Suez Canal and the Red Sea than one that passes through the Bab el-Mandeb Strait, which has been facing instability ever since the outbreak of the war in Yemen. This would also provide the opportunity to enhance Chinese interaction with both Saudi Arabia and Kuwait.[15]

Kuwait enjoys a distinguished geographical location that connects the Persian Gulf with both maritime and overland routes, and this explains why China is so eager to collaborate with it on the Belt and Road Initiative trade network. Beijing also wants to work with Kuwait on infrastructure projects, including the construction of Al-Hareer (Silk City). As part of the PRC's effort to revive the old Silk Road trading route that once connected Europe to Asia, Chinese companies are interested in building up five uninhabited islands in Kuwait's eastern coast and connecting them to the Belt and Road Initiative.[16]

Five years after Chinese President Xi Jinping first unveiled the Belt and Road Initiative, in September 2013, the Persian Gulf region is now emerging as one of the project's most important partners. Chinese infrastructure and construction projects in the Persian Gulf, which were spearheaded under the framework of the Belt and Road Initiative, were extended to include Oman and UAE.[17] In Kuwait, China signed an agreement to cooperate on the $86 billion Silk City project. The Silk City and the five islands will serve as a huge economic free zone that will link the Arabian Gulf to central Asia and Europe. Beijing is also holding talks to link Kuwait with a planned network of railways that will make the country a major commercial center and a base for a network of railways which starts from China and passes through Central Asia and Gulf states.[18]

The Silk City and the five northern islands (Failaka, Warba, Boubyan, Miskan, and Awha) project are set to accommodate 700,000 residents within a designated urban area of 250 square kilometers, with the first phase expected to be completed by 2023. The Sheikh Jaber Al Ahmad Al Sabah Causeway (a bridge that links Kuwait City to Silk City) is now one of the largest infrastructure ventures in Kuwait. Currently 73 percent complete, the route will eventually be 37.5 km in length, extending from the Al Doha region, west of Kuwait City, to Al Shuwaikh Port in the capital and Al Sabiyah in the northeast. One of the main developments will be the Mubarak Seaport with a capacity of 24 berths that will help to increase trade through the Red Sea to Europe. The port, when completed, will be Kuwait's largest commercial trading hub.[19]

The Silk City mega-project has been under development since 2014 when the Kuwaiti government approved its final master plan and signed a cooperation MoU with the PRC for its development as a major component of China's Belt and Road Initiative.[20] The head of the Silk City project, Faisal Al Medlej, signed the agreement with China's National Development and Reform Commission, a government-run economic management agency, at its headquarters in Beijing.[21]

The Silk City, a $100 billion project, is the cornerstone of the Kuwait 2035 Vision and will play an important role in the country's diversification efforts to transform the country into a commercial and cultural hub for the region. It will also include a 1,000-metre skyscraper, a wildlife sanctuary, a new airport, a duty-free shopping zone, and media and conference facilities.[22] According to the Kuwaiti Ambassador to China, Samih Hayat, "There is a mutual and substantial consensus between New Kuwait 2035 vision and the Belt and Road Initiative to revive the Silk Road and establish a commercial center to serve the world."[23]

As part of the Silk City and five islands development projects, Kuwait signed an MoU with the Huawei Company in July 2018 to implement the smart cities strategy in the country. (A "smart city" is an urban area that uses different types of electronic data collection sensors to supply information to efficiently manage assets and resources. For example, the strategy includes developing apps, such as to manage urban flows and provide real-time responses). The Huawei–Kuwait government MoU was divided into four sections that are connected with the development of intelligent infrastructure networks, security, virtual systems, and the digital transformation of various industries and central managements in Kuwait. In November 2018, the Kuwait National Fund for Small and Medium Enterprise Development (SMEs) signed an MoU with the Huawei company to encourage and develop small- and medium-size enterprises and to enhance companies' advanced services in information technology and communications, as part of the Kuwait Vision 2035.[24]

However, there is some skepticism about the implementation of the Silk City and the five islands development projects. This is not unexpected, given the uncertainty surrounding the Persian Gulf where ambitious leaders' mega-project proposals can come unstuck due to financial or political hurdles. There is also uncertainty regarding how many of these MoUs that were signed between Kuwait and China will be implemented. According to the International Monetary Fund, reform and project delays are major risks to Kuwait's outlook, alongside lower oil prices and regional security challenges. Kuwait's history of stop-start reforms and tardy project development sustains concerns about the ability to push the Silk City and the five islands development projects through the bureaucracy and the legal changes necessary to ease business procedures and open up the economy.[25]

Policy coordination

According to China's strategic partnership with Kuwait, promoting political cooperation between countries, creating mechanisms for dialogue and consensus-building on global and regional issues, developing shared interests, deepening political trust and reaching a new consensus on cooperation are important to integrate the Kuwait Vision 2035 into the Belt and Road Initiative framework.[26]

In July 2018, during the state visit of Kuwaiti Emir Sheikh Sabah Al-Ahmad Al-Jaber Al-Sabah in China, both countries agreed to establish a strategic partnership between the two countries in order to inject new impetus into bilateral ties and open up new prospects in the new era. President Xi Jinping called the two countries "tried and true friends".[27] Under the strategic partnership framework, China and Kuwait will synergize the Belt and Road Initiative with Kuwait Vision 2035 and work to promote the establishment of a China–GCC free trade area at an early date.[28]

China plans to set up free trade zones with members of the GCC, which are an essential part of the Belt and Road project. In that respect, as long as the Qatar–Gulf crisis prevails and diplomatic and economic ties remain strained, if not fully cut off, the creation of free-trade zones seems impossible. Though Chinese investments will not be directly affected by the current GCC conflict, the growing instability in the region could still harm China's economic cooperation with the Gulf states and will undoubtedly impact Beijing's regional trade prospects.[29]

Energy cooperation

In China's strategic partnership with Kuwait, investment in energy infrastructure is considered one of the critical areas of cooperation to integrate Kuwait into the Belt and Road Initiative framework. Therefore, the new Silk Road can provide a new framework for more extensive Chinese investments in the Kuwait energy industry. Beijing is Kuwait's largest source of imports, and Kuwait is China's fourth-largest crude oil supplier in the Arab world. They are, obviously, linked together by their common interests in that their energy industries supplement and complement each other.

According to the U.S. Energy Information Administration (EIA), Kuwait was the world's tenth-largest producer of oil and other petroleum liquids in 2017, and it was the fifth-largest producer of crude oil among the OPEC members. Despite its relatively small geographic size (about 6,900 square miles), in terms of production it trailed only behind Saudi Arabia, Iraq, Iran, and the UAE in the production of oil and other petroleum liquids in 2017.[30] Kuwait holds the world's sixth-largest oil reserves and is one of the top ten global producers and exporters of total petroleum liquids (about 102 billion barrels, 6% of world reserves), and had an estimated 63 trillion cubic feet (Tcf) of proved natural gas reserves.[31]

In 2013, China became the world's largest net importer of total petroleum and other liquid fuels, and by 2017 China had surpassed the US in annual gross crude oil imports by importing 8.4 million barrels per day (b/d) compared with 7.9 million b/d of US crude oil imports. In that year, an average of 56 percent of China's crude oil imports came from countries within OPEC. New refinery capacity and strategic inventory stockpiling, combined with declining domestic production, were the significant factors contributing to its increase in imports.[32]

The year 2017 also highlighted some changes in the global oil market. First, despite the increase in production of this raw material in the United States, its stored reserves were decreasing rapidly on an annual basis. Second, a sharp increase in oil imports from the United States to China contributed to the fact that Beijing became the world's largest importer of oil. Third, forecasts indicate that before 2025, the Middle Kingdom will overtake the US as the largest consumer and will be responsible for 18–20 percent of the world's oil consumption.[33] According to the International Energy Agency's (IEA) World Energy Outlook 2017, China will overtake the US as the largest oil consumer around 2030, and its net imports are forecast to reach 13 million barrels per day (mb/d) in 2040 (its oil import dependence will rise to 80 percent).[34]

China's dependence on crude oil imports from the Persian Gulf, a leading oil-producing region, has been increasing gradually since 1993 when it became a net importer of oil.[35] In 2017, the value of crude oil imported into China totaled $162.2 billion (18.6 percent of total crude oil imports). Forty-five countries supplied crude petroleum oil to China, but close to half (44 percent) of Chinese imported crude oil originates from just nine Middle Eastern nations, and six Persian Gulf states are among the top 15 crude oil suppliers to China. Kuwait is ranked in eighth place, exporting some $7.1 billion (4.4 percent) worth of oil to China.[36]

The PRC is Kuwait's largest source of imports, and Kuwait is China's fourth-largest crude oil supplier in the Arab world.[37] Kuwait's crude oil wealth and Beijing's heavy dependence on crude oil are the underlying keys to the rapidly growing energy relationship between the two countries. They are, obviously, linked together by their common interests in that their energy industries supplement and complement each other. The energy relationship between the two countries includes cooperation in building oil refineries and petrochemical plants, in oil supplies, oil field services, and exploration, and oil services and equipment in the oil drilling sector.

In 2011, Kuwait Petroleum Corporation, China Petroleum and Chemical Corporation Limited (Sinopec) signed a $9 billion deal to build an oil refinery and petrochemical plant, with the completion date scheduled by 2017, in the southern coastal city of Zhanjiang.[38] In August 2014, Kuwait concluded a new ten-year deal with China's Sinopec Corp to nearly double its supplies by offering to ship the crude oil and sell it on a more competitive cost-and-freight basis. Under the deal, Kuwait will increase the volume of its crude oil exports to China up to 500,000 bpd over the next three years.[39]

In recent years, China has become one of the biggest oil drilling contractors in Kuwait. Chinese enterprises have won contracts for 64 projects in Kuwait, covering such sectors as oil field services and exploration, infrastructure and telecommunications, with a total value of $13.7 billion. New contracts reached $3.01 billion in the oil drilling sector that are becoming landmark projects in China–Kuwait cooperation. Kuwait has so far bought Chinese-made rig equipment worth more than $635 million. The Sinopec International Petroleum Service Corp (SIPSC) owns 53 drilling rigs, taking up more than 45 percent of the Kuwait market.[40]

In July 2018, the Chinese oil services and equipment company Kerui Petroleum won $100 million worth of contracts for two ultra-deep well drilling rigs from Kuwait AREC. The contract follows another ultra-deep well drilling rig contract valued at $50 million concluded earlier this year, from Kuwait National Drilling Company.[41] In October 2018, Kuwait signed an MoU with Chinese NOC Sinopec to build a new refinery in south China. The new refinery unit will be constructed in partnership with Chinese NOC Sinopec.

In July 2018, Kuwait Petroleum Corporation (KPC) signed on a cooperation agreement with China's ShanDong Refining and Chemical Group to market Kuwaiti crude oil. This Chinese company is one of the leading oil industry bases in the country and is known for hosting a large number of private and state-owned oil refineries. The deal aims to expand joint investment platforms in the oil and logistics industries.[42] In November 2018, PetroChina, Sinopec, China's Sinochem Group (one by one) signed a 2019 crude oil supply deal with Kuwait, with volumes unchanged from this year.[43]

Trade and investments

According to the PRC's strategic partnership with Kuwait, the aim is to mitigate as much as possible the barriers to free trade, investment, industrial cooperation, and technical and engineering services in order to facilitate the integration of Kuwait Vision 2035 within the Belt and Road Initiative framework. Both countries should take a series of measures, such as expanding free-trade zones, improving trade structures, seeking new potential areas for trade and improving the trade balance, devising new initiatives for the promotion of conventional forms of trade, developing trans-border electronic trade and other advanced models of business, creating a system for supporting trade in services to strengthen and expand conventional trade, increasing customs cooperation, and regularly sharing information in these areas.[44]

Although Beijing's rapidly increasing energy demand, especially for petroleum and other liquid fuels, has made Kuwait an important business partner, the cooperation goes well beyond oil and gas. Chinese companies are also investing in building infrastructure and construction projects under the framework of the BRI that become a crucial theme of the bilateral relations and could create new opportunities for partnerships in promising sectors between the Chinese companies and Kuwait.[45] More important, Kuwait's signature on the agreement to establish a strategic partnership in July 2018 with China was an essential step in implementing and fulfilling the economic Vision 2035 and subsequent projects.

China views Kuwait as a key partner for cooperation in the Belt and Road Initiative, and maintenance of regional peace and stability in the Gulf region. During his seventh visit to China in July 2018, the Kuwaiti Emir Sheikh Sabah Al-Ahmad Al-Jaber Al-Sabah and Chinese President Xi Jinping agreed to promote the Belt and Road initiative and incorporate it with the Kuwait Vision 2035. They also agreed to work together to establish a free trade area between China and the GCC. The two leaders found a consensus between the Kuwait Vision 2035 and China's Belt and Road Initiative to revive the old Silk Road for creating a vibrant trade region and to restore Kuwait to its leading role in the commercial and economic fields within the region.[46]

Since the establishment of diplomatic relations between the two countries, bilateral economic and trade exchanges have become more frequent, and bilateral trade volume has been on the increase. The relationship commerce between the two countries has expanded rapidly over the years, and today, China is one of Kuwait's key trade partners.[47] According to official statistics, the two-way trade between the countries jumped from $642 million in 2001 to $9.5 billion in 2016 and $12.04 billion in 2017 (recording year-on-year growth of 28 percent). According to China Customs Statistics (export–import), China's trade volume with Kuwait grew from $12.04 billion in 2017 to about $18.3 billion in 2018.[48] There are currently more than 40 Chinese companies operating in Kuwait with about 80 projects in progress in the sectors of oil, infrastructure, communications, and banking.[49]

According to the Chinese ambassador to Kuwait, Wang Di, the collective value of construction projects involving Kuwait and China in 2017 has hit $8.2 billion, the most lucrative deal Beijing has ever forged with a Gulf country.[50] In July 2018, a Chinese firm signed a $709 million contract with the Kuwaiti government to build infrastructure and roads for a new 18,000-unit housing project in Kuwait's South Matlaa, located west of the capital. Chinese technology and smartphone giant Huawei will execute the second phase of a fiber optics project after signing a $72 million contract.[51] Since the Kuwaiti government needs foreign investment to diversify its economy, they have urged Chinese companies to increase their investments in the country.[52]

The high-level contacts and the bilateral visits reflect the state of economic relations between the two countries. During these visits, several bilateral economic, trade, oil, and gas agreements were signed to boost bilateral trade and mutual investment. For instance, during the state visit of the Kuwaiti ruler Sheikh Sabah Al-Ahmad Al-Jaber Al-Sabah several agreements and MoUs were signed, aimed at boosting bilateral ties. The two countries have thus sealed a cooperation protocol to boost defensive industry cooperation, an MoU to encourage investment and upgrade cooperation between the Kuwait Direct Investment Promotion Authority (KDIPA) and the China Council for the Promotion of International Trade (CCPIT), and a cooperation agreement between Kuwait Petroleum Corporation (KPC) and China Export and Credit Insurance Corporation (Sinosure).

Moreover, an MoU on developing smart applications for Kuwait's Al-Hareer (Silk City) and Boubyan Islnds projects was also signed between Kuwait's Communication and Information Technology Regulatory Authority (CITRA) and Huawei Technology. Kuwait and China also inked an MoU on e-commerce, aimed to boost cooperation through facilitating trade between the two countries and achieving sustainable development in the field.[53]

Nevertheless, the signing on several wide agreements/MoUs represents a significant step forward in China's commercial relationship with Kuwait business community, and will only serve to strengthen the strong and longstanding economic and commerce ties between the two countries. Although it is unclear how many of these agreements/MoUs represent completely new projects and how many mark incremental progress in deals struck over the past two years between Kuwait and China, one thing is clear: the test of these declared agreements/MoUs will be in their implementation and in the promotion of follow-up transactions.

Tourism and Cultural Ties

According to China's strategic partnership with Kuwait, enabling the people of the two countries to bond along the Silk Road is also vital to integrate the Kuwait Vision 2035 within the Belt and Road Initiative framework. The promotion of extensive cultural and academic exchanges are aimed to win public support for deepening bilateral and multilateral cooperation, as well as providing scholarships, holding yearly cultural events, increasing cooperation in science and technology, and establishing joint laboratory or research centers and international technology transfer centers.[54]

In recent years, tourism and cultural cooperation have become another important aspect of the China–Kuwait strategic partnership, and both nations have outlined their intention to expand collaboration in these areas in the coming years. As Chinese Ambassador to Kuwait Li Minggang said, "People-to-people exchanges is a key factor to consolidate the foundation of relations between the two countries and the two governments have been actively engaging in visa issues to facilitate personnel exchanges."[55]

China's links with the GCC states have strengthened due to the introduction of additional and direct airline routes, the steady growth of the Chinese economy, and Chinese tourists' increasing disposable income. According to data from Colliers International published ahead of Arabian Travel Market (ATM) 2019, the number of Chinese tourists traveling to the GCC is expected to increase 81 percent from 1.6 million in 2018 to 2.9 million in 2022, and Kuwait will steadily increase their Chinese visitor arrivals with a growth of 7 percent. The GCC countries currently attract just one percent of China's total outbound market, but positive trends are expected over the coming years, to as many as 400 million tourists.[56] Cultural cooperation has become another important aspect of the China–Kuwait strategic partnership, and both nations have outlined their intention to expand the collaboration in this area in the coming years. In March 2018, Kuwait opened a Chinese center in its capital, Kuwait City, to promote cultural exchanges and deepen economic and trade cooperation. According to the director of the Chinese Center, Yao Jian, tea art, traditional Chinese medicine, and Chinese food are famous in Kuwait and the hope that more Kuwaitis and people from neighboring countries will enjoy the rich and colorful Chinese culture in this center.[57]

Summary

The Persian Gulf is in a unique geopolitical position, as it connects three continents Asia, Africa, and Europe, giving it a vital strategic significance in the realization of the Belt and Road Initiative. In the last five decades, Kuwait and China have developed dense and multi-faceted relations. Trade and economic relations have been foundational in developing these ties, with energy playing an important role. Increasingly, commercial relations are becoming more diverse and formalized, with foreign direct investment, and infrastructure and construction projects featuring heavily. Since China announced the Belt and Road Initiative in 2013, Kuwait has regarded it as an engine to enhance bilateral cooperation.

Economic relations between Gulf countries and China have rapidly expanded, and the region's strategic importance to Beijing's infrastructure and energy-driven Belt and Road vision are clear although the Gulf region is not classified as a key corridor in the Belt and Road Initiative architecture. This suggests China's determination to avoid being sucked into the region's multiple conflicts, with Beijing preferring to take a non-intervention position, allowing it to remain neutral in most inter-regional disputes and to take advantage of the strategic and economic opportunities available. China is also switching its focus on energy in the region, which accounts for half of its imported oil, to more investments in trade and infrastructure construction projects that have risen substantially

This chapter has investigated various aspects behind the establishment of the China–Kuwait strategic partnership and examined the synergies between the Belt and Road Initiative and the Kuwait Vision 2035 in order to understand the extent of economic engagement and bilateral relationship between the two nations. The findings show that the strategic partnership between Kuwait and China is contributing to the development of trade relations that have become diversified beyond the energy industry, and the two sides have economic interests that are increasingly complementary. Policy coordination, connectivity, trade and investments, energy cooperation, tourism, and cultural ties are all areas where commercial relations have strengthened in recent years. The Belt and Road Initiative complements Kuwait's Vision 2035 and could help the Kuwait government to achieve its national development strategy.

Nevertheless, despite the potential economic opportunities for Kuwait's Vision 2035 to collaborate in the China Belt and Road Initiative, there are some internal obstacles and external challenges. First, regional turbulence and political rivalry among major powers add to the challenges and uncertainties of cooperation between China and Kuwait. Second, some economic risks and barriers include susceptibility to the US and European influence, the high barrier of market access, bureaucratic corruption and royal monopoly, fierce competition with other countries, bottlenecks in project funding, and local labor and commercial disputes.

Third, although state-owned companies remain the dominant investors in Belt and Road Initiative projects, mainly in energy and transport, the Chinese private sector is less enthusiastic about investing in Kuwait's vast trade and infrastructure strategy. Beijing is also becoming more wary of throwing money at the Belt and Road Initiative project as it comes under pressure from the trade war with the United States; the decline in its foreign exchange reserves have further complicated its efforts to finance the new Silk Road.[58] Finally, as the Belt and Road Initiative proceeds, there is a possibility that extremist groups and criminals might hijack or attack Chinese citizens and assets, as has taken place elsewhere in the region.[59]

6
Qatar

China–Qatar ties have strengthened considerably in recent years. The relationship between the two countries has seen steady and smooth bilateral development in the political, economic, and cultural fields, in trade, energy and other areas, and has given active play to the complementarities between the two economies. This chapter examines the motivation behind Beijing's measures to formalize a strategic partnership with Qatar in order to understand the impact and the extent of the Qatar–Gulf crisis on Doha engagement and integration within the Belt and Road Initiative (BRI).

Since the establishment of diplomatic relations in 1988, the PRC and Qatar have enjoyed friendly relations, marked by the opening of embassies, mutual visits and exchanges of high-ranking official visits, and signing agreements in the field of investment and energy co-operation aimed at strengthening commerce and trade relations.[1] In recent years, the bilateral relations between Beijing and Doha have witnessed a significant development to further bilateral cooperation in the political, economic, cultural, trade, energy, and other fields, and have given active play to the complementarities between both economies.[2]

The $1 trillion Belt and Road Initiative, put forward in October 2013 by Chinese President Xi Jinping, seeks to connect Beijing to the global market by linking Asia and Europe via a set of land and maritime trade routes. The concept took shape over a period of several years and has now become a cornerstone of President Xi's foreign policy. The preeminent position of Qatar in the Gulf and extensively in the Middle East has a key role to play in the realization of China's Silk Road Initiative, especially with its economic and geographical components.

This chapter analyzes the motivation behind China's measures to formalize strategic partnerships in order to understand the impact and the extent of the Qatar–Gulf crisis on Doha engagement and integration in the implementation of the Belt and Road Initiative. The main argument is that China's measures to formalize strategic partnerships with Qatar are based on shared or mutual complementary economic and strategic interests. Doha discovered that more in-depth Sino–Qatari cooperation can brighten the prospects for Qatar's National Vision 2030 and could help it to escape from diplomatic and economic isolation. At the same time Beijing finds Qatar a critical partner to promote the Belt and Road project, especially with its economic and geographical components which play a vital role in the creation of China–GCC free-trade zones.

Qatar National Vision 2030

The Qatar National Vision 2030 (QNV2030) is a master vision and roadmap towards Doha becoming a forward-thinking society capable of sustainable development with the goal of providing a high standard of living for all citizens by the year 2030. Through defining long-term outcomes for Doha, it provides a framework within which national strategies and implementation plans can be developed. It assists Qatari government-led strategies, policy, planning, and allocation of funds and resources towards a unified goal. It also provides private sector companies and, to an extent, individuals, with a shared direction and purpose. The Qatar National Vision 2030 foresees development in four interconnected fields: human development, social development, economic development, and environmental development.[3]

There is a point of convergence of interests that can be built upon to forge a basis for cooperation between the Qatar National Vision 2030 and development of the Belt and Road Initiative by linking these two projects in a way to set up a unified development strategy to the advantage of both. Qatar Vision 2030 is pretty much in line with the concept of development upheld by the Belt and Road vision, primarily in terms of the pursuit of economic, human, social, cultural, and environmental development. As Chinese Foreign Minister Wang Yi said, Qatar should take part in the realization of China's Silk Road Initiative since the Belt and Road project shares common cooperative opportunities with the Qatar National Vision 2030.[4]

Qatar and the Belt and Road Initiative

China's measures to formalize strategic partnerships with Qatar includes seven major areas for cooperation within the Belt and Road Initiative. These areas are policy coordination, connectivity, trade and investments, energy cooperation, financial cooperation, military ties, tourism and cultural ties. However, each country views the BRI framework and reacts to it according to its perspective and the consequences for its own national interests and international status. Therefore, the two countries have very different attitudes regarding how to realize the vision. The Qatar's National Vision 2030 and China's Belt and Road vision have converged on a common economic development path, and their synergetic strategy will bring new opportunities for both sides. As a result, the realization of the BRI will provide new momentum for Doha's economic transformation.

Policy coordination

China's measures to formalize strategic partnerships with Qatar involve: promoting political cooperation between countries, creating mechanisms for dialogue and consensus-building on global and regional issues, developing shared interests, deepening political trust and reaching a new consensus on cooperation. These are the important goals in order to integrate the Qatar's National Vision 2030 into the Belt and Road Initiative framework.[5]

In November 2014, the historic visit of the Emir of Qatar, Tamim bin Hamad Al-Thani, to China was a crucial milestone in the course of building the strategic partnership framework. The visit opened a new era of cooperation between the two countries and produced a clear and complete understanding to upgrade their relationship, as well as recognizing Qatar's regional role as an economic and security partner. As Chinese President Xi Jinping said, "Qatar is an important country that plays a unique role in the Middle East and Gulf region, and is a major partner of China in the region."[6]

The deep relations and strong economic ties in a wide range of cooperation areas that extend from the ongoing export of Qatari gas to Beijing, to joint infrastructure construction projects and Chinese investments in Doha, through constructive and positive exchanges in the domains of finance, tourism and culture, have helped to build a solid foundation for cementing these relations and to formalize a comprehensive strategic partnerships in the future. As the Ambassador of the State of Qatar to the People's Republic of China, Sultan bin Salmeen al-Mansouri, said, "There has been comprehensive development. We have witnessed that since 2014."[7]

In January 2019, the Qatari Amir Sheikh Tamim bin Hamad Al-Thani arrived for a two-day state visit in China, and both countries agreed to deepen the bilateral strategic partnership and create a strategic dialogue between the governments. The last visit drew a roadmap to boost strategic partnership between the two countries in the fields of politics, economics, investment, energy, technology, and security cooperation. The Chinese President also called the two sides to further synergize their development strategies and jointly build the Belt and Road Initiative.[8]

Connectivity

As part to China's measures to formalize strategic partnerships with Qatar, facilitation of connectivity is one of the important ways to integrate the Qatar National Vision 2030 into the BRI framework. Qatar, which has a preeminent position in the Gulf and extensively in the Middle East, has a key role to play in the realization of China's Silk Road Initiative, especially with its economic and geographical components.[9]

Qatar is also in a position to benefit substantially from the implementation of the Silk Road Initiative since deeper Sino–Qatari cooperation can brighten the prospects for its National Vision 2030. In April 2017, the Qatar Chamber and the China Council for the Promotion of International Trade (CCPIT) signed an agreement to promote cooperation ties between the two sides to maximize the benefit for Qatari and Chinese private sectors and create more partnerships. The two sides also signed an MoU for Qatari Chamber of Commerce to join the Silk Road Chamber of International Commerce.[10] In November 2018, China and Qatar signed an MoU to identify global maritime investment opportunities; the document serves both Qatar's National Vision 2030 and China's Belt and Road Initiative.[11]

Nevertheless, in the synchronization process between the implementation of the Belt and Road projects with its Qatar National Vision 2030, Doha is unquestionably competing with other GCC members to establish itself as a regional business hub that attracts Chinese and global trade, investment, and tourism. And there are several obstacles that can prevent Qatar from achieving their goal. First, with the sudden diplomatic isolation from its direct neighbors and supposedly close GCC allies, and with land, sea, and air barriers in place, Doha cannot possibly hope to be of regional economic centrality.[12]

Second, Qatar is highly unlikely to develop into a leading Gulf business hub since it will not be able to rival the UAE, Saudi Arabia, or Oman as the major maritime trade route on Beijing's 21st century Maritime Silk Road Initiative. The UAE currently enjoys hub status in West Asia due to its advanced infrastructure, business-friendly regulatory environment, diversified economy, vast international human resource pool, and level of touristic attraction. The Chinese have long realized this, which is why most of their exports to the GCC, wider West Asia, and even Africa and Europe go through the UAE, the third largest re-export hub in the world; approximately 60 percent of China's pass-through trade is via this hub.[13]

Finally, China plans to set up free trade zones with members of the GCC, which are an important part of the Belt and Road project. In that respect, as long as the Qatar–Gulf crisis prevails and diplomatic and economic ties remain strained, let alone fully cut off, the creation of free-trade zones seems impossible. Though Chinese investments will not be directly affected by the current conflict, the growing instability in the region could still harm China's economic cooperation with the Gulf states and will certainly impact Beijing's regional trade prospects.[14]

Trade and investments

As part of China's measures to formalize strategic partnerships with Qatar, they are attempting to mitigate as much as possible the barriers to free trade, investment, industrial cooperation, and technical and engineering services in order to facilitate the integration of Qatar's National Vision 2030 within the Belt and Road Initiative framework. Both countries should take a series of measures, such as expanding free-trade zones, improving trade structures, seeking new potential areas for trade and improving the trade balance, devising new initiatives for the promotion of conventional forms of trade, developing trans-border electronic trade and other advanced models of business, creating a system for supporting trade in services to strengthen and expand conventional trade, increasing customs cooperation, and regularly sharing information in these areas.[15]

Qatari trade and investments with China are significant, especially in light of the ongoing blockade imposed on it by its neighbors. Qatar also needs to boost economic cooperation and trade exchange with various countries, including China, in order to diversify the national economy from reliance on oil and gas export in order to become a global financial and commercial hub. Likewise, Doha needs technologies and the experience of Chinese companies which have great potentials in management and production.[16] Thus, the Qatari government is trying to promote strategic partnerships with China to incorporate the Belt and Road Initiative into its national development plan. As the Qatari Amir Sheikh Tamim bin Hamad Al-Thani said, Qatar attaches importance to ties with China and vows to promote cooperation in the

Belt and Road Initiative, as well as areas such as trade, sports, and tourism.[17]

Although the Qatar–Gulf crisis has directly undermined and threatened Beijing's economic cooperation and trade exchange in numerous ways, the diplomatic row has also represented available investment opportunities for China to gain influence in the oil-rich Gulf and to support a rapid expansion of conventional energy trade and investments with Doha, particularly as regards natural gas, as well as to promote the BRI. China is Qatar's third-largest trading partner (accounting for 10.92 percent of the country's total trade volume) and the second largest source of imports.[18]

The trade volume between the two countries has increased from less than $50 million in 1988 at the beginning of bilateral diplomatic relations to $10.6 billion in 2017.[19] According to China Customs Statistics (export–import), China's trade volume with Qatar grew to $11.5 billion in 2018.[20] More than 14 fully owned Chinese companies are currently operating in Qatar, in addition to 181 joint Qatari–Chinese firms. According to Minister of Commerce and Industry Ali bin Ahmed al Kuwari, China represents an attractive destination for Qatari investments in the fields of shipbuilding, manufacturing, petrochemicals, technology, hospitality, tourism, and financial services among other vital industries. Qatar also allows foreign investors 100 percent ownership across various sectors and industries.[21]

Beijing and Doha are also connected through a network of cooperation arrangements in various investment and infrastructure projects, and other areas. According to the China Global Investment Tracker, Beijing investments and contracts in Qatar from 2013 to 2018 reached $3.9 billion.[22] Chinese enterprises have participated in the construction of several strategic projects in Doha, such as the Hamad port, the 2022 World Cup main stadium, and other infrastructure works across the country, while Qatari companies are entering the Chinese market. The private sector in both countries could play a bigger role in the future of economic relations, especially given abundant investment and business opportunities.[23]

The Hamad port is located between the municipalities of Al Wakrah and Mesaieed, 40 km south of Doha, 14 times the size of the existing Doha port. The new port is one of the largest ports in the Middle East and considered to be the world's largest port development project built on unused land. The new $7.4 billion port replaced the existing Doha port, partly built and operating by China Harbor Engineering Company (CHEC) that constructed the port basin, the quay walls, and the inner breakwaters.[24]

In January 2017, Qatar launched the first-ever regular direct service between Hamad Port and Shanghai, which helps reduce the sailing time and increases the handling volume of containers coming to Doha from the Far East, Southeast Asia, and Southeast India. The Hamad container port forms part of the Qatar National Vision 2030, which aims at converting Qatar into a developed country and promoting trade and investment by bringing in machines, boilers, and electrical equipment. These new trading lines are helping Qatar diversify its economy by boosting its manufacturing capacity and breaking its dependence on its neighbors.[25]

In November 2018, CHEC signed an MoU with Qterminals to create joint employment opportunities and investments between the two sides around the world. In the signing ceremony, the Ambassador of China to Qatar, Li Chen, said "Qatar and China have a strategic partnership that is conducive to cooperation in all fields, and ports are one of those important areas. We have well-experienced companies in many fields and are fully prepared to participate in the field of investment in ports or other fields related to infrastructure".[26]

Furthermore, China is extensively involved in the infrastructure and construction of the Lusail Stadium for the 2022 FIFA World Cup. The stadium is located on a one-square kilometer precinct plot along the Al Khor Expressway in the western edge of Lusail City, 20 km north of Qatar's capital Doha. The construction of the Lusail Football Stadium is one of the most important Chinese projects in Qatar. The iconic 80,000-seater stadium, which is currently under construction in cooperation with China Railway Construction Corporation Limited (CRCC), is expected to be the largest in the world and will be used for the opening and final matches of the 2022 FIFA World Cup to be held in Qatar.[27]

Huawei Technologies, a leading global provider of communications and information technology (ICT) infrastructure and smart devices, become one of the first fully owned technology companies in Qatar. Over the past few years, the Chinese company has launched several major projects in Qatar, as the telecom giant is working on developing the fifth-generation technology, which is expected to provide better communication services between individuals, vehicles, homes, and appliances.[28] The Chinese, together with Qatar's leading communications operator (Ooredoo), launched a fifth-generation (5G) network through the 3.5 GHz Spectrum in Qatar, the first in the world to launch the service commercially.[29]

Khalifa bin Jassim Al-Thani is chairman of Qatar Chamber that organizes business interests and represents the Qatari private sector locally and globally as well as supports the country's economic actors and productivity. He reports that since 2015, Qatar Chamber has been hosting an annual "Made in China" expo, a platform that enables Chinese companies to display their products in Qatar. It also aims to build commercial alliances to enhance Qatar–China trade relations. Qatar Chamber also organized joint meetings between businesspeople from both sides, to explore opportunities to set up joint projects and build business alliances between Chinese and Qatar companies.[30]

Qatari companies are also engaged in the investment business in China under the state-run Qatar Investment Authority (QIA), one of the world's most aggressive investors with an investment value estimated at approximately $15 billion. These include joint investments with Chinese companies in the sectors of finance, e-commerce, and the Internet, including those with privately owned companies such as Alibaba and Baidu.[31] In 2014, Qatar's sovereign wealth fund (QIA) signed an MoU with the Chinese state-owned China International Trust and Investment Corporation (CITIC) Group to set up a $10 billion fund to invest in China's property, infrastructure, and healthcare sectors.[32] In September 2018, according to Bloomberg, the Qatar Investment Authority was negotiating the potential purchase of a minority stake in Lufax (about $500 million to $1 billion), which is an arm of China's Ping Insurance (Group) Co.[33]

In January 2019, Qatar's National Airline acquired a 5 percent stake in China Southern Airlines, in a move to gain access to the fast-growing mainland Chinese, one of the world's largest aviation markets. The Sino–Qatari deal came as Doha seeks new partners and routes for the national airline due to the ongoing diplomatic dispute in the Gulf. Qatar Airways' stake in China Southern is valued at roughly $530 million based on current stock prices, and Chief Executive Akbar Al Baker said in a written statement that there is "massive potential for cooperation in the future".[34]

Financial cooperation

Under China's measures to formalize strategic partnerships with Qatar, the formation and promotion of financial integration between the two countries are considered one of the essential cooperation areas to integrate Qatar's National Vision 2030 into the BRI framework. There are a number of measures for the realization of financial integration between the two countries: including deepening financial cooperation and building a stable currency system, establishing an investment and financing system and a credit information system in Asia, expanding the scope and scale of bilateral currency swaps between the two countries, developing the bond market in Asia. In addition, making joint efforts to establish the Asian Infrastructure Investment Bank (AIIB), and financial institutions with good credit ratings to issue RMB-denominated bonds in China, and encouraging qualified Chinese financial institutions and companies to issue bonds in both RMB and foreign currencies outside China and use the funds thus collected in countries along the Belt and Road route.[35]

Doha has engaged in all the financial mechanisms underpinning the foundation of the initiative and was among the first countries to join the AIIB. Qatar's Renminbi clearing center in its capital is one of the most important steps taken to promote the implementation of the Belt and Road project.[36] Qatar, which is one of the primary shareholders in the AIIB,[37] and one of the first countries in the region that joined; this will assist in their aim to synergize the implementation of the BRI projects with its National Vision 2030.[38]

In April 2015, China established a renminbi (RMB) clearing center in Qatar, the first of its kind in the Middle East and North Africa, with capital of RMB 30 billion. The center offers local financial institutions access to Chinese renminbi and foreign exchange markets. It also aims to help promote trade, encourage expanded investment in the Chinese currency, and to facilitate financial transactions between Beijing and Doha on the one hand and between China and Gulf Arab economies and the rest of southwestern Asia, on the other. Moreover, over the long run, the center could help Gulf oil exporting countries reduce their dependence on the US dollar, another step in China's goal of becoming a significant economic player in the region and beyond.

China's electing to establish a renminbi clearing center in Doha is not surprising since according to the Qatar central bank, the country is presently sitting on around $340 billion of reserves, some $40 billion-plus gold at the central bank, and $300 billion at the Qatar Investment Authority, the sovereign wealth fund.[39] More broadly, Beijing accounts for more than 15 percent of all goods exported to the Middle East, and Chinese companies and investors are becoming increasingly active in the region. Through currency swap agreements and the RMB clearing center, Beijing is ensuring that a growing share of that trade will be cleared in Chinese currency. The RMB center in Qatar, in providing access to RMB-based financial products and exchanges, is strengthening financial ties between Beijing and the Middle East and fostering the widespread use of the renminbi in the region, thus enabling China to do business with the region on its terms.[40]

Qatar has also benefited from the establishment of the clearing center since it will bolster its position as a regional and international financial hub. In bilateral terms, Beijing is the third-largest trading partner of Doha, which makes it quite reasonable for the latter to diversify part of its large pool of foreign reserves away from American dollars and to strengthen links that already exist with China. In regional terms, the clearing center in Qatar also makes new financial products in RMB currency accessible to Qatar and other Gulf investors. According to recent data by global payment system provider Swift, more countries in the Middle East are turning towards the yuan, while Qatar and the UAE are the most active in using the yuan for direct payments with China and Hong Kong.[41]

In addition, there is Sino–Qatari bilateral cooperation in the financial services sector, including the banking and insurance sectors and capital markets, as well as opening branches of Chinese banks in Qatar, such as the Industrial and Commercial Bank of China (ICBC), and the People's Bank of China (PBOC).[42] The ICBC has been appointed as the clearing bank for yuan deals in Qatar; this will increase the strong ties between the two countries and Doha's position as the regional center for renminbi clearing and settlement. Qatar investment in China financial sector, banks and real estate fields has increased and is considered to be effective investments of a developmental nature. For example, the State of Qatar is represented by QIA (its sovereign wealth fund) as a shareholder of the Agricultural Development Bank of China with a 13 percent holding. The bank is currently one of the most important Chinese banks at this time, and there are many investment opportunities for Qatari businessmen in various parts of China.[43]

Energy Cooperation

As part of China's measures to formalize strategic partnerships with Qatar, investment in energy infrastructure is considered one of the important cooperation areas to integrate Qatar's National Vision 2030 into the BRI framework. Therefore, the new Silk Road can provide a new framework for more extensive Chinese investments in the Qatar energy industry. Beijing offers Doha a market for its Liquefied Natural Gas (LNG) export; Qatar enables China to diversify its energy sources to natural gas, so as not to be overly reliant on, for instance, Saudi Arabia or Russia.

The central theme of China's measures to formalize a comprehensive strategic partnership between the two nations is the energy sector; Qatar is the second-largest exporter of Liquefied Natural Gas (LNG).[44] Here the strategic significance of Qatar to China's energy security will be shaped by Qatar's uninterrupted supply of natural gas to China's rising demand for energy. According to Minister of Commerce and Industry Ali bin Ahmed al Kuwari, Qatar is the second largest supplier of liquefied natural gas to China and Doha is also home to numerous Chinese companies in the engineering, consulting, contracting, information technology, trade and services sectors.[45]

According to EIA (U.S. Energy Information Administration), in 2018 China became the world's top importer of natural gas and second-largest buyer of LNG, accounting for over one-third of net growth, an increase of 12 billion cubic feet per day (Bcf/d).[46] Doha is already the second largest supplier of LNG to Beijing, and the volume of LNG imports from Qatar is expected to rise substantially as the demand for energy is growing at a rapid pace in Beijing.[47]

According to EIA, like many of its neighbors, Qatar's economy is largely based on oil and gas production and processing. The Qatar National Bank (QNB) reported that earnings from the hydrocarbon sector accounted for nearly half of the country's total government revenues in 2014, a figure that has declined over the past four years. Qatar's recoverable reserves of oil and gas are reported to be 25 billion barrels (bbl) and 872 trillion standard ft3 (scf), respectively. This puts Qatar behind only Russia and Iran in terms of natural gas reserves, with the ninth largest reserves in the Organization of the Petroleum Exporting Countries (OPEC), and 13th largest in the world in terms of crude oil reserves.[48] Qatar's North Field and its geological extension of Iran's South Pars Field have the world's largest non- associated gas reserves. Most of Qatar's natural gas production comes from the North Field, which at current gas production rates is expected to last another century.[49]

The PRC plan to cover its growing needs to diversify energy sources and shift to clean and renewable energy makes Qatar the world's largest exporter of LNG, essential to energy-hungry China, which has stepped up efforts to combat air pollution. Beijing's increasing inclination to reduce dependence on traditional sources of energy and achieve green, sustainable economic development makes Doha's supply of natural gas that more vital. As the Ambassador of the State of Qatar to the People's Republic of China, Sultan bin Salmeen al-Mansouri said, "Qatar's [has shown] constant readiness to meet China's gas needs, even beyond what is agreed upon."[50]

According to SIA Energy forecasts, China's LNG imports may surge by 70 percent over the next three years to 65 million tonnes in

2020. In 2017, China imported a record of 38.1 million tonnes, 46 percent more than the previous year. Beijing's imports are bound to grow as the country has only secured 43 million tonnes per year of imports and is expected to need 65 million tonnes per year of imports by 2020, rising to 87 million tonnes per year by 2020. Given China's growing appetite for imported LNG and Qatar's plan to expand its LNG capacity to 100 million tonnes per year, these mutual interests create a natural framework for strategic partnership in the liquefied natural gas industry.[51]

In September 2018, state-owned Qatargas, the world's largest liquefied natural gas producer with a production capacity of 77 million tonnes per year, agreed on a 22-year deal with PetroChina International, a wholly owned subsidiary of PetroChina Company Limited, to supply China with some 3.4 million tonnes of LNG annually. The Qatari state-owned company will supply LNG from the Qatargas 2 project to receiving terminals across China. The deal allows flexibility in delivering LNG to Chinese terminals, including those in Dalian, Jiangsu, Tangsha, and Shenzhen, using the Qatargas fleet of 70 conventional Q-Flex and Q-Max vessels.[52]

In October 2018, Qatar Petroleum (QP) and China's Oriental Energy (Singapore), a subsidiary of China's largest Liquefied Petroleum Gas (LPG) player Oriental Energy, signed a sale and purchase agreement to directly supply PRC with 600,000 metric tons of LPG per year for five years.[53] The contract with QP underscores the urgency faced by China to lock in stable and diversified energy supply, considering the trade war with the US and the sanctions on Iran. This deal also aims to improve QP's energy partnership with China, which is now the world's largest growing LPG market. QP also has joint ventures with several Chinese counterparts, including exploration, production, and refining projects in Qatar and China.[54] Eventually, Qatar can remain a significant player in the China gas industry as long as natural gas continues to be an essential energy source for achieving ecologically-sound economic development.

Beijing's dependence on crude oil imports from the Persian Gulf, a leading oil-producing region, has been increasing gradually since 1993 when it became a net importer of oil.[55] In 2018, the value of crude oil imported into China totaled $239.2 billion (20.2 percent of total crude oil imports). Forty-five countries supplied crude petroleum oil to China, but close to half (44.1 percent) of Chinese imported crude oil originates from just nine Middle Eastern nations, and six Persian Gulf states are among the top 15 crude oil suppliers to Beijing.[56] Qatar's oil output is about 2 percent of OPEC (accounts for around 44 percent of global oil production and 81.5 percent of the world's oil reserves), and a modest contribution to the oil market. Thus, since Qatar is not among the top 15 crude oil suppliers to China and its oil industry is small in regional and international terms, the energy partnership between the countries takes place mainly in the gas industry.

Military ties

Under China's measures to formalize strategic partnerships with Doha, defense cooperation has become an increasingly significant part of integrating Qatar's National Vision 2030 into the BRI framework. Even though it remains modest, since 2014 it has been maintaining a good momentum of development in the fields of personal training and academic exchange, and the transfer of military technology as well as high-level leadership visits.[57]

China–Qatar cooperation in security, anti-terrorism, and the military have also been strengthened in recent years. During the period of turmoil in GCC-Qatar relations, Beijing decided to upgrade its security partnership with Doha. Although China's security ties with Qatar remain significantly less than those with Saudi Arabia or UAE,[58] the timing of its expanded security partnership with Doha's can be explained by the shared or mutual complementary economic and strategic interests between the two countries.

The relative decline of US hegemony and power in the Middle East and the emergence of a risen China that seeks significant roles in the region might affect the stability of the balance of power.[59] Within this context and the tension with its neighbors, Qatar has started to seek ways to invest in stronger military ties with China, as well as other powers, to strengthen its position in an increasingly vulnerable geopolitical balance of power. Although Doha is determined to preserve its strategic alliance with the US, it is also seeking to hedge itself against the economic and trade embargo that has isolated it by air, land, and sea from its neighbors.[60]

For Beijing, the strengthened security partnership with Qatar is motivated by economic considerations. China is a significant importer of Qatari liquefied natural gas, and through military technology exports it can improve its balance of trade with Doha.[61] According to the Stockholm International Peace Research Institute (SIPRI), Qatari arms imports have drastically increased by 282 percent from 2012 to 2016, and Qatar became the world's third biggest importer, despite only having entered the top ten for the first time in 2015.[62] Moreover, Beijing's strengthened security partnership with Qatar is also motivated by strategic considerations. China views Qatar as a highly useful partner in the Arab world and the GCC, and can thereby bolster its own bid to act as mediator in the rapidly intensifying Middle East security crisis.[63] China wants to preserve the GCC's cohesion and is supportive of a peaceful resolution to the Gulf–Qatar standoff. Instability in the Persian Gulf is a worrisome prospect for China's Belt and Road vision that includes the promotion of trade across the Arabian Peninsula.[64]

The security ties and the transfer of military technology must be interpreted within the context of Beijing's grander objectives in the Middle East pertaining to the ambitious Belt and Road Initiative. Qatar and the other Gulf countries play essential roles in PRC's vision for a multicontinental trade corridor that positions China at the center of the 21st-century global economy.

For Qatar, the growing defense ties with China are motivated by strategic considerations. The closer security ties to China may enable Doha to strategically hedge against future tensions from its more extensive and more powerful neighbors that are encouraging the US to limit ties to the tiny gas-rich nation,[65] including discussing the possibility (even if remote) of Washington relocating the US military presence at Qatar's al-Udeid to another Arab state. Notwithstanding this ever-present threat, in January 2019 the US and Qatar signed an MoU regarding the expansion and renovation of al-Udeid Air Base, which hosts the forward headquarters of the US military's Central Command and some 10,000 American troops.[66]

Besides, Qatar's deeper security ties with Beijing will further diversify its alliances away from Washington and other Western countries which will give it greater leverage in its relationship with the Trump administration. China has offered and will continue to offer Doha an opportunity to counter-balance the geopolitical interests of its Western allies. In particular, China's non-interventionist approach to arms sales makes it an attractive security partner for Doha during a period of tensions and unprecedented economic isolation.[67] Qatar, like the other GCC states which have conducted foreign policies closely aligned to Washington, has embraced a "Look East" approach, taking stock of the global shift in economic prosperity from North America and Europe to the Far East.[68] Thus, the Chinese-Qatari security partnership is expected to continue to deepen, strengthened by a complex network of interdependence based on energy, investments, and political cooperation.

The most significant Chinese defense sales and military technology export to Qatar was the SY-400 short-range ballistic missile system, with a range of 400 kilometers. Beijing's sale of the SY-400 missile system to Doha underscores how the Chinese security partnership with Qatar has reached its strongest point and how it is now balancing two adversaries – the Saudi-UAE-led coalition – to its own geopolitical and strategic advantage.[69] The sale of the SY-400 system enables Doha to assert greater clout as its geographically larger neighbors continue their siege. Qatar unveiled the missiles and accompanying launch systems during its 2017 National Day parade, and the media in Saudi Arabia and UAE warned that the new missiles could potentially strike targets in their countries.[70]

Tourism and Cultural Ties

As part of China's measures to formalize strategic partnerships with Qatar, enabling the people of the two countries to bond along the Silk Road is also vital to integrate the Qatar's National Vision 2030 within the Belt and Road Initiative framework. The promotion of cultural and academic exchanges are aimed to win public support for deepening bilateral and multilateral cooperation; these ventures provide scholarships; increase cooperation in science and technology; and establish joint laboratory or research centers, and international technology transfer centers.[71] As Chinese President said in a meeting with Qatari Emir Sheikh Tamim Bin Hamad Al-Thani, the two countries need to advance cooperation in such areas as tourism, culture, sports, and media, especially by supporting each other in hosting the 2022 Beijing Winter Olympic Games and the 2022 World Cup in Qatar.[72]

China's links with the GCC states have strengthened due to the introduction of additional and direct airline routes (Qatar Airways flights from seven destinations in mainland China), the steady growth of the Chinese economy, and Chinese tourists' increasing disposable income. According to data from Colliers International published ahead of Arabian Travel Market (ATM) 2019, the number of Chinese tourists traveling to the GCC is expected to increase 81 percent from 1.6 million in 2018 to 2.9 million in 2022. The GCC countries currently attract just one percent of China's total outbound market, but positive trends are expected over the coming years, to as many as 400 million tourists.[73]

In recent years tourism and cultural cooperation have become another important aspect of the China–Qatar strategic partnership, and both nations have outlined their intention to expand the collaboration in these areas in the coming years. Qatar has seen the potential and huge market in China, especially in the tourism industry. Thanks to the broad economic development of the PRC in recent years, the Chinese have been able to see their purchasing power increase considerably and can now aspire to new experiences. More and more Chinese are traveling abroad every year, and Qatar is becoming a particularly popular destination for them. In 2017, the number of Chinese tourists who visited Qatar reached nearly 45,000, a sharp increase of 26 percent compared to the previous year.[74] According to Akbar Al Baker, Secretary-General of Qatar National Tourism Council (QNTC) and Group Chief Executive of Qatar Airways, the number of Chinese tourists to Qatar in 2018 has growth 38 percent from the previous year.[75]

Qatar's tourism agencies are making efforts to create a Chinese-friendly environment at hotels and other tourism facilities to make it more appealing to the unique taste and culture of Chinese tourists and travelers, including providing services in the Chinese language, accepting payment by China UnionPay cards, providing hot water kettles to make Chinese tea, and carrying the channels of CCTV, the predominant state television broadcaster in China.[76] Beijing is also a desirable tourist destination for the Qataris, who mainly head to Shanghai and southern Chinese cities to enjoy the various tourist attractions.[77]

As part of Doha's desire to attract the travel and leisure-loving Chinese to the Qatari tourism market, both countries reached an agreement on comprehensive visa exemption for the citizens of both countries.[78] Qatar Airways currently operates 45 weekly direct flights to seven cities in China, and the Qatar Tourism Authority has also set up representative offices in several Chinese cities along with an exclusive project to welcome Chinese people.[79]

Currently, there are approximately 6000 Chinese citizens living and 10,000 working in Qatar (working in Qatar Airways, Oil and Gas, and some in constructions companies).[80] As Chinese companies win tenders for development projects in Qatar, there is an increasing back-and-forth of Chinese workers, both professionals and non-professionals. The two countries have also signed an agreement regulating the employment of Chinese workers in Qatar. This agreement is not surprising, due to the growing presence of Chinese workers taking part in the construction of facilities for the FIFA World Cup in 2022 and because of the development and extensive infrastructure constructions plans in Qatar.[81] It is expected that more Chinese tourists and workers will be visiting Qatar shortly with recent developments in the bilateral ties between the two countries.

Meanwhile, China's Belt and Road initiative, which cuts through the Middle East, has the potential to put the region on the map for adventurous Chinese travelers who are seeking new destinations off the beaten path. The Middle East is also becoming a hotspot for China's growing group of luxury travelers. Many have already gone to Asia, Europe, and America and are seeking more unique getaways that blend great hospitality, unique culture and experiences, shopping and local cuisine.[82]

The cultural ties between China and Qatar include academic and educational cooperation, language teaching and cultural activities. The academic and educational cooperation is perhaps the most visible element of China's cultural ties with Qatar. China has exerted various efforts to bolster its academic and language and culture. For instance, the Translation and Interpreting Studies (TII) of Hamad bin Khalifa University (HBKU) have signed an MoU with the Chinese Embassy in Qatar to collaborate in the areas of language teaching and cultural activities.[83] There are student and academic exchange programs between Qatar University and some Chinese universities (e.g., Peking University, and other universities in Shanghai).[84] In 2014, the Qatari government decided to grant $10 million to establish a Qatar Chair for Middle East Studies at Peking University.[85]

The most important Beijing–Doha cooperation in cultural exchanges was the great success of the celebration of the 2016 China–Qatar Year of Culture, when Chinese arts and silk exhibitions, open-air Chinese festivals, movie weeks, and educational programs were featured, among other activities. This cultural initiative aimed to connect the people of China and Doha through exploring the contemporary and traditional cultures of both countries, innovative cultural exchange activities, exhibitions, festivals, and educational programs.[86] In the same year, Qatar organized cultural activities and exhibitions in China, foremost, the Pearl Jewelry Exhibition held at Beijing National Museum, and the Al Thani Jewelry Exhibition held in the Forbidden City in Beijing, featuring a dazzling collection of royal pieces from around the world, spanning various periods.[87]

Summary

Qatar is a small emirate located on the Persian Gulf's northeast coast in the Middle East, sharing a land border with Saudi Arabia in the southeast and sea borders on the Persian Gulf with the UAE and Iran. The motivation behind China's measures to formalize a strategic partnership reflects multiple issues and aspirations. Not least from the Qatar side is to better position the country given the Qatar–Gulf crisis on Doha engagement and integration in the implementation of the Belt and Road Initiative. China's measures to formalize strategic partnerships with Qatar include seven aspects: policy coordination, connectivity, trade and investments, energy cooperation, financial cooperation, military ties, tourism and cultural ties.

The findings indicate that China has skillfully used its sophisticated foreign policy to take advantage of strategic opportunities and unique situations to formalize a comprehensive strategic partnership with the Qatari government. This is based on shared or mutual complementary economic and strategic interests, such as synergizing the implementation of BRI projects with the Qatar National Vision 2030, in light of the Qatar–Gulf crisis. The Chinese-Qatari strategic partnership is expected to continue to deepen, strengthened by a complex network of interdependence based on the seven areas identified.

Economic relations between Gulf countries and China have rapidly expanded and the region's strategic importance to Beijing's infrastructure and energy-driven Belt and Road vision is clear, although the Gulf region is not classified as a key corridor in the BRI architecture. This suggests China's determination to avoid being sucked into the region's multiple conflicts, with Beijing preferring to take a non-intervention position, allowing it to remain neutral in most inter-regional disputes and to take advantage of the strategic and economic opportunities available. China is also switching its focus on energy in the region, which presently accounts for half of its imported oil, to more investments in trade and infrastructure construction projects that have increased substantially.

7
Oman

This chapter examines the Sino–Oman strategic partnership, and the synergy between the Belt and Road Initiative and the Oman Vision 2020 in order to understand the extent of economic engagement and bilateral relationship between the two nations. From the Chinese perspective, Oman is an attractive addition to the implementation of the Belt and Road Initiative. The 21st century Maritime Silk Road Initiative (MSRI), part of the wider Belt and Road Initiative, primarily seeks to create a continuous link of Chinese-controlled ports and industrial facilities throughout Southeast Asia, Oceania, the Indian Ocean, and East Africa. Nevertheless, there are certain constraints and barriers in the Sino–Omani strategic partnership that could prevent or disrupt the engagement between the two countries.

On May 2018, the occasion of the China–Oman 40th anniversary of diplomatic relations, both countries' leaders decided to establish the strategic partnership, and active Omani participation in the Belt and Road Initiative. These relations have witnessed significant progress towards strengthening and deepening the fields of cooperation between the two countries.[1] From the Chinese perspective, Oman is attractive to the implementation of the Belt and Road Initiative. The 21st century Maritime Silk Road Initiative (MSRI), part of the wider Belt and Road Initiative, essentially seeks to create a continuous link of Chinese-controlled ports and industrial facilities throughout Southeast Asia, Oceania, the Indian Ocean, and East Africa. Oman forms a crucial potential link in this chain, given its strategic location between India and East Africa outside the volatile Strait of Hormuz.

The past two decades have seen substantial changes in the global economy and geopolitical trends, with the PRC on the global and regional stage. These developments are creating new opportunities for the Middle East (West Asia) countries as they look to diversify their economies, increase trade, and seek investment opportunities in emerging markets; this includes schemes such as forging strategic partnerships with China to promote the Belt and Road Initiative and to incorporate it into their national development plan. All of this reflects a growing tendency in Oman and other GCC states to seek benefits from the favorable business conditions in China, as well as China's expertise and experience in its rapid path to economic development.

The $1 trillion One Belt, One Road Initiative (BRI), put forward in October 2013 by Chinese President Xi Jinping, seeks to connect Beijing to the global market by linking Asia and Europe via a set of land and maritime trade routes. The concept took form over several years and has now become a cornerstone of President Xi's foreign policy. The BRI has become a key theme of bilateral relations, and could also create opportunities for partnerships in the many promising emerging markets between China and the countries in the Persian Gulf region. Although the Gulf region is not directly along Belt and Road Initiative's trade routes, the Gulf countries have high economic and geopolitical stakes in Beijing's planned multicontinental trade corridor.

More important, PRC's goal of securing oil and natural gas reserves from as many diverse sources as possible has brought it close to the Persian Gulf states, which are China's top energy suppliers.[2] A stable Gulf region is vital for Beijing's sustainable growth, and with the completion of the Gulf Pearl Chain, China can achieve effective management and control the flow of its energy needs. Consequently, it can open new markets and trade routes for the Gulf Countries, as the Silk Road would connect Gulf economies with the Southeast and East Asian economies to enhance economic integration and cooperation.[3]

This chapter examines the Sino–Oman strategic partnership, and the synergy between the Belt and Road Initiative and the Oman Vision 2020 in order to understand the extent of economic engagement and bilateral relationship between the two nations. As Chinese President Xi Jinping said, at the jointly announced establishment of Sino–Oman's strategic partnership, Beijing is willing to establish a strategic partnership with Oman in order to elevate ties between the two countries, and this will lead to achievements in the Belt and Road cooperation and safeguard the common interests of both sides in international and regional affairs.[4]

The chapter's main argument is that Beijing's strategic partnership framework with Oman is based on shared or mutual complementary economic and commercial interests, especially Oman Vision 2020 integration within the implementation of the Belt and Road Initiative. The Sino–Oman strategic partnership is contributing to the development of trade relations that have become diversified beyond the energy industry, and the two sides have economic interests that are increasingly complementary. Policy coordination, connectivity, trade and investments, energy cooperation, financial integration, and tourism and cultural ties are all areas where commercial relations have strengthened in recent years. The Belt and Road Initiative complements Oman's Vision 2020 and could help Muscat to achieve its national development strategy.

Oman Vision 2020

The Oman Vision 2020, a plan for Oman's economic future up to the year 2020, was announced in 1995 and provided a roadmap for the achievement of the country's economic and social goals over the fifth five-year plan period (1996–2000). The first phase took place between 1970 and 1995, and Oman Vision 2020 is the second phase. The key objectives include Economic and financial stability; changing the role of government in the economy and broadening private sector participation; diversifying the economic base and sources of national income; globalizing the Omani economy; and upgrading skills of the Omani workforce and developing human resources.[5]

The primary aim of the vision for Oman's economy in the next quarter of a century is to, at least, maintain the current level of per capita income in real terms and to strive to double it by 2020. The vision also aims at providing suitable conditions for economic take-off. The government will strive to use the proceeds of oil and gas for sustainable economic diversification, and will accept full responsibility for promoting basic health education training for Omani citizens, in addition to adopting policies which promote their standard of living. The following three main strategies also assist the vision for Oman's Economy: Human Resources Development, Economic Diversification, and Private sector Development.[6] Oman's Vision 2020, despite its limited achievements, is paving the way for further and bolder reforms to be attempted under Vision 2040.[7]

Oman and the Belt and Road Initiative

The PRC's strategic partnership with Oman includes six major areas for cooperation within the Belt and Road Initiative. These areas are policy coordination, connectivity, trade and investments, energy cooperation, financial integration and tourism, and cultural ties. However, each country views the Belt and Road Initiative framework and reacts to it according to its perspective and the consequences for its national interests and international status. Therefore, the two countries have very different attitudes regarding how to realize the vision.[8] The Oman Vision 2020 and China's Belt and Road vision have converged on a common economic development path, and their synergetic strategy will bring new opportunities for both sides. As a result, the realization of the Belt and Road Initiative will provide new momentum for Oman's economic transformation.

Connectivity

As part of China's strategic partnership with Muscat, facilitation of connectivity is one of the essential ways to integrate the Oman Vision 2020 into the BRI framework. Muscat should attempt to optimize its infrastructural connections and also to adapt its technical systems to those of the other countries in initiative. This would lead Beijing–Oman to jointly contribute to the development of international transport maritime and overland routes, and the creation of an infrastructural network that could in time connect all the regions in Asia and also specific points in Asia, Africa, and Europe. In addition, there should be serious attempts to create low-carbon and green infrastructure.[9]

The Persian Gulf forms a unique geopolitical position, as it connects three continents: Europe, Asia, and Africa; this geographical position gives it a vital strategic significance and value to the materialization of China's BRI.[10] On this basis, Beijing seeks to strengthen the mutual interdependency with Muscat in various sectors such as energy, trade, and investments in construction and infrastructure projects, to leverage its economic capabilities to realize the successful implementation of the MSRI.

Oman is situated closer to East Africa, India, Iran, Pakistan, Yemen, and the greater Indian Ocean region than other GCC states; it will be of immense strategic value to China's efforts to revive ancient maritime trade routes. Oman's strategic location (on the axis of the Indian Ocean and Arabian Gulf) enables it to act as a regional hub between Asia and GCC states and boasts accessible trade routes and speedy transit times to the world's most attractive emerging markets.[11]

In this context Oman's port, Duqm, the most significant economic project in the Middle East region and one of the largest in the world, with a $10.7 billion Chinese investment, constitutes a vital link in Beijing's Belt and Road Initiative. On Oman's central eastern seaboard, the port town of Duqm hopes to become a critical Middle East logistics hub, connecting the Gulf to the world's busiest maritime trade route. Duqm's economic zone comprises several projects, including a multi-purpose harbor, a refinery that aims to process 230,000 barrels of crude oil per day, and the largest dry dock in the Middle East, which will have a capacity of 200 ships per year.[12]

Duqm is strategically located outside the Strait of Hormuz, the sole passageway into the Gulf for a third of all oil traded by sea. The strait is the doorway to the Persian Gulf, and with Iran frequently threatening to block sea traffic passing through it, the Omani port is geographically well positioned to be an alternative hub for shipping. Duqm also offers primary port access to the main sea lanes between the Red Sea and the Gulf. The port could provide unhindered access to the Indian Ocean for gas, oil and other bulk products arriving overland from the Gulf states. Moreover, the Duqm economic zone is expected to host the first refinery in the Middle East to process crude from another Middle Eastern country on a long-term contractual basis. Duqm is aiming to emerge as a regional transshipment hub, docking large boats from Asia to offload cargo that will be re-shipped to the Gulf and East Africa.[13]

Oman has also started to build a regional rail network linking Duqm to other ports, industrial areas and free zones at Sohar and Salalah with their wider GCC coverage.[14] There is an accelerated infrastructural program to boost the supply of power and water to meet rising demands from growth and development. For example, natural gas supply to the industrial estates in Sohar and Salalah has helped to promote such industries as petrochemicals and bitumen refinery.[15]

The Omani government responded positively to the Chinese invitation to cooperate in the MSRI projects. China–Oman cooperation is a win-win model because the investment and trade fit into the fields of infrastructure construction, finance, and capacity so that China can provide strong support for Oman's economic restructuring. China's investments are essential for Oman to achieve the robust logistics and infrastructure links needed to promote the downstream diversification goals outlined in its Vision 2020 strategy to diversify its economy away from a reliance on oil and gas. Due to economic problems stemming from cheap oil, as well as the major challenge of youth unemployment, the Omanis welcome China's growing investment.

Furthermore, the related financial mechanism of BRI will provide much-needed financial support for the economic restructure and infrastructure construction of Oman.[16] As Yu Fulong, China's Ambassador to Oman, said at the eighth ministerial meeting of the China–Arab States Cooperation Forum (CASCF) held in Beijing in July 2018, "in the next five years, China will make outbound investments of $750 billion worldwide, and Oman is among the countries that will benefit from such investment. Arab countries, including Oman, should grasp these opportunities. Being strategically located, huge investments are ideal for Oman, which will come from both the Chinese government and the private sector. Oman has played an important role in the Belt and Road Initiative due to its strategic geographical location in the region."[17]

Policy coordination

As part of China's strategic partnership with Oman, promoting political cooperation between the two countries, creating mechanisms for dialogue and consensus-building on global and regional issues, developing shared interests, deepening political trust and reaching a new consensus on cooperation are important to integrate the Oman vision 2020 within the Belt and Road Initiative framework. Beijing appreciates the sultanate's unique climate of stability and peaceful sectarian co-existence, making it a reliable regional key player in realizing the MSRI and expanding its maritime presence in the Indian Ocean and the Arabian Sea for economic, political, and security reasons.[18]

According to Yu Fulong, Ambassador of the People's Republic of China to the Sultanate, China considers Oman an important country in the region, and acknowledges and appreciates its peaceful foreign policies and its unique and constructive role in maintaining the security and safety of the region. The Sultanate is an important station along the Belt and Road Initiative, and it enjoys geographical advantages, including the ease of maritime transport and its proximity to many promising markets. The two sides seek to combine the advantages of the Sultanate with the potential of Chinese companies to turn them into a driving force that benefits both countries.[19]

In May 2018, Beijing and Oman issued a joint statement on the establishment of a strategic partnership between the two nations. Both countries agreed that since the establishment of their diplomatic ties, political mutual trust and traditional friendship have continued to increase and cooperation in the areas of energy, economy, and trade, connectivity, and culture has yielded fruitful results. They also agreed to strengthen exchanges and consultations between leaders of both countries, maintain regular communication and coordination on bilateral relations as well as international and regional issues of common concern, continuously expand consensus, and consolidate and deepen mutual political trust.[20]

More important, according to the joint statement, Oman welcomes and supports the China-proposed Belt and Road Initiative and is willing to participate actively in projects under this framework. It will continue to support and participate in the Belt and Road Forum for International Cooperation. Beijing appreciates Oman's active participation in the Belt and Road construction and welcomes Oman to become a partner under the initiative. The two countries are willing to strengthen policy communication further, enhance alignment of the Belt and Road Initiative and Oman's "Ninth Five-Year Plan" and actively implement the cooperative documents on the Belt and Road construction. The two sides will synergize their development strategies and focus on cooperation in such areas as the exploitation of energy resources, chemical industry, manufacturing, and marine industries.[21] During the meeting between Chinese Foreign Minister Wang Yi and Omani Foreign Minister Yousef Bin Alawi Bin Abdullah, they signed an MoU on the joint construction of the Belt and Road Initiative. Thanks to this agreement, Oman is committed to participating in the realization of the new Silk Road.[22]

In December 2018, Hatem al-Tai, a member of the State Council of Oman, said during the Omani–Chinese Business Forum in the capital Muscat, "The Belt and Road Initiative not only helps China but also aims to help the world to achieve common benefits. Beijing and Oman signed a strategic partnership agreement early this year, and there are many projects to be achieved between the two countries as a result of the agreement. Omani–Chinese relations are witnessing progress and prosperity of civilization, economy, and culture."[23]

Energy cooperation

In China's strategic partnership with Muscat, investment in energy infrastructure is considered one of the critical areas of cooperation to integrate Oman Vision 2020 into the Belt and Road Initiative framework. Therefore, the new Silk Road can provide a new framework for more extensive Chinese investments in the Omani energy industry. In 2017, China was Oman's largest export market, receiving 70 percent of Oman's crude oil exports. They are, obviously, linked together by their common interests in that their energy industries supplement and complement each other.

In 2013, China became the world's largest net importer of total petroleum and other liquid fuels, and by 2017 China had surpassed the US in annual gross crude oil imports by importing 8.4 million barrels per day (b/d) compared with 7.9 million b/d of US crude oil imports.

In that year, an average of 56 percent of China's crude oil imports came from countries within OPEC. New refinery capacity and strategic inventory stockpiling, combined with declining domestic production, were the significant factors contributing to its increase in imports.[24]

Beijing's dependence on crude oil imports from the Persian Gulf, a leading oil-producing region, has been increasing gradually since 1993 when it became a net importer of oil.[25] In 2018, the value of crude oil imported into China totaled $239.2 billion (20.2 percent of total crude oil imports). Forty-five countries supplied crude petroleum oil to China, but close to half (44.1 percent) of Chinese imported crude oil originates from just nine Middle Eastern nations, and six Persian Gulf states are among the top 15 crude oil suppliers to Beijing. In 2018, Oman was ranked in fifth place (up 40 percent), exporting some $17.3 billion (7.2 percent) worth of oil to China.[26]

According to the EIA (US Energy Information Administration), Oman is the largest oil and natural gas producer in the Middle East that is not a member of OPEC. According to the *Oil & Gas Journal*, in 2018 Oman had 5.4 billion barrels of estimated proved oil reserves, ranking Oman as the seventh largest proved oil reserve holder in the Middle East. In 2017, Oman held 23 trillion cubic feet (Tcf) of proved natural gas reserves.[27] Like many countries in the Middle East, Oman is highly dependent on its hydrocarbon sector. According to the Central Bank of Oman, in 2017 the hydrocarbon sector accounted for 30 percent of Oman's nominal GDP, an increase from 27 percent from last year, and natural gas accounted for 68 percent of Oman's domestic energy consumption.[28]

Beijing's growing reliance on oil imports from the Middle East is a crucial reason for its substantial investment in its twin trade and infrastructure initiatives (SREB and MSRI); these are likely to become linked through ports or pipeline developments, with growing naval access and support facilities to help protect China's energy security. This is also a powerful driver to China's blue-water naval development and power projection capacity through the Indian Ocean, and development of a whole set of strong diplomatic ties with the littoral Indian Ocean countries. Hence, the oil trade is significant and will become increasingly so in Sino–Omani relations.[29]

Since the early 1980s, Oman has been an essential source of imported energy and became the first Arab nation and member of the GCC to export oil directly to China.[30] Indeed, over the years, energy cooperation has been the primary axis around which the Sino–Oman partnership revolves.[31] According to the Oman Ministry Oil & Gas, China remained Oman's largest export market and procured 87.2

percent of the Sultanate's crude oil exports in 2018, thanks to the perceived compatibility between the quality of the Sultanate's crude oil and the needs of Chinese refineries.[32]

As the Ambassador Extraordinary and Plenipotentiary of the People's Republic of China to Oman, Yu Furlong, said: Oman is one of the principal oil suppliers to China because the quality of Oman's oil is very good, and most importantly because it suits the (needs of) Chinese refineries.[33] According to Fitch Solutions, a part of the Fitch Rating report, China is also important for Oman as it is the largest customer of Omani oil. In the first eleven months of 2018, Beijing took 82.8 percent of Oman's total crude exports, and this percentage has broadly increased over the past several years.[34]

According to the Sino–Oman joint statement on the establishment of strategic partnership, the two countries will synergize their development strategies and focus on cooperation in such areas as the exploitation of energy resources, the chemical industry, manufacturing, and marine industries. The two sides believe that energy cooperation is an important pillar of pragmatic cooperation and support further cooperation in such fields as crude oil trading, exploration and development of oil and gas resources, service engineering, refining, and the chemical industry. They agreed to strengthen cooperation in new energy and renewable energy.[35]

China's numerous objectives in the Persian Gulf region, mainly securing access to energy supplies, drive Beijing's growing interest in Oman because as China moves forward with MSRI, the sultanate is uniquely positioned to facilitate Chinese companies' ability to better access markets throughout the Middle East and beyond. As a strategically situated and leading natural gas producer, Oman will play an increasingly important role in the materialization of Beijing's MSRI.

Trade and investments

As part of the PRC's strategic partnership with Muscat, both sides will mitigate as much as possible the barriers to free trade, investment, industrial cooperation, and technical and engineering services in order to facilitate the integration of Oman Vision 2020 within the Belt and Road Initiative framework. Both countries should take a series of measures, such as expanding free-trade zones, improving trade structures, seeking new potential areas for trade and improving the trade balance, devising new initiatives for the promotion of conventional forms of trade, developing trans-border electronic trade and other advanced models of business, thereby creating a system for supporting trade in services to strengthen and expand conventional trade, increasing customs cooperation, and regularly sharing information in these areas.[36]

Although petroleum exports serve as the foundation of Sino–Omani relationships, recent Chinese bilateral trade and massive investments in construction and infrastructure projects will certainly help grow relations further. According to China Customs Statistics (export–import), China's trade volume with Saudi Arabia grew to about $21.4 billion in 2018.[37] According to the Sino–Oman joint statement on the establishment of a strategic partnership, the two countries agreed to make full use of the mechanism of the China–Oman Joint Committee of Economics and Trade, expand mutually beneficial cooperation in infrastructure construction, industrial parks, railways, ports, power stations and logistics, and promote the all-round development of bilateral economic and trade relations.[38]

As Yu Fulong, China's Ambassador to Oman, said at the eighth ministerial meeting of the CASCF held in Beijing in July 2018, Oman is an attractive country to foreign investment as it is characterized by a stable political situation and legal system. In addition to having natural resources, Oman is currently implementing the Ninth Five-Year Plan and National Program for Economic Diversification, which is an ambitious program launched for foreign investors to invest in Oman. The country has taken many measures to facilitate the work of foreign companies within the sultanate, with a sophisticated investment law indicating that the volume of investments between Oman and China will increase in the coming years. The Omani and Chinese sides will form a joint working group to discuss ways of developing investment between the two countries. Chinese investment in the Sultanate will not be limited to Duqm but will also include Muscat, Salalah, Sohar, and other areas".[39]

In recent years, China has boosted its investment activity in the Sultanate, most prominently in Duqm where numerous Chinese firms are funding a $10 billion China–Oman Industrial City.[40] Over the past years, China has become the key to Oman's efforts to transform Duqm, a fishing settlement about 550 km south of the Omani capital Muscat, into an industrial center aimed to diversify its economy beyond oil and gas. The Duqm Industrial Park is the most important foreign cooperation project in Al Duqm Special Economic Zone.[41] Such investments could be the key for Oman as it looks to diversify its economy away from reliance on oil and gas. According to Li Lingbing, Ambassador of the People's Republic of China to the Sultanate, the volume of Chinese investments in the Sultanate was over $6 billion in 2018.[42]

Within the framework of Beijing's Belt and Road initiative, Chinese firms are planning investments as well as already investing in the construction of large industrial parks and special economic zones along the tendrils of the MSRI across Asia, the Middle East, and Africa. Duqm, a remote and underutilized Omani port situated 550 km south of the capital, Muscat, is one of Beijing's more ambitious projects, transforming it into a vital nerve center of Sino–Omani global trade and manufacturing.[43] Oman Wanfang, a consortium of six private Chinese firms, the main developer of the China–Oman Industrial Park at Duqm Special Economic Zone (SEZ), intends to invest $10.7 billion in building an industrial city there. The Chinese consortium has promised to develop at least 30 percent of the Oman Industrial Park in Duqm within five to seven years, and ten Chinese firms signed land lease agreements for building various projects, totaling an investment of $3.06 billion.[44]

There will be some 35 SEZ projects implemented in the China–Oman industrial park: twelve projects in the field of heavy industries including the production of commercial concrete, building materials and related industries, production of glazed glass, methanol and other chemicals. In the light industrial zone, there will be twelve projects, including the production of 1 GW of solar power units, production of oil and gas tools, as well as products for pipelines and drilling.[45] For Oman, the SEZ projects success is essential for its quest to diversify its economy beyond its traditional hydrocarbon sector, and is in line with Vision 2020.[46]

If the SEZ projects materialize, which is by no means certain, given the multi-year timeframe and the many pressures on Chinese companies, it will be equivalent to over half of Oman's current stock of foreign direct investment. Duqm is marketing its location as a major attraction, lying on the Arabian Sea between the Gulf of Oman and the Gulf of Aden; the location of the port and SEZ combo at Duqm fits into the development and realization of China's MSRI.[47]

According to Yu Fulong, Ambassador of the People's Republic of China to the Sultanate, the Industrial Park at Duqm Special Economic Zone has received much attention from the business community and the governments of the two countries. The construction work in the project is underway, as the general design of the first phase of the project is currently under approval by the concerned authorities in the Sultanate. The industrial city will play a major role in supporting trade cooperation between the two countries by taking advantage of the potentials of Chinese companies in industry and capital on one side, and the Sultanate's potentials on the other side, in terms of the strategic position and the proximity to promising markets and policies to facilitate and attract investments to the Duqm region, which contribute to the acceleration of the growth of non-Omani oil sectors and the diversification of the economic structure and the national income of the Sultanate.[48]

Financial integration

Under China's strategic partnership with Muscat, the formation and promotion of financial integration between the two countries are considered one of the essential cooperation areas to facilitate the integration of Oman Vision 2020 within the Belt and Road Initiative framework. There are a number of measures for the realization of financial integration between the two countries: including deepening financial cooperation and building a stable currency system, establishing an investment and financing system and a credit information system in Asia, expanding the scope and scale of bilateral currency swaps between the two countries, and developing the bond market in Asia. In addition, making joint efforts to establish the Asian Infrastructure Investment Bank (AIIB), and financial institutions with good credit ratings to issue RMB-denominated bonds in China, and encouraging qualified Chinese financial institutions and companies to issue bonds in both RMB and foreign currencies outside China and to use the funds thus collected in countries along the BRI.[49]

As part of the joint statement on the establishment of a strategic partnership in May 2018, the two countries are willing to promote financial cooperation. They support discussion on the possibility of developing monetary cooperation and the role of their own currency in bilateral trade and investment. They encourage financial institutions of the two sides to provide financial support for bilateral trade and investment cooperation.[50]

The Sino–Omani financial cooperation is still at an initial stage. In October 2014, Oman, represented by the State General Reserve Fund (SGRF), signed an MoU with 21 other Asian countries in preparation for the establishment of the Asian Infrastructure Investment Bank. According to Abdulsalam Al Murshidi, Executive President of SGRF, the Sultanate will have an opportunity to benefit from the facilities which the bank will provide for financing the ambitious infrastructural projects in the country. Furthermore, there will be job opportunities for qualified Omani candidates in the banking sector to work in AIIB.[51]

In March 2019, a delegation from the board of directors of AIIB visited in Oman to meet with key officials from both the public and private sectors. The AIIB visit's agenda focuses on Oman's Vision 2040, a flagship program adopted by the Sultanate. The visit aims to bring together infrastructure experts and support effective and project-driven networking, with a focus on utilizing innovative financing to address critical infrastructure needs. The program also includes field visits to Duqm port to familiarize themselves with the project and future development plans. During the visit, AIIB learned how to further support the Omani government to achieve its priorities for economic development.[52]

Besides, in August 2017, the Omani government has raised $3.55 billion through a loan from a group of Chinese financial institutions with a five-year maturity. The transaction – the largest ever for a regional borrower in the Chinese market – was increased from an initial target of $2 billion because of the keen interest received.[53]

Tourism and Cultural Ties

As part of China's strategic partnership with Muscat, enabling the people of the two countries to bond along the Silk Road is also vital to integrate the Oman Vision 2020 within the Belt and Road Initiative framework. The promotion of cultural and academic exchanges helps win public support for deepening bilateral and multilateral cooperation; the means include providing scholarships, holding yearly cultural events, increasing cooperation in science and technology, and establishing joint laboratory or research centers and international technology transfer centers.[54]

In recent years, tourism and cultural cooperation have become another important aspect of the China–Oman strategic partnership, and both nations have outlined their intention to expand the collaboration in these areas in the coming years. According to the Sino–Oman joint statement on the establishment of a strategic partnership, the two countries will carry out cultural exchanges in various forms to increase understanding and friendship between the two peoples. Beijing will provide more opportunities for Oman students to study in China and support Chinese language teaching in Oman. Both parties are willing to actively study the establishment of a Chinese cultural center in Oman.[55]

Cultural cooperation has become an important aspect of the China–Oman strategic partnership, and both nations have outlined their intention to expand the collaboration in this area in the coming years. For instance, the China–Oman Duqm Industrial Park, a project under the Belt and Road Initiative, which plays a critical role in boosting

Chinese-Omani cooperation, has been sponsoring Omani students' studying trips to China. In cooperation with the Omani government, the park selects high-school graduates every year and sends them to study in China. The park plans to help train 1,000 students for Oman in the next eight to ten years. In June 2018, the first batch of 39 students returned to Oman after completing vocational training. They will finish their internships and then work for the industrial park.[56]

In September 2018, Omani Minister of Information, Abdul Munim bin Mansour Al Hasani, visited China to participate in a cultural media event held in Beijing on the occasion of the 40th anniversary of the establishment of diplomatic relations between the two countries, in addition to the unveiling the plaque of the Sohar Vessel Memorial in the famous Chinese City of Guangzhou. The Omani–Sino Media and Cultural Festival includes many media, cultural, artistic, and musical events, which last for several days, and it reflects the importance of these relations at present and in the future.[57]

In addition, China's links with the GCC states have strengthened due to the introduction of additional and direct airline routes, the steady growth of the Chinese economy, and Chinese tourists' increasing disposable income. According to data from Colliers International published ahead of Arabian Travel Market (ATM) 2019, the number of Chinese tourists traveling to the GCC is expected to increase 81 percent from 1.6 million in 2018 to 2.9 million in 2022, and Oman will steadily increase their Chinese visitor arrivals with a growth of 12 percent. The GCC countries currently attract just one percent of China's total outbound market, but positive trends are expected over the coming years, to as many as 400 million tourists.[58]

According to Li Lingbing, ambassador of the People's Republic of China to the Sultanate, at the second Oman–China Tourism Forum, 22 major Chinese tourism companies participated. This is a positive sign for the promotion of the Sultanate in China to be carried out by these companies which have a presence in all parts of their country. The ambassador was confident that the number of Chinese tourists visiting Oman would increase in coming years as the Ministry of Tourism of the Sultanate was taking a keen interest in promotional efforts in this huge market. Meanwhile, the number of Chinese tourists who visited the Sultanate has reached 20,476 in the first quarter of 2019. In 2018, the number of Chinese tourists who visited the Sultanate was 44,580, which was a huge jump from 19,470 of 2017.[59]

Summary

The Sultanate of Oman is a strategic partner (in terms of geopolitics, commerce, energy security, and non-traditional security) of China in the Persian Gulf, the Arab world, the Middle East, and the Indian Ocean. Beijing's strategic partnership framework with Oman is based on shared or mutual complementary economic and commercial interests, especially Oman Vision 2020 integration within the implementation of the Belt and Road Initiative. The Sino–Oman strategic partnership contributes to the development of trade relations that have become diversified beyond the energy industry, and the two sides have economic interests that are increasingly complementary. The Belt and Road Initiative complements Oman's Vision 2020 and could help Muscat to achieve its national development strategy.

Li Lingbing, Ambassador of the People's Republic of China to the Sultanate, has reaffirmed the Sultanate's important role in the Belt and Road Initiative. Oman enjoys an important geographical location and excellent ports, such as Duqm, Salalah, and Sohar that have a natural advantage in participating in building the BRI.[60] More broadly, Oman can offer its geographical location (situated strategically at the juncture of the overland and seaborne routes), its important influence in international energy markets, and its record as a politically stable country. Unlike other Gulf Arab states, Oman, which follows the more moderate form of Ibadi Islam, has been spared sectarian unrest, radical Islamist terrorism, and unstable post-revolution transitions.[61]

However, there are certain constraints and barriers in the Sino–Omani relationship that could prevent or disrupt the engagement between the two countries. First, Oman is seeking to benefit from its geographical location to become a vital maritime global trade route but is forced to compete with other GCC countries that are also keen on capitalizing on their logistic hubs to play a more pivotal role in global trade via the region.

Second, geopolitical turmoil in the Persian Gulf in recent years may affect the investment security of Chinese companies. Oman is located between two regional powers: Saudi Arabia and Iran. Muscat, together with Tehran, shares the exit of the Strait of Hormuz, which is one of the world's major oil chokepoints. This strategic location involves more geopolitical risks to Oman (e.g., Iran has frequent conflicts with Saudi Arabia; the Trump government's tough policy against Iran). There are risks of a sudden outbreak of war in the entire Gulf region, which may influence Oman and hinder normal economic development and production in the region.[62]

Furthermore, India is likewise determined to take advantage of Omani trade networks to gain access to more markets in African and Middle Eastern markets and continues to compete for geopolitical influence across the Indian Ocean.[63] Oman and India have a tradition of close diplomatic, cultural, and economic ties that include extensive cooperation in the military and defense spheres. Oman's tendency to play on both sides of the line in order to protect its economic arrangements and to keep its options open is a fact that China will not ignore.

More important, Oman plays an important role in helping the US realize its wide-ranging stability goals for the Persian Gulf region. Oman's longstanding partnership with the United States is critical to its mutual national security objectives, which include countering terrorism, increasing economic diversification and development opportunities, and halting Iran's pursuit of nuclear weapons. Oman has been a strategic ally of the US since 1980 when it became the first of the Persian Gulf states to sign a formal accord permitting the US military to use its facilities. Oman has hosted US forces during every US military operation in and around the Gulf since then, and is a partner in US efforts to counter regional terrorism and related threats.[64]

During the Obama administration, Oman played a critical role in securing U.S interests in the Middle East; the Sultanate was a fruitful broker of Washington's diplomacy in areas where traditional lines of communication were unavailable. Most importantly, Oman's role in facilitating the Iran nuclear negotiations, starting secretly in 2013 and completed in 2015, vindicated the level of trust that the Obama government placed in its ally.[65] However, the Trump administration watered down the relationship due to accusations that Oman has been complicit in arms smuggling from Iran to Houthi rebels in Yemen.

There are no indications to suggest that Oman is contemplating either a shift in its traditionally pro-US foreign policy orientation or replacing its Washington ally with China. Nevertheless, strained relations with the Trump administration on the one hand, and China's intention to invest billions of dollars in the Duqm industrial complex, and to construct storage facilities, refineries, and other transportation infrastructure to connect another link in the Belt and Road Initiative, on the other hand, might change this picture. The Trump administration would be wise to repair its fraying relations with Oman, which is a valuable player in the complex Middle East; it would be a mistake to sideline such a critical strategic partnership and strengthen China's presence and influence in the region.

8
Bahrain

Recent years have witnessed the expansion of Beijing's economic ties with Manama because of Bahrain's fast-evolving startup ecosystem and the country's willingness to play a vital role in China's flagship One Belt, One Road Initiative. This chapter examines the various aspects that underlie the friendly cooperative relations between China and Bahrain and the synergies between the Belt and Road Initiative and Bahrain's Economic Vision 2030. An overview is presented of the shared or mutual complementary economic and commercial interests that power the relationship, as a result of the integration and implementation of the Belt and Road Initiative and Bahrain's Economic Vision 2030. Under these conditions, it can be expected that the growth of positive relations between China and Bahrain will continue over the next few years.

In 2019, the PRC and Bahrain will celebrate the 30th anniversary of the establishment of their diplomatic ties. Ever since the establishment of diplomatic ties on April 15, 1989, bilateral relations have maintained a favorable momentum of development. While many have documented China's ties with the GCC countries, Beijing's relations with the Kingdom of Bahrain remain undocumented. Although China's relations with Bahrain have been kept out of the limelight, they have developed well beyond diplomatic and political affairs.[1]

The $1 trillion One Belt, One Road Initiative (BRI), put forward in October 2013 by Chinese President Xi Jinping, seeks to connect Beijing to the global market by linking Asia and Europe via a set of land and maritime trade routes. The concept took form over several years and has now become a cornerstone of President Xi's foreign policy. The BRI has become a key theme of bilateral relations, and could also create opportunities for partnerships in the many promising emerging markets between China and countries in the Persian Gulf region. Although the Gulf region is not directly along the BRI's trade routes, the Gulf countries have high economic and geopolitical stakes in

Beijing's planned multicontinental trade corridor. This is due to the strategic location of Bahrain as the gateway to the Arabian Gulf, and the fact that it is one of the key countries along the new Silk Road route, enabling it to serve as a transportation hub for the region.

Bahrain, known as 'the Pearl of the Gulf', is an important port on the ancient Maritime Silk Road. The kingdom is also one of the most open and dynamic countries within the top-ranking business environment in the Middle East. Its open and liberal lifestyle, unique market access, world-class regulatory environment, and highly competitive taxation system combined with the lowest operating costs in the region, high quality of life, and a technologically literate population makes the Kingdom the ideal location from which Chinese companies can access this $1.5 trillion GCC market.[2]

Since Bahrain is ideally positioned to play a vital role in China's Belt and Road Initiative, it is important to examine some of the aspects behind the friendly cooperative relations between China and Bahrain, and the synergies between the Belt and Road Initiative and the Bahrain's Economic Vision 2030 in order to understand the extent of economic engagement and bilateral relationship between the two nations. As the Chinese ambassador to Bahrain, An Wa'er, pointed out, Manama is a member of the Arab League and GCC and an important partner to Beijing; it has played an important role as a bridge between China and other countries in the GCC.[3] The central thesis of this chapter is that China's friendly cooperative relations framework with Bahrain is based on shared or mutual complementary economic and commercial interests, especially with the integration and implementation of the Belt and Road Initiative and Bahrain's Economic Vision 2030.

Bahrain's Economic Vision 2030

In 2008 the kingdom developed a national roadmap for government strategy (called the Economic Vision 2030) for the country's future, which was based on the three guiding principles of sustainability, fairness, and competitiveness. The country's national plan is aimed at growing and diversifying the economy by enhancing private sector growth and government investment in infrastructure, affordable housing, and human resources. Bahrain wants to attract foreign investment in five sectors: logistics, light manufacturing, financial services, digital technology, and tourism. The Economic Development Board (EDC) has led a program of coordinated economic and institutional reform intended to transform Bahrain from a regional pioneer to a global contender. The ultimate aim of the plan is to ensure that every Bahraini household has at least twice as much disposable income, in real terms, by 2030.[4]

In the past, oil has been the main force behind economic growth in Bahrain, accounting for over 70 percent of GDP and 80 percent of government revenue. While the hydrocarbon sector remains the dominant industry in Bahrain, continuing efforts to boost trade growth and industrial diversification bode well for the economy in the medium- to long-term. Non-oil industrial development is still at an early stage, but the country's strong logistics profile and supportive industrial policies may provide a base for stronger manufacturing growth and less reliance on oil revenues.[5]

According to the World Bank's "Doing Business 2018" report, Bahrain ranked 66th out of 190 countries on ease of doing business and fifth in the paying taxes category.[6] In the World Economic Forum's 2017–18 Global Competitiveness Index, Bahrain ranked 44th out of 137 economies, mainly due to its strong institutions, growing and stable infrastructure, market efficiencies, and business sophistication.[7] According to the International Monetary Fund, the kingdom's GDP was $31.86bn in 2016, increasing to $33.9bn in 2017.[8] According to the quarterly report produced by the Bahrain Economic Development Board (EDB), the pace of growth in Bahrain "accelerated markedly" in 2017 compared to 3.2 percent in 2016, making it the fastest growing country in the GCC.[9]

The BRI has become a key theme of bilateral relations, and could also create opportunities for partnerships in the many promising emerging markets between China and countries in the Persian Gulf region. Although the Gulf region is not directly along BRI's trade routes, the Gulf countries have high economic and geopolitical stakes in Beijing's planned multicontinental trade corridor. More important, the PRC's pursuit of securing oil and natural gas reserves from as many diverse sources as possible has brought it close to the Persian Gulf states, which are China's top energy suppliers.[10] A stable Gulf region is vital for Beijing's sustainable growth, and with the completion of the Gulf Pearl Chain, China can achieve effective management and control the flow of its energy needs. This will open new markets and trade routes for the Gulf Countries, as the Silk Road would connect Gulf economies with the Southeast and East Asian economies which will enhance economic integration and cooperation.[11]

The past two decades have seen substantial changes in the global economy and geopolitical trends, with the rise of China on the global stage. These developments are creating new opportunities for the GCC countries as they look to diversify their economies, increase trade, and seek investment opportunities in emerging markets; this includes schemes such as forging strategic partnerships with China to promote the Belt and Road Initiative and to incorporate it into their national development plan. This reflects a growing tendency among the GCC states which seek to benefit from the favorable business conditions in China, as well as Beijing's expertise and experience in its rapid path to economic development.[12]

The Gulf countries have strongly embraced and benefitted from a network of cooperation lines in various investment and infrastructure projects and other fields with China. Hence, they have much to gain from the realization of the Belt and Road vision as the project aims to enhance the PRC's diplomatic and economic relations with countries that maintain a positive view of Beijing's global economic and political ascendancy, and can provide the energy resources that it needs to fuel its economy.[13]

Bahrain and the Belt and Road Initiative

The PRC's friendly cooperative relations with Bahrain include four major areas for cooperation within the Belt and Road Initiative. These areas are policy coordination, connectivity, trade and investments, tourism and cultural ties. Inevitably, each country views the Belt and Road Initiative framework and reacts to it according to its own perspective and the consequences for its own national interests and international status. Therefore, in realizing the shared vision, the two countries have very different attitudes.[14] Nonetheless, Bahrain's Economic Vision 2030 and China's Belt and Road vision have converged on a common economic development path, and their synergetic strategy will bring new opportunities for both sides. As a result, the realization of the Belt and Road Initiative will provide new momentum for Bahrain's economic transformation.

Policy coordination

China's friendly cooperative relations with Bahrain are being translated into promoting political cooperation between countries, creating mechanisms for dialogue and consensus-building on global and regional issues, developing shared interests, deepening political trust, and reaching a new consensus on cooperation. These are all important in order to integrate the Bahrain's Economic Vision 2030 into the Belt and Road Initiative framework.[15]

Bilateral relations have gathered momentum since the King of Bahrain Sheikh Hamad bin Isa Al-khalifa visited China in 2013 when he strengthened the ties between both sides and opened new channels of cooperation at several levels. Major agreements were signed in the areas of education, health, culture, and investment which boosted relations and bilateral cooperation.[16] Chinese President Xi Jinping said in talks with King Hamad that Bahrain is an important cooperative partner of China in the Middle East and Gulf region, and "the two countries should be jointly committed to building friendly cooperative relations of long-term stability."[17]

The friendly cooperative relations (友好 合作 关系) framework between the two nations has further strengthened over the past couple of years because of Bahrain's fast-evolving startup ecosystem and the country's willingness to play a vital role in China's flagship Belt and Road Initiative. According to Chinese Ambassador to Bahrain, Qi Zhenhong, China and Bahrain have become friendly partners of mutual understanding and trust, a cooperative partner of the win-win result and a respectable partner of learning from each other and deriving mutual benefit. He added that a further strengthening of the friendly cooperative relations between China and Bahrain will not only bring benefits to the two peoples, but also promote the strategic cooperation between China and GCC countries, and safeguard regional peace, stability, and prosperity.[18]

Connectivity

The facilitation of connectivity is one of the important ways to integrate the Bahrain's Economic Vision 2030 into the Belt and Road Initiative framework. Bahrain should attempt to optimize its infrastructural connections and also to adapt its technical systems to those of the other countries in the Belt and Road Initiative framework. This would lead Beijing–Manama to jointly contribute to the development of international transport maritime and overland routes and the creation of an infrastructural network that could gradually connect all the regions in Asia and also at specific points in Asia, Africa, and Europe. In addition, there should be serious attempts to create low-carbon and green infrastructure.

In the past, Bahrain traded pearls, dates, and copper, while it imported silk and musk from China. Now in the 21st century, Beijing has a reinvigorated interest in the kingdom and the broader GCC because of its Belt and Road Initiative. Bahrain was a trading outpost along the old Silk Road connecting the Gulf to the world for thousands of years, and traces of the history of this long trading relationship between Bahrain and China can be found at many of the archaeological sites around the kingdom.[19]

The kingdom's location in the heart of the Arabian Gulf makes accessibility and entry into any Middle East market (whether by land, sea, or air) fast and economically feasible. Bahrain's geographic location is a key strategic asset, enabling it to serve as a transportation hub for the region. The Khalifa Bin Salman Port (KBSP), the premier transshipment hub for the Northern Gulf, has enhanced the country's role as a primary supplier of goods to Saudi Arabia, the region's largest market. KBSP's strategic location in the middle of the Arabian Gulf, together with its deep-water berths and approach channel which enable it to accept the largest oceangoing container vessels, and its direct overland links to the mainland (Saudi Arabia and Qatar) position the port as a major regional distribution center.[20]

The kingdom is also linked to Saudi Arabia, the Gulf's largest economy, via the 25-kilometer King Fahd Causeway, which is being expanded to handle increased traffic. From 2014, a 45km causeway has linked Bahrain to Qatar, which has the world's third-largest natural gas reserves. The link will complete a single trans-Gulf highway, connecting the entire $1.1 trillion Gulf Market, with Bahrain at its center. By 2030, this causeway will also carry a freight railway, thus increasing its capacity. Additionally, Bahrain International Airport is undergoing an extensive expansion and modernization program, which is expected to further improve the country's status as a tourist destination and a center for logistics by 2020.[21] Hence, Bahrain can be considered a great regional transportation hub and a good place for fulfillment centers for Chinese companies that operate along the Silk Road.

There is a convergence of interests that can be built upon to forge a basis for cooperation and integration between the Bahrain Economic Vision 2030 and development of the Belt and Road Initiative by linking these two projects in a way to set up a unified development strategy to the best objectives of both countries. As the Ambassador of China to Bahrain, Qi Zhenhong, said, "I do believe under this big picture, the comprehensive cooperation between China and Bahrain is bound to face great and historical opportunity, especially with the integration and implementation of the Belt and Road Initiative and Bahrain's Economic Vision 2030."[22]

Moreover, according to Bahrain Minister for Transportation and Telecommunications Kamal bin Ahmed Mohammed, the BRI could become a great opportunity for the Gulf nations. The Gulf region, which is the central location of the Belt and Road Initiative, is a prime market for China and vice versa. "We think that China always will look for a new market for their services, they are manufacturing goods, every day they are increasing their production and we can be the market for these goods. We also have a lot of projects [going on] and . . . there will be a need for Chinese goods and products. There is a great opportunity for the GCC countries; the infrastructure already exists, already we have the routes and the [trade] corridor available, a politically stable region, a resilient financial sector, and there are many areas in which both regions, China and the GCC, can benefit from each other."[23]

In July 2018, the foreign ministers of Bahrain and China signed a memorandum of understanding (MoU) to advance the construction of the Belt and Road project jointly. "The two sides would continue to firmly support each other on issues concerning each other's core interests and promote pragmatic cooperation across the board under the Belt and Road framework. According to Bahrain Foreign Minister, Shaikh Khalid bin Ahmed Al Khalifa, the kingdom highly applauds and supports the Belt and Road Initiative and stands ready to strengthen all-round cooperation with China and boost bilateral ties."[24] In the end, Bahrain's central location in the Gulf and its transportation links to the rest of the Middle East, with rapid access by road, sea, and air, make it a unique partner in the implementation of the Belt and Road Initiative. Potentially, Bahrain could serve as a regional hub for the growing GCC trade flows and the economic expansion in the Middle East.

Trade and investments

Part of Beijing's friendly cooperative relations with Manama include attempts to mitigate as much as possible the barriers to free trade, investment, industrial cooperation, and technical and engineering services, so as to facilitate the integration of Bahrain's Economic Vision 2030 within the Belt and Road Initiative framework. Measures must be taken by both countries, such as expanding free-trade zones, improving trade structures, seeking new potential areas for trade and improving the trade balance, devising new initiatives for the promotion of conventional forms of trade, developing trans-border electronic trade and other advanced models of business, creating a system for supporting trade in services to strengthen and expand conventional trade, increasing customs cooperation, and regularly sharing information in these areas.[25]

Economic relations have gathered momentum since King Hamad's visit to China in 2013. Since then, the two sides have launched a large number of commerce and trade investments. For example, foreign investments in Bahrain have increased from $142 million in 2015 to $810 million in the first three quarters of 2018.[26] The kingdom has already attracted some big Chinese names to invest in the country, including Huawei Technologies, CPIC Abahsain Fiberglass, China Machinery Engineering Corporation, and China International Marine Containers Company (CIMC). For example, in 2009, Huawei moved its headquarters to Bahrain, and it is now creating and accelerating Bahrain's 5G mobile networks ecosystem.[27]

According to China Customs Statistics (export–import), China–Bahrain trade volume increased to nearly $1.3 billion by 2018.[28] Although the kingdom has fewer natural resources to offer compared to other Gulf states, the country offers Beijing a way to access untapped consumer markets for its exports, as well as lucrative investment opportunities. Leading Chinese companies such as Huawei have established operations in Bahrain, since Bahrain offers a favorable business environment in the Gulf, with attractive policies for foreign direct investment. Currently, about 600 Chinese companies are registered in Bahrain, and the total investment has increased from $50 million to $400 million.[29] According to the 2019 Index of Economic Freedom, Bahrain's economic freedom ranked 54 among the 178 countries in the world and ranked 5th among 14 countries in the Middle East and North Africa region, and its overall score is above the regional and world averages.[30]

In addition, the kingdom is one of the largest financial service centers in the Middle East, with more than 400 well-regulated financial services companies and many financial institutions that have regional headquarters in the country. Investors have a great number of opportunities in Bahrain's mature and sizeable business system and its global, transparent mechanism and strong regulatory system also provide strong support.[31] In 2010, the Bahrain-China Joint Investment Forum (BCJIF) was formed to facilitate the growth of economic links between the two countries, and 18 Chinese commercial agencies, including the Bank of China, opened operations in Bahrain.[32]

Moreover, China is playing an increasingly significant role in several of Bahrain's major construction and infrastructure projects. In January 2014, Chinese construction companies signed an agreement with the Bahraini government to help build 40,000 new residential units across the country.[33] In February 2014, Bahrain announced its plan to open a vast, China-themed mall similar to that of Dragon Mart in Dubai, which it calls it 'Dragon City'; this is a 115,000 square meter mega-mall with more than 780 shops, which raise the profile of Chinese goods in the GCC.[34]

Chinese companies are actively developing business in the kingdom covering all fields of cooperation, including information and communication, high-end manufacturing, environment protection, and project contracting. Some 3,000–4,000 Chinese nationals are living and working in Bahrain. Most of them are tenants of Dragon City or staff of Huawei. CPIC Abahsain Fiberglass is planning to invest 500 million to extend to four production lines that are estimated to be complete in 2020. China Machinery Engineering Corporation (CMEC) is negotiating with the Ministry of Housing over guaranteed financing clauses for a social housing project. Once the agreement is reached, the amount of investment in the first phase will be a rather huge $550 million.[35]

The vigorous development of logistics in Bahrain and the central position of the Gulf allows Chinese companies to quickly and easily connect with other markets and attract more opportunities. The kingdom boasts a unique location, good transport links, large numbers of professional workers, rich natural resources, a highly-developed financial industry, and beautiful scenery. To better develop and utilize its advantages and increase its competitiveness in the Middle East, Bahrain is focusing on the development of its manufacturing, finance and high-tech industries, providing lower investment costs, and a free business environment for companies.[36] For example, in September 2019, Bahrain Tourism and Exhibitions Authority (BTEA), together with Hilal Conference and Exhibitions (HCE), will host the region's largest Chinese trade expo in the kingdom. More than 60 companies from China will showcase their latest offerings at the China Heavy Machinery and Industry Exhibition to be held in Bahrain.[37]

One of the important areas that has been gaining momentum in the trade relations between the two countries is e-commerce. Chinese tech companies are recognizing that Bahrain is a great regional hub for e-commerce. The Kingdom has been receiving more attention from Chinese e-commerce companies because like many other Middle Eastern economies, it is focusing on building a digital economy to reduce overreliance on revenues from energy.[38]

In September 2018, Bahrain-listed Investcorp agreed to invest $250 million, its first investment in China, in a Hong Kong-listed tech fund. Investcorp will partner with China Everbright Limited, a sovereign-backed cross-border asset manager publicly listed on the Hong Kong Stock Exchange, to invest up to $150 million in the second round of the China Everbright Limited New Economy Fund. The company has also agreed to an additional co-investment right of up to $100 million. In the first round, the fund received an aggregate commitment of $313 million from other investors that have been deployed into Chinese technology companies working in a wide variety of segments, including e-commerce, smart retail, and artificial intelligence. The fund's portfolio comprises investments in several high-profile companies in greater China, including one of the largest unlisted mobile e-commerce platforms in the world, one of the largest online-to-offline consumer services companies, and a popular long-form online video platform.[39]

In November 2018, a high-level business delegation from Bahrain led by the Capital Governor Sheikh Hisham Bin Abdulrahman Al Khalifa and organized by the Bahrain Economic Development Board visited China's leading commercial centers in cities such as Beijing, Shenzhen, Hebei, Hangzhou, Zhejiang, and elsewhere. Such high-level visits across China emphasized the continuing interest of the Kingdom in fostering deeper economic ties with Beijing; and the spirit of collaboration is growing over the years. These visits also highlight the mutual desire to expand cooperation between the two nations at all levels, from financial services to Information and Communication Technology (ICT), tourism, manufacturing, transportation and logistics services.[40] The agreements and MOUs that were signed represent an important step towards stronger economic ties between China and Bahrain.

In Shenzhen, the Bahrain business delegation signed eight landmark agreements in the areas of technology and transportation which include: An MoU between the EDB and the artificial intelligence (AI) firm, Intellifusion Technologies to advance AI dynamic portrait recognition that can benefit China, Bahrain, and the Middle East. EDB partnered with Shenzhen FinTech company, IAPPPAY, to establish a full mobile payment gateway in Bahrain and explore opportunities in cryptocurrency, and the potential for the establishment of a Mobile Internet Incubator in the Kingdom. This will accelerate regional digital economic development, the promotion of investment opportunities in Bahrain to leading industrial players in China, as well as the establishment of a FinTech ecosystem between MENA (the Middle East and North Africa region) and China. An MoU was also signed between EDB and Shenzhen Outbound Alliance, aimed at strengthening economic cooperation, information exchange, and establishing a regular communication channel for business information and investment opportunities.

An MoU was signed between EDB and Softbank China Capital –

Wonder News aiming to encourage Softbank China Capital and their investment portfolio companies to establish a presence in Bahrain and use the Kingdom as a regional hub to cover the Middle East. EDB and 4PX signed an MoU exploring the possibility of 4PX initiating and establishing funds together with Bahraini companies in order to invest in entrepreneurship in China and Bahrain. EDB and Shenzhen Coolhi Network Culture Technology partnered to promote the development of E-sports between the Middle East and China including hosting E-sports events and exploring investment opportunities in E-sports downstream supply chain between MENA and China. The Bahrain Chamber of Commerce and Industry (BCCI) signed an MoU with the China Council for the Promotion of International Trade Shenzhen Branch (CCPITSZ) to harness and enhance collaborative initiatives to promote trade and investments between the two countries. EDB and CCPITSZ signed an MoU to harness and enhance collaborative initiatives between Bahrain and Shenzhen, strengthening information exchange and cooperation in economic and business activities.[41]

In Hebei, the delegation from Bahrain signed three strategic business partnerships with Hebei Business Forum, an essential region of China's economy, to explore opportunities to drive growth together. Hubei province ranks second among the six provinces in central China and eighth among all provinces in China. Being the largest comprehensive transportation hub in central China, Hubei possesses strong regional advantages, including having strong scientific and educational institutions, being rich in natural resources, having good transport and communication infrastructures and a strong industrial bases. Hubei is focused on the development of advanced and emerging manufacturing industries; the promotion of smarter networking and digitization of the manufacturing industry; encouraging privately-owned businesses with the help of advanced technologies and the Internet;, and the build-up of "household brands." In 2016, Hebei established a free trade zone to ensure orderly industry migration toward central regions, and the setting-up of a group of industrial bases for strategic and high-tech industries.[42]

The Bahrain–Hebei Business Forum witnessed the signing of several MoUs: An MoU between the EDB and Hebei Provincial Department of Commerce to strengthen information exchange, establish a regular investment information exchange, and strengthen cooperation in economic and trade activities; an MoU between the EDB and CNBM International Corporation to explore opportunities for CNBM International to expand its presence in Bahrain, mobilize

Chinese building material manufacturers, and promote high-level visits between the two parties; an MOU between the EDB and Baoding Hanyang Technology to explore the possibility of establishing a Middle East management office in Bahrain, assess Bahrain's demand for 3D printing and the possibility of Hanyang partnering with local companies to develop the MENA market, and explore opportunities to construct a platform that can facilitate exchanges in 3D printing.[43]

In Hangzhou, Bahrain and China signed several agreements to expand co-operation in the sectors of e-commerce, logistics, transportation, financial services, and tourism as the two countries deepen economic ties. Among major agreements signed during the delegation's visit to Hangzhou, Capital Governorate signed a pact on Friendly Cooperation with Hangzhou to enhance cooperation in the areas of logistics, transportation, financial services, tourism, and training.[44]

In Zhejiang, EDB and the Department of Commerce of Zhejiang Province signed a deal to strengthen information exchange, establish a channel for regular investment information exchange and strengthen cooperation in economic and trade activities. EDB also reached an agreement with Chinese e-commerce retailer JollyChic to explore the potential of using Bahrain as its Middle East hub. Bahrain Chamber of Commerce and Industry (BCCI) signed an agreement with the Zhejiang International Investment Promotion Centre to establish cooperation between Bahraini and Zhejiang companies and develop the private sector in both countries.[45]

Tourism and Cultural Ties

China's friendly cooperative relations with Bahrain, enabling the people of the two countries to bond along the Silk Road, are also vital to integrate the Bahrain's Economic Vision 2030 within the Belt and Road Initiative framework. Extensive cultural and academic exchanges are being promoted in order to win public support for deepening bilateral and multilateral cooperation, as well as providing scholarships; holding yearly cultural events; increasing cooperation in science and technology; and establishing joint laboratory or research centers and international technology transfer centers.[46]

In recent years, China's links with the GCC states have strengthened due to the introduction of additional and direct airline routes, following the strong growth of the Chinese economy and Chinese tourists' increasing disposable income. According to data from Colliers International published ahead of Arabian Travel Market (ATM) 2019, the number of Chinese tourists traveling to the GCC is expected to increase 81 percent, from 1.6 million in 2018 to 2.9 million in 2022. The GCC countries currently attract just one percent of China's total outbound market, but positive trends are expected over the coming years with forecasts for as many as 400 million tourists in 2030.[47]

Bahrain already has a large tourism industry (12 million visitors per year),[48] due to its vibrant history, rich culture, and diverse population, and attracts a large number of tourists, particularly from other GCC states. In October 2018, China and Bahrain signed a mutual visa exemption policy for diplomatic and special passport holders. The agreement allows diplomatic and special passport holders to stay for a 90-day duration from their date of entry. Such a move reflects the desire by both the countries to consolidate their ties at various levels and shows their efforts towards the development of political, economic and trade cooperation.[49]

The Chinese tourist arrivals in Bahrain as total arrivals to the GCC grew from 2012 (0.3 percent) to 2016 (0.4 percent), and the annual growth forecasted for Chinese tourist arrivals to the Kingdom is 7 percent. Given the desire of the Bahraini government to implement its Economic Vision 2030, this trend is expected to continue as more and more Chinese travelers are seeking to explore newer, unexplored cities, and cultures. The opening of new leisure attractions and business opportunities in the Kingdom, and falling visa barriers for Chinese travelers to Bahrain, will contribute to this trend.[50]

Bahrain has a long history, splendid culture, and rich tourism resources, which it is vigorously promoting to attract Chinese tourists who can experience Arab history and culture, Islam, and the charm of the F1 Grand Prix and various international conferences and exhibitions. With a stable society and hospitable people, Bahrain is an oasis of harmonious coexistence between different religions and civilizations. In March 2018, Bahrain Tourism and Exhibition Authority set up a representative office in Beijing, and actively cooperates with the Ministry of Culture and Tourism of China, major travel agencies and airlines, to launch direct flights to China via Bahrain's Gulf Air.[51] These measures will undoubtedly further facilitate personnel exchanges and promote tourism cooperation between the two countries.

Cultural cooperation has become another important aspect of the China–Bahrain friendly cooperative relations, and both nations have outlined their intention to expand the collaboration in this area in the coming years. In mid-2013, a Chinese painting and calligraphy exhibition, hosted by the China International Culture Communication Center, was held in Bahrain, featuring over 70 works from more than

30 renowned contemporary Chinese artists. The Kingdom has also participated in China at the Arabic Arts Festival in 2014, an important event to improve understanding between Chinese and Arab people.[52] In 2018, Bahrain also participated in the Fourth Arabic Arts Festival in Chengdu that shows the latest achievements of cultural exchanges and cooperation between the two states under the framework of the BRI Initiative.[53]

In April 2014, China established the Confucius Institute at the University of Bahrain in collaboration with Shanghai University, which is dedicated to promoting the Chinese language and culture in Bahrain and furthering the understanding of contemporary China.[54] By the end of 2018, 548 Confucius Institutes and 1,193 Confucius classrooms and 5,665 teaching sites had been established in 154 countries and regions, receiving more than 9 million students. In 54 countries involved in the Belt and Road Initiative, there are 153 Confucius Institutes and 149 primary and high-school Confucius Classrooms.[55] In the Middle East there are fifteen Confucius institutes and one of them is in Bahrain. The Confucius Institute at the University of Bahrain is the 431st in the world, and Bahrain is the 105th among countries which have established one.[56] In education, the Chinese Government Scholarship Program (Bahrain) offers annually five full scholarships for Bahraini students who wish to study abroad in China. The program was founded by China's Ministry of Education and aims to increase mutual understanding between the two nations.[57] According to the Chinese embassy in Bahrain, throughout the past decade a few dozen Bahraini students have studied at different universities across China. Going forward, a strong focus on tourism, culture, and education is set to strengthen the bonds of the friendly cooperative relations between China and Bahrain.[58]

Summary

As the Persian Gulf region becomes increasingly essential for Beijing's Belt and Road Initiative, the Chinese are expected to strengthen their friendly cooperative relations with the Bahraini government in the coming years. Although the kingdom has fewer natural resources compared to other Gulf states, the country offers China a way to access untapped consumer markets for its exports, as well as lucrative investment opportunities. Bahrain also could potentially serve as a regional hub for economic expansion in the Middle East and a logistics center for the growing GCC trade flows.

This chapter emphasizes the role of Bahrain in China's Belt and Road Initiative and the synergies with Bahrain's Economic Vision 2030, as well as the increasing mutual interdependency and economic interests in China's friendly cooperative relations with the Kingdom in major areas: policy coordination, connectivity, trade and investments, tourism and cultural ties. Bahrain's Economic Vision 2030 and China's Belt and Road Initiative have converged on a joint economic development path, and their strategic synergy will bring brand new opportunities for both sides. As a result, the realization of the Belt and Road Initiative will provide a new momentum for Bahrain's economic transformation.

Conclusion

Challenges and Prospects

Located at opposite ends of Asia, China and the Gulf states have developed dense and multifaceted relations in recent years. Trade, investment, infrastructure and construction projects are all areas where commercial relations have strengthened.Chinese state and private firms, banks, and financial institutions have embarked on efforts to advance the Belt and Road Initiative (BRI) in the Gulf, particularly in the energy sector. Increasingly, commercial relations are becoming more diverse and formalized, with foreign direct investment, infrastructure and construction projects featuring heavily.[1]

The central theme of China's measures to formalize strategic partnerships with the Gulf states is the energy sector. Energy cooperation has long been at the heart of China–Gulf states partnerships. While Western countries had been the primary export market for Gulf energy products, East Asian states have recently become the largest importers of Gulf oil and natural gas, a trend that is set to continue as the shale revolution and the push for greater diversification and development of alternative energy sources grow in the West. Despite Chinese efforts to diversify its imports of energy sources, oil consumption is projected to grow. At the same time, domestic production, while forecast to increase modestly, will not be able to meet China's growing energy needs. As such, the Persian Gulf will play a substantial role in Beijing's energy security.

In 2018, the Persian Gulf was home to six of China's main suppliers of crude oil imports, accounting for 44 percent: Saudi Arabia (12.4%), Iraq (9.4%), Oman (7.2%), Iran (6.3%), Kuwait (5%), and the United Arab Emirates (2.8%).[2] Five of the ten largest proven oil reserves in the world are located in the Persian Gulf region. Saudi Arabia had the world's second-largest proven oil reserves at the end of 2017, at 268.5 billion barrels.[3] Iran ranks fourth (158.4 billion barrels), Iraq ranks fifth (142.5 billion barrels), Kuwait ranks sixth (101.5 billion barrels), and the UAE ranks seventh (97.8 billion barrels).[4] In 2018 Qatar was the world's largest exporter of Liquefied Natural Gas (LNG).[5]

China, by necessity rather than by choice, could become even more dependent on the Persian Gulf crude oil for a long time to come. This is because oil from other sources is expected to decline much faster than Middle Eastern oil, which may lead to fierce, if not violent, competition to obtain it.[6] As such, imported oil and natural gas will be an important feature of Chinese energy security in the coming decades, while the Gulf producers see a reliable customer in China. Energy is also one of the crucial pillars of the BRI, and huge China-led investments will be devoted to it within and across BRI countries. Energy plays a key role within the BRI, mainly because of supply issues related to China's necessary transition to new energy sources, but also for national security reasons.[7]

Bilateral trade between China and the Gulf states has also seen significant growth in recent years, with the Gulf representing a large proportion of Chinese trade in the Arab world. According to the China Global Investment Tracker, Beijing's investments and construction in the Gulf states from 2013 to 2018 reached $72 billion.[8] According to China Customs Statistics (export–import), the China–Gulf states trade volume increased to nearly $227 billion by 2018. Saudi Arabia ($63.2 billion) has become China's most important trade partner in the Middle East, and the UAE ranks second ($45.8 billion), Iran ranks third ($35 billion), Iraq ($30.3 billion), Oman ($21.4 billion), Kuwait ($18.3 billion), Qatar ($11.5 billion), and Bahrain ($1.3 billion).[9]

Beyond trade, there are other areas where economic ties have increased. Capital cooperation between China and the Gulf countries includes mutual investment, project contracting, labor cooperation, and design consultation which have also witnessed steady growth.[10] As part of GCC countries' efforts to diversify their economies and in line with their national development plans, they have been implementing a large number of transportation, communications, and infrastructure construction projects, as well as special economic zones such as Dubai's Jebel Ali Free Zone (JAFZA),[11] and the China–Oman Industrial Park at Duqm Special Economic Zone (SEZ).[12] At the same time, China is implementing its Belt and Road strategy. Chinese construction and engineering expertise are thus becoming important features in developing economic ties with the Gulf states. Many Chinese state-owned enterprises (SOEs) have been using the UAE's JAFZA, the third largest re-export hub in the world, to establish regional headquarters there to service projects across the peninsula (approximately 60 percent of China's pass-through trade).[13]

This book has emphasized the significance of China's strategic partnerships with the Gulf states in its BRI framework, as well as setting out the increasing mutual interdependency between both sides in various sectors such as energy, construction, and infrastructure building, political ties, trade and investments, financial integration, culture and tourism, and defense ties. A stable Gulf region is vital for China's sustainable growth, and with the completion of the Gulf Pearl Chain, the PRC can achieve effective management and control the flow of its energy needs. This will open new markets and trade routes for the Gulf countries, as the BRI will connect Gulf economies with the Southeast and East Asian economies, thus enhancing economic integration and co-operation.

China's relationship with the nations of the Persian Gulf is based on a two-dimensional approach: the implementation of the new Silk Road strategy and the emerging partnerships between them. China's levels of interdependence with these states have increased dramatically in recent years, spanning a wide range of interests (e.g., energy security, trade cooperation, and infrastructure construction). The individual country chapters have shed light on China's BRI complexities and challenges, and revealed how the synergy between the new Silk Road strategy and the local, national development plan will shape the Persian Gulf in the future. The balance of global politics will be critically affected by these powerful emerging partnerships and convergence of interests.

China's partnership diplomacy has provided a platform for deepening and expanding the cooperation between China and the Gulf states under the framework of the BRI. Since 2013 China has forged special political relations (i.e., signed either a strategic or comprehensive strategic partnership) with every state in the Gulf region except Bahrain. There is a clear and direct connection between China's emerging strategic partnerships with the Gulf states and the implementation of the new Silk Road strategy. Therefore, the key to understanding China's upgraded involvement in the Persian Gulf must be in the context of the successful implementation of the BRI. The new Silk Road is an essential guide to China–Gulf states' strategic partnership diplomacy, since the region holds a unique position in the PRC's new policy framework.

The central thesis of the book is that the Persian Gulf region has a significant and unique role in the successful implementation of China's BRI strategy, as well as the emerging partnerships between them (e.g., comprehensive strategic partnerships and strategic partnerships). These partnerships help the PRC to achieve effective management and control the flow of its energy, goods and product needs and to open new markets and trade routes. Beijing has been mostly successful in employing strategic partnerships, a prominent instrument in its limited diplomatic toolkit, in order to guarantee integration between the national development plan of the Gulf monarchies or economic reconstruction plan (e.g., Iraq and Iran) and China's Belt and Road vision.

The national development plan of the Gulf states and China's BRI have converged under common economic interests and a common development path that complement each other, bringing new opportunities for both sides. As a result, the realization of the BRI strategy will also provide new momentum for the Gulf states' economic transformation. The implementation of the new Silk Road strategy will unleash a regional infrastructure boom by connecting China with Asia, Europe, and Africa by land and sea, and boost renminbi internationalization by encouraging its use in both trade and financial transactions.

Challenges and Risks of the BRI Construction in the Gulf Region

Despite China's increasing engagement in the Persian Gulf, it lacks a clear, consistent, and comprehensive strategy for the successful implementation of the new Silk Road. Currently, Beijing's BRI framework cooperation with the Gulf states consists of strategic flexibility and maximizing opportunities, but that may prove insufficient. As China and the Gulf states become more integrated, they will also share risks and face certain challenges in the near term. These challenges range from geopolitical rivalry with both great powers and local powers to financial problems and religious and cultural complexities.

Geopolitical rivalry

Since the turn of the 21st century, West Asia has been experiencing the most profound transformation, which exposes the region to geopolitical risks and instability. As regional order and international relations are yet to reach a new equilibrium in the process of disintegration, such restructuring could easily trigger geopolitical conflicts, even wars, and lead to increased uncertainty and risk in the Belt and Road construction.

First, great power (US–Russia) competition in the BRI region will follow a normal trend, the essence of which is the shift between emerging powers and conservative powers. Russia, taking advantage of the US eastward strategic rebalancing, dispatched its troops to Syria and involved itself in regional conflicts. The Trump administration has been taking a tough stance against Tehran, by withdrawing from the JCPOA and re-imposing sanctions on Iran, which created barriers in the new dynamic in Sino–Iranian trade and obstacles to integrate Iran as part of the realization of the Belt and Road Initiative.[14]

Therefore, China should address the security risks in the Gulf region while strengthening cooperation and appropriately coordinating its relations with the great powers. As a hegemonic country, the US has a wide range of interests in the region, while Russia, as a regional, traditional country, still has a particular influence on the various security issues in the region. Beijing and Washington share compatible and complementary interests in the Middle East security governance and conflict de-escalation, which forges structural dynamics for the two sides to seek common ground for partnership. It is possible for China and the US to join forces in the Belt and Road construction, since Washington has acquired a great deal of experience in similar ventures all over the world, including in the Middle East, and because it would be challenging, perhaps practically impossible, for Beijing to accomplish its new Silk Road alone.

The second geopolitical rivalry is the all-out confrontation between Saudi Arabia and Iran. As two regional powers in the Gulf region, Riyadh and Tehran not only represent the Arab and the Persian ethnic groups respectively but are also the leaders of the Sunni and Shia in the Islam world. Therefore, the rivalry between the two sides is competition for ideological influence, aimed at gaining regional hegemony. The two powers' proxy battles in Iraq, Syria, Yemen, and Lebanon, among other regional conflicts, have exacerbated regional tensions and the breakdown of the Islamic world.[15]

There are concerns in the Gulf states about the BRI's geopolitical implications because Iran will likely benefit over all Gulf countries. Tehran plays a crucial role in the new Silk Road as an integral country in China's Eurasian overland route. Given Iran's geographical role linking Central Asia and the Middle East (and by extension Europe), untapped natural resource wealth, and the fact that Tehran and Beijing maintain positive bilateral relations, it is difficult to imagine Sino–Iranian relations not improving in the future.[16] Hence, the Gulf states' concern about the new Silk Road is that the initiative, if successful, could weaken Saudi Arabia's role in the Middle East's geopolitical order by advancing Tehran's strategic interests and deepening its trade links with the rest of the world. This imbalance will have geopolitical ramifications for the Gulf region, and as the BRI progresses this would make China's initiative more complicated and expensive.

Third, the BRI also faces threats from terrorist organizations which are active in the Gulf region. The activities of the 'three forces' (terrorist forces, religious extremists, and national separatist forces), which are the core of terrorism, are an essential factor threatening the implementation of the BRI, increasingly becoming the largest non-traditional security threat in the region.[17] Further escalation of certain hotspot issues in the region (e.g., Iraq, ISIS, Qatar–GCC crisis, and the Iranian nuclear issue) have added significantly to an already tense situation in the Gulf region, and posed threats to cooperation in bilateral trade, investment, and engineering contracts.[18]

The Gulf region has long been the base camp for Al Qaeda, ISIS, and other terrorist groups. Though ISIS has been heavily defeated, thanks to joint efforts of the international community, it is unlikely to be wiped out in the short term as its outward expansion is still underway, which poses threats to regional security. As the Belt and Road Initiative proceeds, there is a possibility that extremist groups and criminals might hijack Chinese people for their own political or economic goals.[19]

As Beijing's economic involvement in the Gulf region grows, the safety of Chinese workers and businessmen has become a growing concern. The hundreds of Chinese fighters, mostly Uighurs who joined ISIS in Iraq and Syria, significantly increased Chinese counter-terrorism concerns, and Beijing increasingly feels the need to better protect the thousands of Chinese employees in the Iraqi oil and construction sectors.[20] As Chinese President Xi Jinping declared, China is committed to working with all countries involved with the initiative to address both the symptoms and causes of extremism and terrorism, including poverty.[21] In the counterterrorism sphere, Beijing will rely on its partnerships with the Gulf states to enhance security along the BRI's routes.[22]

Finally, there are various territorial and island disputes in the Middle East, and the results of dispute settlement directly affect the security guarantee for the implementation of the BRI. Maintaining secure access is an essential consideration in the implementation of the 21st Century Maritime Silk Road Initiative, which will ensure that the sea channel stays open rather than cut off. Ninety percent of global commercial trade and sixty-five percent of the world's total oil volume go through ocean shipping, with the Indian Ocean providing half of the world's container shipments and 70 percent of the transportation of petroleum products from the Middle East to the Pacific. The Indian

Ocean routes are strategically crucial for global trade, such as the Strait of Mendoza, the Strait of Hormuz, and the Strait of Malacca, with 40 percent of the world's trade flows through the Strait of Malacca and 40 percent of crude oil trade flowing through the Hormuz Strait.[23]

Financial problems

Most of the Gulf states are governed by monarchies, at the primary stage of industrialization, and they are susceptible to US and European influence. Therefore, the Belt and Road construction faces both internal and external restraints. First, the countries in the Persian Gulf welcome the PRC's economic investment, but five years into the Belt and Road Initiative some signs of concern are emerging. Echoing concerns heard in Asia, critics are pointing out that the Belt and Road projects often seem to bring more significant benefits to China than to the host countries. In addition to calling on China to hire local workers instead of Chinese workers, Beijing's partners and outside observers also raise questions about debt sustainability, environmental impact, corruption, and the PRC's overall motives. President Xi Jinping's muted tone at the Second Belt and Road Forum in Beijing made it clear that his government was conscious of the widespread criticism leveled by developed countries, and complaints from Asian partners of the China-controlled BRI.[24]

Second, the depletion of foreign currency reserves and uncertainty about future oil prices have forced the Gulf states to adopt restraint in economic policy, including streamlining and cost-cutting measures. As part of the economizing measures, various government agencies were instructed to cut their spending on new projects and return unused budget allocations to the Ministry of Finance. The Gulf states seek increasingly to escape their profound dependence on oil revenues through streamlining, diversification of revenue sources, and adoption of the principles of a modern economy. The main difficulty in converting the oil-based Gulf economies to diversity is that political and social stability in these countries is directly related to the high standard of living of their citizens, which is supported by oil money.[25] Economic or social instability in the Gulf states could influence or threaten the implementation of the BRI.

Third, 62 percent of the Gulf countries scored below 50 on the 2018 Corruption Perceptions Index, which is a failing grade. Only three countries have managed to remain above this average (the UAE and Qatar declined to provide figures, compared to the 2017 Index). Iran's ranking in Transparency International's annual corruption report has dropped from 130 to 138 among 180 countries surveyed; Iran's score in 2017 was 30, while in 2018 it dropped to 28. Iraq was ranked the 12th most corrupt state in the world, scoring 18 points out of 100 on the 2018 Corruption Index.[26] These countries are under-going political instability, internal conflicts, war, terrorism, and economic collapse. These phenomena feed corruption and it, in turn, also fuels them. In these respects, the BRI may become a risky gamble for government investments and Chinese investors. As President Xi Jinping said at the second Belt and Road Forum in Beijing 2019, "Everything should be done transparently, and we should have zero tolerance for corruption."[27]

The fourth financial problem is the high barrier to market access in the Gulf region. Business and foreign investments in the Gulf states have been struggling due to bureaucratic corruption and royal monopoly. On the one hand, red tape in the government's approval process jeopardizes the progress and profitability of projects. On the other hand, the government has kept imports under control. Chinese enterprises have no distinct price advantage in the ratings and evalua-tion of foreign enterprises and in contracted projects. Fifth, there is fierce competition with other countries. The Gulf states, having dealt with the US and European countries for a long time, tend to recognize Western standards in planning and design, production and operation, and quality supervision. In the traditional civil engineering field, China is also facing competition from other developing countries like India and Turkey. The comparative advantage of Chinese enterprises is relatively weak.[28]

From 2013 to 2018, China's direct investment in Belt and Road countries surpassed $90 billion, realizing a turnover of $400 billion in foreign contracted projects in these countries. In 2018 Chinese busi-nesses made a total of $15.6 billion in non-financial direct investment, growing by 8.9 percent year on year and accounting for 13 percent of China's total non-financial Foreign Direct Investment (FDI) during the same period. The turnover of foreign contracted projects in Belt and Road countries reached $89.3 billion, or 53 percent of the total turnover of foreign contracted projects in the same period.[29] The BRI total estimated cost is going to increase day by day; hence it will be the responsibility of all the partners in the Gulf region to finance this project as per their capabilities with a combination of public and private, domestic and international financing sources, customized to the specific circumstances of countries and projects.[30]

An additional concern is the bottleneck in project funding in the Gulf region. Infrastructure projects generally feature low profitability, a long period for return on investment, and strict government moni-toring; accordingly, private investment and available financing channels are limited. As most Gulf states are under enormous fiscal pressure, their investment capabilities are so weak that it is hard to meet their financing demands only by relying on the Asian Infrastructure Investment Bank (AIIB) and the Silk Road Fund.[31]

Finally, the BRI lacks central coordination, as many routes and local construction projects are to be carried on by local or regional govern-ments which may create delays and hurdles if the states will not cooperate. Currently, China tends to rely on bilateral relations with each country to help secure its investments, but transnational infra-structure investment in the BRI might suggest a transition to more of a regional and multilateral engagement strategy.[32]

Religious and cultural complexities

The Middle East is a region where most of the global hot issues and conflicts are concentrated. Since the Arab Spring in the Middle East, with its ethnic, religious, and sectarian conflicts, the region has remained in constant turmoil. Thanks to its unique geopolitical position, the Gulf region has been a global energy base and a continent of hope, but it is also a region rife with ethnic, religious, and political conflicts. Regional turbulence and political rivalry among major powers add to the challenges and uncertainties of cooperation between China and the Gulf states.

First, in the Gulf region, Islam holds a dominant position. As a religion and a cultural value system, Islam has profound bearings on local society and economy. With the expansion of Belt and Road construction, there would be inevitable interactions between Chinese and Islamic cultures. The two sides' relatively significant cultural and cognitive differences due to discrepancies in religion and language would affect people-to-people exchanges and the development of bilat-eral relations. For instance, through the BRI, Islam might penetrate eastwards and reinforce the religious awareness of local Muslims in China's northwestern region.[33]

Second, the principal key for the success of the BRI is stability in the Middle East, a goal that appears to be far beyond China's geopolitical capacity. Most of the countries in the Gulf region are developing countries which are affected by complicated factors such as social class contradictions and ethnic and religious problems. The more Beijing engages economically in the Gulf region, the more vulnerable and exposed the Chinese are to the consequences of regional and local instability. To guarantee the success of the BRI, China should contribute to the settlement of Middle Eastern conflicts.[34] Beijing can play a constructive role by bringing relevant parties together to resolve and maintain regional stability peacefully and yet adhere to the principle of non-intervention in internal affairs.[35] In terms of costs and benefits, China's non-intervention policy is essential for the success of its BRI, by maintaining neutrality, i.e., taking no sides and alienating no one.

Third, Chinese companies, as they go global, need more and more local labor. However, their lack of knowledge of local regulations and deficiencies at the operational level have led to the rise of labor and commercial disputes.[36] Finally, given the current regional instability, unrest, and obstacles, Beijing's BRI is facing severe challenges. China's ability to achieve its new Silk Road objectives in the Persian Gulf depends mostly on the security and economic situation in the region, but also on the accumulated knowledge from China's historical experience in the Middle East.[37]

In the end, the BRI has all the marks of a complicated foreign policy challenge. It is a slow-moving development that will unfold in decades rather than days. It is functionally and geographically vast, spanning the responsibilities of many Chinese agencies. It requires grappling with both economics and security issues. It will be tempting to delay action and to try to coordinate an effective response. The key question is whether China will know how to deal with the geopolitical rivalry, financial problems, and religious and cultural risks in the successful implementation of its BRI. Nevertheless, for now it seems that the challenges and risks outweigh the opportunities and possibilities.

Prospects and Opportunities in China–Gulf states

Despite the challenges to China's BRI, risks can be turned into opportunities as long as Beijing faces them squarely and responds positively. The new Silk Road has become the main focus of China's strategic partnerships with the Gulf states. Despite the risks deriving from regional turbulence and geopolitical rivalry among major powers, there remains room for a turnaround in the situation. China–Gulf states cooperation has grown significantly in recent years, and the structure of these strategic partnerships dovetails with China's BRI cooperation priorities of policy coordination, facilities connectivity, financial integration, trade and investment, and people-to-people and cultural exchange.

Policy coordination

China needs to promote political cooperation with the Gulf states, create mechanisms for dialogue and consensus-building on global and regional issues of core interest and major concern, develop shared interests, deepen political trust, and reach a new consensus on cooperation to assist the Belt and Road construction.[38] First, the two sides should strengthen coordination on regional affairs (e.g., Syria, Yemen, and the Iranian nuclear program), and continue to promote political solutions to hotspot issues. Second, China and the Gulf states should improve bilateral and multilateral mechanisms (e.g., China–GCC free trade and the China–Arab States Cooperation Forum), and make full use of bilateral high-level joint committees and sub-committees to implement strategic synergy. Third, the two sides need to establish dialogue mechanisms with countries outside the Gulf region, thereby transforming the cooperation momentum of individual parties into an assurance for sustained stability.[39]

Facilities connectivity

Connectivity, as the basis of the BRI, aims at linking land, sea, air, and cyberspace environments of countries along the routes. Through six major economic corridors of China–Mongolia–Russia, New Eurasian Continental Bridge, China–Central Asia–West Asia, China–Indochina Peninsula, China–Pakistan and Bangladesh–China–India–Myanmar, China will be closely connected with Europe, Africa and the rest of Asia. While the Gulf states are well funded and in urgent need of infrastructure construction, China's experience and technology, accumulated in its own development process, could offer vital assistance.[40]

With the extension of the BRI, the China–Central Asia–West Asia economic corridor will continue to extend to the Gulf countries (e.g., Saudi Arabia, Iraq, and Iran). With the construction of the Gulf corridor and connection with the China–Pakistan Economic Corridor to form the West Asian Silk Road, China's energy security will enjoy maximum protection. This West Asian Silk Road will further stretch along the Mediterranean coast and beyond through the Arabian Peninsula, enriching and extending the connotation and space of the new Silk Road and perfectly linking Asian, European and African economic circles.[41]

Trade and investments

China and the Gulf states must take a series of additional measures, such as expanding free-trade zones, improving trade structures, seeking new potential areas for trade and improving the trade balance, devising new initiatives for the promotion of conventional forms of trade, developing trans-border electronic trade and other advanced models of business, and regularly share information in these areas in order to create a system for supporting trade in services to strengthen and expand conventional trade and increase customs cooperation.[42]

The PRC is the most important trade partner of the Gulf region, but commerce between the two sides is still at a low level. Energy holds a high proportion in trade while the export of China's high value-added and technology-intensive products is small, and there are few landmark cooperation projects. Although cooperation between Beijing and the Gulf countries has extended from traditional industries and infrastructure construction to retail, finance, telecommunications, and tourism, there is still great room for development in policy, layout and the cultivation of key industries. First, China and the Gulf states need to expand areas of industrial capacity cooperation and focus on major projects (e.g., ports, logistics, and industrial parks). Second, Chinese projects should not concentrate its investments only in the Gulf countries with rich energy resources, strong consumption capacity, and great regional influence. It is important that the PRC invest also in the industrial development of the entire region. Third, Beijing should avoid competing alone in the bidding and construction of major projects; cooperating with other international companies or local enterprises would reduce the burden and share the benefits.[43]

Financial integration

There are a number of measures for the realization of financial integration between China and the Gulf states, including: deepening financial cooperation and building a stable currency system, establishing an investment and financing system and a credit information system in Asia, expanding the scope and scale of bilateral currency swaps between the two countries, and developing the bond market in Asia.[44]

The Gulf countries are among the most important long-term sources of capital in the international community. China and the Gulf states could explore cooperation in the following areas. First, diversifying financing to break the funding bottleneck. There are multilateral institutions (e.g., AIIB, the Silk Road Fund, and the BRICS New

Development Bank) which were created to establish a benefit and risk-sharing decision-making mechanism. There are also a variety of financial products (e.g., external guarantee, mixed loan, and the Silk Road bonds) to open up financing opportunities through innovation.

Second, increasing business outlets to improve the geographical deployment across the Gulf region. The number of branches of Chinese commercial banks in the Gulf region is seriously lagging behind the expansion of Chinese enterprises. It is difficult for Chinese financial institutions to provide comprehensive services to the enterprises, and thus, assistance from the Gulf countries is essential. Third, understanding financial regulations and training qualified professionals. The Gulf region is the core area of Islamic finance, which requires compatibility with the teachings of Islam. In order to integrate with the Islamic financial model, familiarity with Islamic teachings and commercial regulations in Islamic countries is necessary, and this is besides the professional knowledge and skills which are required.[45]

People-to-people and cultural exchange

The PRC must enable the people of the two sides to bond along the new Silk Road because this is also vital for integrating the Gulf region into the BRI framework. This can be accomplished, inter alia, by promoting extensive cultural and academic exchanges to win public support for deepening bilateral and multilateral cooperation, as well as providing scholarships, holding annual cultural events, increasing cooperation in science and technology, and establishing joint laboratory or research centers and international technology transfer centers.[46] First, regular exchanges among members and leaders of the various religions are not only crucial for people-to-people bonds but are also useful in dealing with the spread of extremism. Second, Beijing should build a solid foundation of public opinion regarding the principles guiding its engagement with the Gulf states.

Third, domestic think tanks should try to go beyond the traditional departmental and regional divisions and carry out joint research, and at the same time develop interactions and exchanges with foreign think tanks.[47]

Risk prevention and crisis management

In order to address the risks associated with the BRI, it is necessary to set up issue-specific security and risk assessment mechanisms to be forewarned of possible crises and prevent unnecessary setbacks.[48] First,

China should further its understanding of the situation in the Gulf countries, analyze the political and security risks therein; grasp the direction of policy changes, the commercial and cultural environment, and the fiscal and taxation system as well as the legal regime of target countries; and establish a knowledge system of risk prevention. Second, the PRC should establish mechanisms to carry out successful counter-terrorism campaigns in hotspots along the BRI routes. It is necessary to strengthen intergovernmental exchanges of intelligence through bilateral or multilateral channels, and share the responsibility with relevant countries to build a long-term win-win security mechanism.

Third, Beijing should enhance security protection and promote corporate governance by law. Chinese overseas enterprises could employ local or international lawyers, and insist on payment with letters of credit or the combination of prepayment and collection. They should also take advantage of foreign aid to promote payment in renminbi currency and cooperate with overseas security companies to reduce legal and payment risks, and to safeguard the property and personal safety of overseas enterprises.[49]

Over the last five years, China has acquired extensively rich and indispensable experience in investing in infrastructures (e.g., railroads and roads, pipelines, harbors, trains and underground trains, communication systems, dams, airfields, housing, schools, bridges, hospitals, and sewage systems). The Belt and Road construction could lead to a historical and dramatic transformation in the Persian Gulf region, an act of global significance not less than a regional one. China's BRI strategy will substantially shape its engagements and strategic partnerships with the Persian Gulf region. The new Silk Road has provided a platform for deepening and expanding relations between China and the Gulf states. Without detracting from the importance of the project, one must inject a degree of skepticism: the anticipated investment needs that accompany implementation of the BRI are very high. Albeit that the estimates are not precise, ranging from $1–8 trillion, it is not currently apparent that even the lowest estimate of $1 trillion will be met by available funding. Hence, the risks and challenges exceed the prospects and possibilities.

In summary, there is much uncertainty as well as a range of assessments regarding the chances of success of the Belt and Road construction. A mounting wave of opposition to the BRI can be felt both within and outside of China. Thus, Beijing must demonstrate successful implementation of a BRI project as soon as possible in order to sustain the momentum of the Belt and Road vision. The success of the BRI depends on the cooperation between countries along the Belt and Road route. It has five major goals: Policy coordination, facilities connectivity, free trade, financial integration, and people-to-people bonds. Among these, facilities connectivity – which focuses mainly on transportation and energy infrastructure – is the initiative's top priority. Successful implementation of the Belt and Road construction in the Persian Gulf could be a good example of regional facilities connectivity along the Belt and Road and has the potential to increase motivation for preparing for a successful implementation of the BRI in the wider Middle East.

Notes

Introduction: Opportunity and Strategy

1 Andrew Scobell and Alireza Nader, China in the Middle East: The Wary Dragon (Santa Monica, Calif.: RAND Corporation, 2016).

2 Nicholas Lyall, "China in the Middle East: Past, Present, and Future," *The Diplomat*, February 16, 2019, https://thediplomat.com/2019/02/china-in-the-middle-east-past-present-and-future/.

3 Christopher Layne, "The US-Chinese power shift and the end of the Pax Americana," *International Affairs*, 94 (1), 2018, 89–111.

4 Imad K. Harb, "Self-preservation and Strategic Hedging in the Gulf Cooperation Council," *Policy brief*, no. 23, June 26, 2018, http://ams.hi.is/wp-content/uploads/2018/06/Self-Preservation-and-Strategic-Hedging-in-the-GCC-2.pdf.

5 "Full text: Vision for Maritime Cooperation under the Belt and Road Initiative," *Xinhua*, Jun 20, 2017, http://news.xinhuanet.com/english/2017-06/20/c_136380414.htm.

6 Peter Cai, *Understanding China's Belt and Road Initiative*. Sydney: Lowy Institute for International Policy, 2017.

7 Jeffrey S. Payne, "The G.C.C. and China's One Belt, One Road: Risk or Opportunity?," *Middle East Institute*, August 11, 2016, https://www.mei.edu/publications/gcc-and-chinas-one-belt-one-road-risk-or-opportunity.

8 Frank Umbach, China's Belt and Road Initiative and the Mediterranean Region: The Energy Dimension," *Mediterranean Dialogue Series 14*, June 8, 2018, https://www.kas.de/einzeltitel/-/content/china-s-belt-and-road-initiative-and-the-mediterranean-region-the-energy-dimension1.

9 "Greening the Belt and Road Initiative," *WWF's recommendations for the finance sector – in conjunction with HSBC*," January 1, 2018, file:///C:/Users/moti/Downloads/greening-the-belt-and-road-initiative.pdf.

10 Sumedh Anil Lokhande, "China's One Belt One Road Initiative and the Gulf Pearl Chain," *China Daily*, June 5, 2017, http://www.chinadaily.com.cn/opinion/2017beltandroad/2017-06/05/content_29618549.htm.

11 Jane Perlez and Yufan Huang, "Behind China's $1 Trillion Plan to Shake Up the Economic Order," *The New York Times*, May 13, 2017,

https://www.nytimes.com/2017/05/13/business/china-railway-one-belt-
one-road-1-trillion-plan.html?mcubz=3.

12   Hichem Karoui, "Walking together on the new Silk Road," *China Daily*,
     July 23, 2018,
     http://www.chinadaily.com.cn/a/201807/25/WS5b58444fa31031a351e
     901ca.html?bsh_bid=2255047682.

13   Jean-Marc F. Blanchard and Colin Flint, "The Geopolitics of China's
     Maritime Silk Road Initiative," *Geopolitics*, 22 (2), 2017, 223–225.

14   Sumedh Anil Lokhande, "China's One Belt One Road Initiative and the
     Gulf Pearl Chain," *China Daily*, June 5, 2017,
     http://www.chinadaily.com.cn/opinion/2017beltandroad/2017-
     06/05/content_29618549.htm.

15   Laura Zhou, "Chinese private investment in belt and road projects may
     be losing steam," *South China Morning Post*, 15 November, 2018,
     https://www.scmp.com/news/china/diplomacy/article/2173467/chinese-
     private-investment-belt-and-road-projects-may-be-losing.

16   Guo Han and Zhou Zhan, "China's Strategic Vision: Five Years on and
     Looking Ahead," *ICAS BULLETIN: Institute for China-America Studies*,
     November 1, 2017,
     http://chinaus-icas.org/wp-content/uploads/2017/11/November-1-
     Bulletin.pdf.

17   "Greening the Belt and Road Initiative," *WWF's recommendations for the
     finance sector – in conjunction with HSBC*," January 1, 2018,
     file:///C:/Users/moti/Downloads/greening-the-belt-and
     -road-initiative.pdf.

18   Janne Suokas, "Chinese private firms cut back Belt and Road investment:
     report," *GB Times*, November 16, 2018,
     https://gbtimes.com/chinese-private-firms-cut-back-belt-and-road-
     investment-report.

19   "Annual trade between China, B&R countries reaches 1.3 trln USD,"
     Xinhua, January 24, 2019,
     http://www.xinhuanet.com/english/2019-01/24/c_137771613.htm.

20   Wu Sike,"The Strategic Docking between China and Middle East
     Countries under the "Belt and Road" Framework," *Journal of Middle
     Eastern and Islamic Studies (in Asia)*, 9(4), 2015, 1–13.

21   Chris Zambelis, "China and the Quiet Kingdom: An Assessment of
     China–Oman Relations," *China Brief*, XV (22), 2015, 11–15.

22   Andrew Scobell and Alireza Nader, *China in the Middle East: The Wary
     Dragon*. Santa Monica, Calif.: RAND Corporation, 2016.

23   Shannon Tiezzi, "Why China Won't Lead in the Middle East," *The
     Diplomat*, July 28, 2014,
     https://thediplomat.com/2014/07/why-china-wont-lead-in-the-middle-
     east/.

24   Mordechai Chaziza, "China's Counter-Terrorism Policy in the Middle
     East," In: Clarke M. (ed.), *Terrorism and Counter-Terrorism in China:*

Domestic and Foreign Policy Dimensions (pp. 141–156). New York: Oxford University Press, 2018.

25 Liu Li and Wang Zesheng, "Belt and Road Initiative in the Gulf Region: Progress and Challenges," *China Institute of International Studies*, September 11, 2017, http://www.ciis.org.cn/english/2017-11/09/content_40063037.htm.

26 "China unveils action plan on Belt and Road Initiative," *China Daily*, March 28, 2015, http://www.chinadaily.com.cn/business/2015-03/28/content_19938124.htm.

27 "Vision and actions on jointly building Silk Road Economic Belt and 21st Century Maritime Silk Road," *Chinese National Development and Reform Commission (NDRC)* March 28, 2015, http://en.ndrc.gov.cn/newsrelease/201503/t20150330_669367.html.

28 Wu Sike, "Constructing 'One Belt and One Road' to Enhancing China and GCC Cooperation," *Arab World Studies*, 2, 2015, pp. 4–13.

29 Cui Shoujun, "Sino-Gulf Relations: From Energy to Strategic Partners," *JPC*, 2015, https://www.jewishpolicycenter.org/2015/08/31/china-gulf-relations/.

30 "China's imports of crude oil, natural gas surge in 2018," *Xinhua*, January 21, 2019, http://www.xinhuanet.com/english/2019-01/21/c_137761910.htm

31 John Calabrese, "China and the Persian Gulf: Energy and Security," *Middle East Journal*, 52 (3), 1998, 351–366; Steve Yetiv and Chunlong Lu, "China, Global Energy, and the Middle East," *Middle East Journal*, 61 (2), 2007, 199–218.

32 Daniel Workman, "Top 15 Crude Oil Suppliers to China," *World's Top Exports*, April 12, 2019, http://www.worldstopexports.com/top-15-crude-oil-suppliers-to-china/.

33 Sumedh Anil Lokhande, "China's One Belt One Road Initiative and the Gulf Pearl Chain," *China Daily*, June 5, 2017, http://www.chinadaily.com.cn/opinion/2017beltandroad/2017-06/05/content_29618549.htm.

34 Liu Li and Wang Zesheng, "Belt and Road Initiative in the Gulf Region: Progress and Challenges," *China Institute of International Studies*, September 11, 2017, http://www.ciis.org.cn/english/2017-11/09/content_40063037.htm.

35 Ivan Lidarev, "China and the Saudi–Iran conflict," *Observer Research Foundation*, December 20, 2017, https://www.orfonline.org/expert-speak/china-and-saudi-iran-conflict/.

36 Jonathan Fulton, "The G.C.C. Countries and China's Belt and Road Initiative (BRI): Curbing Their Enthusiasm?," *Middle East Institute*, October 17, 2017, https://www.mei.edu/publications/gcc-countries-and-chinas-belt-and-road-initiative-bri-curbing-their-enthusiasm.

37 Wu Sike, "Constructing 'One Belt and One Road' to Enhancing China and GCC Cooperation," *Arab World Studies*, 2, 2015, pp. 4–13.

38 Sumedh Anil Lokhande, "China's One Belt One Road Initiative and the Gulf Pearl Chain," *China Daily*, June 5, 2017, http://www.chinadaily.com.cn/opinion/2017beltandroad/2017-06/05/content_29618549.htm.

39 Andrew Scobell "Why the Middle East matters to China," In A. Ehteshami and N. Horesh (eds), *China's Presence in the Middle East: The Implications of the One Belt, One Road Initiative* (pp. 9–23). New York: Routledge, 2018.

40 "China issues white paper on peaceful development," *Ministry of Foreign Affairs, the People's Republic of China*, September 7, 2011, http://www.fmprc.gov.cn/mfa_eng/topics_665678/whitepaper_665742/t856325.shtml.

41 Joseph Yu-Shek Cheng, "China's Relations with the Gulf Cooperation Council States: Multilevel Diplomacy in a Divided Arab World," *The China Review*, 16 (1), 2016, 35–64.

42 Feng Zhongping and Huang Jing, "China's Strategic Partnership Diplomacy: Engaging with a Changing World," *European Strategic Partnerships Observatory*, ESPO Working Paper No. 8, June 27, 2014, file:///C:/Users/moti/Downloads/SSRN-id2459948.pdf.

43 Georg Struver, "China's partnership diplomacy: International alignment based on interests of ideology," *The Chinese Journal of International Politics*, 10(1), (2017), 31–65.

44 Su Hao, "Zhongguo Waijiao De 'Huoban Guanxi' Kuangjia" ["The 'Partnership' Framework in China's Foreign Policy"], *Shijie Jishi* [World Knowledge], Vol. 5, 2000.

45 "China, UAE issue joint statement on establishing strategic partnership," *Global Times*, January 18, 2012, http://www.globaltimes.cn/content/692650.shtml.

46 "China, UAE agree to lift ties to comprehensive strategic partnership," *Xinhua*, July 21, http://www.xinhuanet.com/english/2018-07/21/c_137338423.htm

47 "Quick guide to China's diplomatic levels," *South China Morning Post*, January 20, 2016, https://www.scmp.com/news/china/diplomacy-defence/article/1903455/quick-guide-chinas-diplomatic-levels.

48 Avery Goldstein, *Rising to the Challenge: China's Grand Strategy and International Security*. Stanford: Stanford University Press, 2005.

49 Brock, F. Tessman, "System structure and state strategy: Adding hedging to the Menu," *Security Studies* 21(2), 2012, 192–231; Evelyn Goh, *Meeting the China Challenge: The United States in Southeast Asian Regional Security Strategies*. Washington: East-West Center, 2005.

50 Jonathan Fulton, "Friends with Benefits: China's Partnership Diplomacy in the Gulf," *POMEPS Studies 34: Shifting Global Politics and the Middle East*, March 2019,

https://pomeps.org/wp-content/uploads/2019/03/POMEPS_Studies_34_Web.pdf.

51   "China Customs Statistics: Imports and exports by country/region," *The Hong Kong Trade Development Council (HKTDC)*, May 27, 2019, http://china-trade-research.hktdc.com/business-news/article/Facts-and-Figures/China-Customs-Statistics/ff/en/1/1X39VTVQ/1X09N9NM.htm.

52   Jonathan Fulton, "China's growing presence in the Gulf," *East Asia Forum*, March 26, 2019, https://www.eastasiaforum.org/2019/03/26/chinas-growing-presence-in-the-gulf/.

53   Daniel Workman, "Top 15 Crude Oil Suppliers to China," *World's Top Exports*, April 12, 2019, http://www.worldstopexports.com/top-15-crude-oil-suppliers-to-china/.

54   Jonathan Fulton, "Friends with Benefits: China's Partnership Diplomacy in the Gulf," *POMEPS Studies 34: Shifting Global Politics and the Middle East*, March 2019, https://pomeps.org/wp-content/uploads/2019/03/POMEPS_Studies_34_Web.pdf.

55   Cui Shoujun, "Sino-Gulf Relations: From Energy to Strategic Partners," *JPC*, 2015, https://www.jewishpolicycenter.org/2015/08/31/china-gulf-relations/.

56   "Speech by H.E. Wen Jiabao, Premier of the State Council of the People's Republic of China, at the China-EU Investment and Trade Forum," *Chinese Ministry of Foreign Affairs*, May 6, 2004, http://www.chinamission.be/eng/zt/t101949.htm.

57   Georg Struver, "China's partnership diplomacy: International alignment based on interests of ideology," *The Chinese Journal of International Politics*, 10(1), 2017, 31–65.

58   Feng Zhongping and Huang Jing, "China's Strategic Partnership Diplomacy: Engaging with a Changing World," *European Strategic Partnerships Observatory, ESPO Working Paper No. 8*, June 27, 2014, Available at http://dx.doi.org/10.2139/ssrn.2459948

59   Jonathan Fulton, "China's approach to the Gulf dispute," *Asia Dialogue*, 2018, http://theasiadialogue.com/2018/05/03/chinas-approach-to-the-gulf-dispute/.

60   Jonathan Fulton, "Friends with Benefits: China's Partnership Diplomacy in the Gulf," *POMEPS Studies 34: Shifting Global Politics and the Middle East*, March 2019, https://pomeps.org/wp-content/uploads/2019/03/POMEPS_Studies_34_Web.pdf.

61   Jon B. Alterman, "China's Middle East Model," *Center for Strategic and International Studies (CSIS)*, May 23, 2019, https://www.csis.org/analysis/chinas-middle-east-model

62   Sarah Zheng, "China's President Xi Jinping wraps up UAE visit with series of deals to boost presence in Middle East," *South China Morning Post*, July 21, 2018, https://www.scmp.com/news/china/diplomacy-defence/article/2156291/chinas-president-xi-jinping-wraps-uea-visit-series.

63   Mohsen Shariatinia and Hamidreza Azizi, "Iran–China Cooperation in the Silk Road Economic Belt: From Strategic Understanding to Operational Understanding," *China & World Economy*, 25, No. (5), 2017, 46–61.

64   James M. Dorsey, *China and the Middle East: venturing into the maelstrom.* Cham, Switzerland: Palgrave Macmillan, 2019; Andrew Scobell, and Alireza Nader, *China in the Middle East: The Wary Dragon.* Santa Monica, Calif.: RAND, 2016; Guang Yang, *China-Middle East Relations.* UK: Paths International Ltd, 2013; Jon Alterman and John Garver, *The Vital Triangle: China, the United States, and the Middle East.* Washington: Center for Strategic and International Studies, 2008; Jacqueline Armijo, "China and the Gulf: The Social and Cultural Implications of Their Rapidly Developing Economic Ties," In T. Niblock and M. Malik (eds.), *Asia-Gulf Economic Relations in the 21st Century: The Local to Global Transformation* (pp.141–156). Berlin: Gerlach Press, 2013; Marc Lanteinge, *Chinese Foreign Policy: An Introduction.* London: Routledge, 2013; Yitzhak Shichor, *The Middle East in China's Foreign Policy: 1949–1977.* Cambridge: Cambridge University Press, 1979; Jon B. Alterman, "China's Soft Power in the Middle East," in C. Mcgiffert (ed.), *Chinese Soft Power and Its Implications for the United States* (pp. 63–76). Washington, DC: Center for Strategic and International Studies, 2009.

65   Mohamed Bin Huwaidin, *China's Relations with Arabia and the Gulf, 1949–1999.* London: Routledge, 2011; Wu Bingbing. "Strategy and Politics in the Gulf as Seen from China," In B. Wakefield and S. L. Levenstein (eds.), China and the Persian Gulf: Implications for the United States (pp.10–26).Washington: Woodrow Wilson International Center for Scholars, 2011; Joseph Y. S. Cheng, "China's Relations with the Gulf Cooperation Council States: Multilevel Diplomacy in a Divided Arab World," *China Review*, 16 (1), 35–64; Feng Chaoling, "Embracing Interdependence: The Dynamics of China and the Middle East," *Policy Briefing.* Doha, Brookings Doha Center, 2015.

66   James Reardon-Anderson, *The Red Star and the Crescent: China and the Middle East.* London: Hurst Publishers, 2018; Muhamad S. Olimat, *China and the Middle East since World War II: A bilateral approach.* Lanham: Lexington Books, 2014; Tim Niblock and Yang Guang, *Security dynamics of East Asia in the Gulf region.* Berlin: Gerlach Press, 2014; Enrico Fardella, "China's Debate on the Middle East and North Africa: A Critical Review," *Mediterranean Quarterly*, 26, (1), 2015, 5–25; Mo Chen, "Exploring Economic Relations between China and the GCC States," *Journal of Middle Eastern and Islamic Studies (in Asia)*, 5 (4),

2011, 88–105; Niu Xinchun and Haibing Xing, "China's Interest in and Influence Over the Middle East," *Contemporary International Relations*, 24, (1), 2014, 37–58; Sarah Kaiser-Cross and Yufeng Mao, "China's Strategy in the Middle East and the Arab World," in J. Eisenman and E. Heginbotham (eds.), *China Steps Out: Beijing's Major Power Engagement with the Developing World* (pp. 170–192). New York: Routledge, 2018.

67 Jonathan Fulton and Li-Chen Sim, *External Powers and the Gulf Monarchies*. London, Oxon; New York, NY: Routledge, 2019; Steven A. Yetiv, *Challenged Hegemony: The United States, China, and Russia in the Persian Gulf*. Stanford, California: Stanford University Press, 2018; Sun Degang and Yahia H. Zoubir, "China's Economic Diplomacy Towards the Arab Countries: Challenges Ahead?," *Journal of Contemporary China*, 24 (95), 2015, 903–21; Mathieu Duchâtel, Oliver Bräuner, and Zhou Hang, "Protecting China's Overseas Interests: The Slow Shift Away from Non-Interference," *Policy Paper No. 41*, Stockholm, Sweden: Stockholm International Peace Research Institute, 2014; Mordechai Chaziza, "Six Years After the Arab Spring: China Foreign Policy in the Middle East-North Africa," In C. Çakmak and A. O. Özçelik (eds.), *The World Community and Arab Spring* (pp.185–204). Cham: Palgrave Macmillan, 2019.

68 Jonathan Fulton and Li-Chen Sim. *External Powers and the Gulf Monarchies*. London, Oxon; New York, NY: Routledge, 2019; Steven A. Yetiv, *Challenged Hegemony: The United States, China, and Russia in the Persian Gulf*. Stanford, California: Stanford University Press, 2018, Jonathan Fulton, "China's Presence in the Middle East: The Implications of the One Belt, One Road Initiative/The Red Star and the Crescent: China and the Middle East," *The Middle East Journal*, 72 (2), 2018, 341–343; Zhongmin Liu, "Historical evolution of relationship between China and the Gulf Region." *Journal of Middle Eastern and Islamic Studies (in Asia)* 10(1), 2016, 1–25.

69 Michael Hudson and Mimi Kirk, *Gulf Politics and Economics in a Changing World*. Washington DC: Middle East Institute, 2014; Qian Xuming, "The Belt and Road Initiatives and China–GCC Relations," *International Relations and Diplomacy*, 5(11), 2017, 687–693; Mohammed N. Jalal, The China-Arab States Cooperation Forum: Achievements, Challenges and Prospects," *Journal of Middle Eastern and Islamic Studies (in Asia)*, 8 (2), 2014, 1–21.

70 Anoushiravan Ehteshami, and Niv Horesh, *China's Presence in the Middle East: The Implications of the One Belt, One Road Initiative*. London; New York: Routledge, Taylor & Francis Group, 2018; Jonathan Fulton, *China's Relations with the Gulf Monarchies*. Abingdon, Oxon; New York, NY: Routledge, 2019; Yitzhak Shichor, "Vision, provision and supervision: The politics of China's OBOR and AIIB and their implications for the Middle East', in A. Ehteshami and N. Horesh (eds.), *China's Presence in the Middle East: Implications for One Belt, One Road Initiative* (pp. 38–

53). London: Routledge, 2017; Theresa Fallon, "The New Silk Road: Xi Jinping's Grand Strategy for Eurasia," *American Foreign Policy Interests*, 37 (3), 2015, 140–147; Peter Ferdinand, "Westward ho-the China dream and 'one belt, one road': Chinese foreign policy under Xi Jinping," *International Affairs*, 92 (4), 2016, 941–957; Tom Miller, *China's Asian Dream*. London: Zed Books, 2017; Qian, Xuewen, "The New Silk Road in West Asia under 'the Belt and Road' Initiative," *Journal of Middle Eastern and Islamic Studies (in Asia)*, 10 (1), 2016, 26–55; Henelito A. Sevilla Jr., "China's New Silk Route Initiative: Political and Economic Implications for the Middle East and Southeast Asia," *Journal of Middle Eastern and Islamic Studies (in Asia)*, 11 (1), 83–106.

1

Saudi Arabia

1   Xu Wei, "Xi hails Saudi Arabia as good friend," *China Daily*, February 23, 2019, http://www.chinadaily.com.cn/a/201902/23/WS5c7044c2a3106c65c34eaef5.html.

2   "Chinese president meets Saudi crown prince," *China Daily*, February 22, 2019, http://www.chinadaily.com.cn/a/201902/22/WS5c6ff654a3106c65c34eaebd.html.

3   "Our Vision: Saudi Arabia the heart of the Arab and Islamic worlds, the investment powerhouse, and the hub connecting three continents," *Kingdom of Saudi Arabia*, March, 2019, https://vision2030.gov.sa/sites/default/files/report/Saudi_Vision2030EN_2017.pdf.

4   Mohamed Negm, "The Suez Canal axes, Neom and the Silk Road initiative an alliance between Egypt, Saudi and China for a century's project in formation," *The Middle East Observer*, March 13, 2018, http://www.meobserver.org/?p=16092.

5   "Vision and Actions on Jointly Building Silk Road Economic Belt and 21st-Century Maritime Silk Road," *National Development and Reform Commission, Ministry of Foreign Affairs, and Ministry of Commerce of the People's Republic of China*, March 28, 2015, http://en.ndrc.gov.cn/newsrelease/201503/t20150330_669367.html.

6   "Xi begins Middle East tour with elevation of Sino–Saudi ties," *China Daily*, January 20, 2016, http://www.chinadaily.com.cn/world/2016xivisitmiddleeast/2016-01/20/content_23162646.htm.

7   "China, Saudi Arabia ink cooperation deals," *The State Council: The People's Republic of China*, August 30, 2016, http://english.gov.cn/state_council/vice_premiers/2016/08/30/content_281475429522366.htm.

8 "China, Saudi Arabia agree to boost all-round strategic partnership," *China Daily*, March 16, 2017, http://www.chinadaily.com.cn/china/2017-03/16/content 28585346. htm.

9 "Crown Prince meets with Chinese Vice Premier," *Saudi Gazette*, August 25, 2017, http://saudigazette.com.sa/article/515872.

10 "China, Saudi Arabia agree to expand cooperation," *Xinhua*, February 22, 2019, http://www.xinhuanet.com/english/2019-02/22/c 137842899.htm.

11 "Country Reports on Human Rights Practices for 2018: China," *United States Department of State*, 2018, https://www.state.gov/documents/organization/289281.pdf.

12 Lesley Wroughton and David Brunnstrom, "U.S. says China's treatment of Muslim minority worst abuses 'since the 1930s'," *Reuters*, March13, 2019, https://www.reuters.com/article/us-usa-rights/pompeo-says-china-in-a-league-of-its-own-in-human-rights-violations-idUSKBN1QU23W?fee dType=RSS&feedName=worldNews.

13 Phil Stewart, "China putting minority Muslims in 'concentration camps,' U.S. says," *Reuters*, May 4, 2019, https://www.reuters.com/article/us-usa-china-concentrationcamps/china-putting-minority-muslims-in-concentration-camps-us-says-idUSKCN1S925K.

14 Esther Felden, Nina Raddy, Kyra Levine, "Saudi women refugees in Germany: Still living in fear," *Deutsche Welle*, February 19, 2019, https://www.dw.com/en/saudi-women-refugees-in-germany-still-living-in-fear/a-47576575.

15 Declan Walsh and Tyler Hicks, "The Tragedy of Saudi Arabia's War," *The New York Times*, October 26, 2018, https://www.nytimes.com/interactive/2018/10/26/world/middleeast/ saudi-arabia-war-yemen.html.

16 Zahraa Alkhalisi, "Saudi Arabia seeks Asia's support for its economic makeover," *CNN Business*, February 19, 2019, https://edition.cnn.com/2019/02/19/business/mbs-asia-tour-business/ index.html.

17 Helene Fouquet, Jonathan Gilbert and Alex Morales, "Saudi Prince Finds Both Friends and Disapproval at G-20 Summit," *Bloomberg*, December 3, 2018, https://www.bloomberg.com/news/articles/2018-12-01/saudi-prince-finds-both-friends-and-disapproval-at-g-20-summit.

18 Oscar Rousseau, "China wants Saudi as key Belt and Road partner," *Arabian Industry*, July 11, 2018, https://www.arabianindustry.com/construction/news/2018/jul/11/china-wants-saudi-as-key-belt-and-road-partner-5952245/#.W0YMp2LblFQ .twitter.

19 Turki Al Faisal bin Abdul Aziz Al Saud, "Saudi Arabia's Foreign Policy," *The Middle East Policy Council*, XX (4), October 22, 2013, https://www.mepc.org/saudi-arabias-foreign-policy.

20 P. R. Kumaraswamy and Md. Muddassir Quamar, *India's Saudi Policy: Bridging the Gulf*. Singapore: Palgrave Macmillan, 2019.

21 "Saudi Energy Minister Labels 'One Belt, One Road' Initiative as Historic," *Asharq Al-Awsat*, May 15, 2017, https://eng-archive.aawsat.com/asharq-al-awsat-english/business/saudi-energy-minister-labels-one-belt-one-road-initiative-historic.

22 Jean-Michel Valantin, "Saudi Arabia and the Chinese New Silk Road," *The Red (Team) Analysis Society: Strategic Foresight & Warning, Risk Management, Horizon Scanning*, May 15, 2017, https://www.redanalysis.org/2017/05/15/saudi-arabia-and-the-chinese-new-silk-road/.

23 "Saudi Energy Minister Labels 'One Belt, One Road' Initiative as Historic," *Asharq Al-Awsat*, May 15, 2017, https://eng-archive.aawsat.com/asharq-al-awsat-english/business/saudi-energy-minister-labels-one-belt-one-road-initiative-historic.

24 "China, Saudi Arabia sign agreements worth $65bn," *China Radio International*, March 16, 2017, https://gbtimes.com/china-vows-to-deepen-support-for-saudi-arabia.

25 "Saudi Arabia To Build $10 Billion Oil Refinery In Pakistan's Gwadar," *RFE/RL*, January 12, 2019, https://www.rferl.org/a/saudi-arabia-to-build-10-billion-oil-refinery-in-pakistan-s-gwadar/29706488.html.

26 Zamir Ahmed Awan, "New era in Sino–Saudi relations," *China Daily*, February 25, 2019, http://www.chinadaily.com.cn/a/201902/25/WS5c734f98a3106c65c34eb2e8.html.

27 "China's Guarded Response To Pak Bringing Saudi In Trade Corridor Work", *NDTV*, October 08, 2018, https://www.ndtv.com/world-news/chinas-guarded-response-to-pak-bringing-saudi-arabia-in-trade-corridor-work-1928715.

28 Asif Amin, "Why Saudi Arabia's interest in CPEC, BRI is good news," *China Daily*, October 12, 2018, http://www.chinadaily.com.cn/a/201810/12/WS5bc047a4a310eff3032820f6.html.

29 "A Shenzhen for Arabia," *Week in China*, November 3, 2017, https://www.weekinchina.com/2017/11/a-shenzhen-for-arabia/.

30 "NEOM and the BRI," *OBOReurope*, February 28, 2019, https://www.oboreurope.com/en/neom-and-the-bri/.

31 John Calabrese, "China and the Persian Gulf: Energy and Security," *Middle East Journal*, 52 (3), 1998, 351–366; Steve Yetiv and Chunlong Lu, "China, Global Energy, and the Middle East", *Middle East Journal*, 61 (2), 2007, 199–218.

32   Daniel Workman, "Top 15 Crude Oil Suppliers to China," *World's Top Exports*, April 12, 2019, http://www.worldstopexports.com/top-15-crude-oil-suppliers-to-china/.

33   Chris Zambelis, "China and Saudi Arabia Solidify Strategic Partnership Amid Looming Risks," *China Brief*, 17 (3), March 2, 2017, https://jamestown.org/program/china-saudi-arabia-solidify-strategic-partnership-amid-looming-risks/.

34   "Saudi Arabia facts and figures," *Organization of the Petroleum Exporting Countries*, September 23, 2018, https://www.opec.org/opec_web/en/about_us/169.htm.

35   Rania El Gamal, "UPDATE 3-Saudi Arabia announces rise in oil reserves after external audit," *Reuters*, January 9, 2019, https://www.reuters.com/article/saudi-oil-reserves/update-3-saudi-arabia-announces-rise-in-oil-reserves-after-external-audit-idUSL8N1Z93WO.

36   "China see' "enormous potential' in Saudi economy as crown prince visits," *Reuters*, February 22, 2019, https://www.reuters.com/article/asia-saudi-china/china-sees-enormous-potential-in-saudi-economy-as-crown-prince-visits-idUSL3N20H05S.

37   Lyu Chang and Xing Zhigang, "Sinopec, Saudi Aramco sign strategic agreement," *China Daily* January 21, 2016, http://www.chinadaily.com.cn/world/2016xivisitmiddleeast/2016-01/21/content_23174517.htm.

38   "Yanbu's joint venture refinery shines as example for beneficial China–Saudi energy cooperation," *Xinhua*, July 9, 2018, http://www.xinhuanet.com/english/2018-07/09/c_137312287.htm.

39   "Saudi to supply 12 million barrels crude to China's Huajin in 2018 deal," *Reuters*, February 26, 2018, https://www.reuters.com/article/us-saudi-china-crude-huajin/saudi-to-supply-12-million-barrels-crude-to-chinas-huajin-in-2018-deal-idUSKCN1GA0VR.

40   "Saudi's SABIC signs MOU to build petrochemical complex in China," *Reuters*, September 11, 2018, https://www.reuters.com/article/us-sabic-china/saudis-sabic-signs-mou-to-build-petrochemical-complex-in-china-idUSKCN1LR0L8.

41   "China and Saudi Arabia sign 35 cooperation deals worth \$28 bln in Beijing," *China Global Television Network (CGTN)*, 24 February 2019, https://news.cgtn.com/news/3d3d414f306b444f32457a6333566d54/index.html.

42   "Saudi Aramco agrees to \$10 billion joint venture deal in China," *ARAB NEWS*, February 22, 2019, http://www.arabnews.com/node/1456321/business-economy.

43   Florence Tan, Chen Aizhu and Rania El-Gamal, "Saudi Arabia nabs new China oil demand, challenges Russia's top spot," *The Globe and Mail*, November 28, 2018,

https://www.theglobeandmail.com/business/article-saudi-arabia-nabs-new-china-oil-demand-challenges-russias-top-spot/.

44   "Pan-Asia PET Resin (Guangzhou, China) Plans to Invest $3.8 Billion to Build a Polyester Manufacturing Complex at Jazan, Saudi Arabi," *Bloomberg*, July 10, 2017, https://www.bloomberg.com/research/stocks/private/snapshot.asp?priv-capid=30395182.

45   Natasha Alperowicz, "Chinese firm to invest in huge polyester complex in Saudi Arabia," *Borderless*, June 27, 2017, https://www.borderless.net/chinese-firm-to-invest-in-huge-polyester-complex-in-saudi-arabia/.

46   "Beijing, Saudi Arabia agree to more oil cooperation, exports to China," *Reuters*, March 18, 2017, https://www.reuters.com/article/us-china-saudi/beijing-saudi-arabia-agree-to-more-oil-cooperation-exports-to-china-idUSKBN16P055.

47   Hisham Al-Joher, "SABIC and SINOPEC Support Saudi Vision 2030 and China's One Belt, One Road Initiative by Singing a Strategic Cooperation Agreement," *SABIC*, March 16, 2017, https://www.sabic.com/en/news/6098-sabic-and-sinopec-support-saudi-vision-2030-and-china-s-one-belt-one-road-initiative-by-signing-a-strategic-cooperation-agreement.

48   "Saudi-China Tie Up Furthers 'One Belt One Road'," *Port Technology*, Jun 5, 2017, https://www.porttechnology.org/news/saudis_joins_up_on_one_belt_on_e_road.

49   "Saudi Arabia 2018," *The Oil & Gas Year Saudi Arabia 2018*, 2019, https://www.theoilandgasyear.com/market/saudi-arabia/.

50   Dania Saadi, "Saudi Arabia announces rise in oil and gas reserves after independent audit," *The National*, January 9, 2019, https://www.thenational.ae/business/energy/saudi-arabia-announces-rise-in-oil-and-gas-reserves-after-independent-audit-1.811247.

51   Rania El Gamal, Alex Lawler, "Exclusive: China offers to buy 5 percent of Saudi Aramco directly- sources," *Reuters*, October 16, 2017, https://www.reuters.com/article/us-saudi-aramco-ipo-china-exclusive/exclusive-china-offers-to-buy-5-percent-of-saudi-aramco-directly-sources-idUSKBN1CL1YJ.

52   " PowerChina signs marine facilities construction contract in Saudi Arabia," *State-owned Assets Supervision and Administration Commission of the State Council*, December 4, 2018, http://en.sasac.gov.cn/2018/12/04/c_685.htm.

53   "Chinese group launches $1bn Saudi industrial project," *Trade Arabia*, January 31, 2019, http://www.tradearabia.com/news/OGN_350428.html.

54   "Massive Chinese project in Saudi Arabia makes big breakthroughs," China Daily, January 9, 2019,

http://www.chinadaily.com.cn/regional/2019-01/10/content_37425087.htm

55 Global Commission on the Geopolitics of Energy Transformation, "A New World the Geopolitics of the Energy Transformation," *International Renewable Energy Agency (IREA)*, 2019, http://www.geopoliticsofrenewables.org/assets/geopolitics/Reports/wp-content/uploads/2019/01/Global_commission_renewable_energy_2019.pdf.

56 Juergen Braunstein and Oliver McPherson-Smith, "The US–China Trade War and its Implications for Saudi Arabia," *Global Policy*, February 12, 2019, https://www.globalpolicyjournal.com/blog/12/02/2019/us-china-trade-war-and-its-implications-saudi-arabia.

57 Mark Osborne, "LONGi set for agreement to develop major solar manufacturing hub in Saudi Arabia," *PV-Tech*, May 25, 2018, https://www.pv-tech.org/news/longi-signs-agreement-to-develop-major-solar-manufacturing-hub-in-saudi-ara.

58 "Hanergy to set up the region's first thin-film solar power industrial park in Middle East," *EIN Newsdesk*, 2019, https://www.einnews.com/pr_news/475415644/hanergy-to-set-up-the-region-s-first-thin-film-solar-power-industrial-park-in-middle-east.

59 "Saudi Arabia's PIF signs MoU with China's NAE on renewable energy," *ARAB NEWS*, February 22, 2019, http://www.arabnews.com/node/1456326/business-economy.

60 Jason Deign, "Saudi Arabia Looks to China for Solar as Power Politics Shift," *Greentech Media*, February 5, 2019, https://www.greentechmedia.com/articles/read/saudi-looks-to-china-for-solar-as-power-politics-shift#gs.26fdtx.

61 "Shift in Power Politics, Saudi Arabia Courting China for Help in Solar," *Times of Saudia*, February 5, 2019, https://www.timesofsaudia.com/saudi-arabia/shift-in-power-politics-saudi-arabia-courting-china-for-help-in-solar/.

62 Chen Kane, "Why proposals to sell nuclear reactors to Saudi Arabia raise red flags," *The Conversation*, February 23, 2019, https://theconversation.com/why-proposals-to-sell-nuclear-reactors-to-saudi-arabia-raise-red-flags-112276.

63 "Saudi Arabia, Largest Producer of Desalinated Water, to Build 9 More Plants," *Al-bawaba*, January 22, 2018, https://www.albawaba.com/business/saudi-arabia-desalination-plants-red-sea-coast-1077706.

64 "China, Saudi Arabia agree to build HTR," *World Nuclear News*, January 20, 2016, http://www.world-nuclear-news.org/NN-China-Saudi-Arabia-agree-to-build-HTR-2001164.html.

65 "Saudi Arabia signs cooperation deals with China on nuclear energy," *Reuters*, August 25, 2017,

https://www.reuters.com/article/saudi-china-nuclear/saudi-arabia-signs-cooperation-deals-with-china-on-nuclear-energy-idUSL8N1LB1CE.

66 "Vision and Actions on Jointly Building Silk Road Economic Belt and 21st-Century Maritime Silk Road," *National Development and Reform Commission, Ministry of Foreign Affairs, and Ministry of Commerce of the People's Republic of China*, March 28, 2015, http://en.ndrc.gov.cn/newsrelease/201503/t20150330_669367.html.

67 "China Customs Statistics: Imports and exports by country/region," *The Hong Kong Trade Development Council (HKTDC)*, May 27, 2019, http://china-trade-research.hktdc.com/business-news/article/Facts-and-Figures/China-Customs-Statistics/ff/en/1/1X39VTVQ/1X09N9NM.htm.

68 Ibrahim Al-Othaimin, "Win-win cooperation usher in new type of international ties," *Saudi Gazette*, May 4, 2018, http://saudigazette.com.sa/article/534190.

69 Zahraa Alkhalisi, "Saudi Arabia seeks Asia's support for its economic makeover," *CNN Business*, February 19, 2019, https://edition.cnn.com/2019/02/19/business/mbs-asia-tour-business/index.html.

70 "Chinese Investments & Contracts in Saudi Arabia (2013–2018)," *China Global Investment Tracker*, 2019, https://www.aei.org/china-global-investment-tracker/.

71 "China, Saudi Arabia sign multiple deals," *Global Times*, February 22, 2019, http://www.globaltimes.cn/content/1139770.shtml.

72 Ibrahim Al-Othaimin, "Win-win cooperation usher in new type of international ties," *Saudi Gazette*, May 4, 2018, http://saudigazette.com.sa/article/534190.

73 Lindsay Hughes, "China in the Middle East: The Saudi Factor," *Future Directions International*, October 2, 2018, http://www.futuredirections.org.au/publication/china-in-the-middle-east-the-saudi-factor/.

74 Joseph A. Kéchichian, "Saudi Arabia and China: The Security Dimension," *Middle East Institute*, February 9, 2016, https://www.mei.edu/publications/saudi-arabia-and-china-security-dimension.

75 "State Councilor and Foreign Minister Wang Yi gave an interview to Asharq Al-Awsat," *Embassy of the People's Republic of China in the Kingdom of Saudi Arabia*, February 22, 2019, http://www.chinaembassy.org.sa/eng/zsgx/t1640239.htm.

76 "Xi Jinping Holds Talks with King Salman bin Abdulaziz Al Saud of Saudi Arabia: Two Heads of State Jointly Announce Establishment of China–Saudi Arabia Comprehensive Strategic Partnership," *Ministry of Foreign Affairs, the People's Republic of China*, January 20, 2016, https://www.fmprc.gov.cn/mfa_eng/topics_665678/xjpdstajyljxgsfw/t1333527.shtml.

77 Wang Jin, "China and Saudi Arabia: A New Alliance?," *The Diplomat*, September 2, 2016, https://thediplomat.com/2016/09/china-and-saudi-arabia-a-new-alliance/.

78 Catherine Wong, "China, Saudi Arabia sign US$65 billion in deals as King Salman starts Beijing visit," *South China Morning Post*, March 16, 2017, https://www.scmp.com/news/china/policies-politics/article/2079528/china-saudi-arabia-sign-us65-billion-deals-king-salman.

79 "China–Saudi Arabia cooperation to enter more fruitful era, broad consensus reached on key projects," *Xinhua*, August 25, 2017, http://www.xinhuanet.com//english/2017-08/25/c_136554724.htm.

80 Andrew Torchia, "Saudi Arabia, China plan joint $20 billion investment fund," *Reuters*, August 24, 2017, https://www.reuters.com/article/us-saudi-china-funds/saudi-arabia-china-plan-joint-20-billion-investment-fund-idUSKCN1B40KO.

81 "Saudi Arabia, China sign $28 billion worth of economic accords," *Arab News*, February 22, 2019, http://www.arabnews.com/node/1456366/business-economy.

82 "Saudi Arabia and China sign agreements worth $28 billion," *Offshore Technology*, February 27, 2019, https://www.offshore-technology.com/comment/saudi-arabia-and-china-sign-agreements-worth-28-billion/.

83 "Interview: Saudi crown prince's visit to China expected to bring ties to new high: minister," *Xinhua*, February 21, 2019, http://www.xinhuanet.com/english/2019-02/21/c_137837773.htm.

84 Ahmed Al-Quiasy, "Saudi-Chinese Rapprochement and Its Effect on Saudi-American Relations," *The Washington Institute*, February 2, 2018, https://www.washingtoninstitute.org/fikraforum/view/saudi-chinese-rapprochement-and-its-effect-on-saudi-american-relations.

85 Yoel Guzansky and Assaf Orion, "Slowly but Surely: Growing Relations between Saudi Arabia and China," *INSS Insight No. 891*, January 29, 2017, https://www.inss.org.il/publication/slowly-surely-growing-relations-saudi-arabia-china/.

86 Thomas Woodrow, "The Sino–Saudi Connection," *China Brief*, 2 (21), October 24, 2002, https://jamestown.org/program/the-sino-saudi-connection/.

87 Muhammad Saleh Zaafir, "Saudi Arabia planning procurement of JF-17 Thunder, Mashshaks, says Saudi air chief," *The News*, November 7, 2016, https://www.thenews.com.pk/print/163018-Saudi-Arabia-planning-procurement-of-JF-17-Thunder-Mashshaks-says-Saudi-air-chief.

88 Phil Mattingly, Zachary Cohen and Jeremy Herb, "Exclusive: US intel shows Saudi Arabia escalated its missile program with help from China," *CNN*, June 5, 2019,

https://edition.cnn.com/2019/06/05/politics/us-intelligence-saudi-arabia-ballistic-missile-china/index.html.

89   Zamir Ahmed Awan, "New era in Sino–Saudi relations," *China Daily*, February 25, 2019, http://www.chinadaily.com.cn/a/201902/25/WS5c734f98a3106c65c34eb2e8.html.

90   Chen Chuanren and Chris Pocock, "Saudi Arabia Buying and Building Chinese Armed Drones," *AIN online*, April 12, 2017, https://www.ainonline.com/aviation-news/defense/2017-04-12/saudi-arabia-buying-and-building-chinese-armed-drones.

91   "Saudi Arabia imports UAV production line from China: reports," *People's Daily Online*, March 27, 2017, http://www.ecns.cn/military/2017/03-27/250906.shtml.

92   Stephen Clark, "China launches satellites for Saudi Arabia," *Spaceflight Now*, December 7, 2018, https://spaceflightnow.com/2018/12/07/china-launches-satellites-for-saudi-arabia/.

93   "Xi Jinping Holds Talks with King Salman bin Abdulaziz Al Saud of Saudi Arabia," *Embassy of the People's Republic of China in the Kingdom of Saudi Arabia*, January 19, 2016, http://sa.china-embassy.org/eng/zt/2/t1335502.htm.

94   "King receives special envoy of Chinese president," *Saudi Gazette*, November 7, 2016, http://saudigazette.com.sa/article/166742/King-receives-special-envoy-of-Chinese-president.

95   Chris Zambelis, "China and Saudi Arabia Solidify Strategic Partnership Amid Looming Risks," *China Brief*, 17(3), March 2, 2017, https://jamestown.org/program/china-saudi-arabia-solidify-strategic-partnership-amid-looming-risks/

96   "Vision and Actions on Jointly Building Silk Road Economic Belt and 21st-Century Maritime Silk Road," *National Development and Reform Commission, Ministry of Foreign Affairs, and Ministry of Commerce of the People's Republic of China*, March 28, 2015, http://en.ndrc.gov.cn/newsrelease/201503/t20150330_669367.html.

97   "State Councilor and Foreign Minister Wang Yi gave an interview to Asharq Al-Awsat," *Embassy of the People's Republic of China in the Kingdom of Saudi Arabia*, February 22, 2019, http://www.chinaembassy.org.sa/eng/zsgx/t1640239.htm.

98   "China to host its first major cultural relic exhibition in Saudi Arabia," *China Daily*, August 23, 2018, http://www.chinadaily.com.cn/a/201808/23/WS5b7e24dda310add14f387556_4.html.

99   "Saudi Arabia plans to include Chinese language in education curriculum," *Saudi Gazette*, February 22, 2019, http://saudigazette.com.sa/article/559758/SAUDI-ARABIA/Saudi-

Arabia-plans-to-include-Chinese-language-in-education-curriculum.

100 "China, Arab states agree to enhance cooperation under new strategic partnership," *Arab News*, July 10, 2018, http://www.arabnews.com/node/1336746/saudi-arabia.

101 Yang Feiyue, "Program helps young Saudis study abroad," *China Daily*, January 21, 2016, http://www.chinadaily.com.cn/world/2016xivisitmiddleeast/2016-01/21/content_23177839.htm.

102 "Interview: Saudi crown prince's visit to China expected to bring ties to new high: minister," *Xinhua*, February 21, 2019, https://edition.cnn.com/2019/02/21/asia/saudi-arabia-china-mohammed-bin-salman-intl/index.html.

103 Sam Bridge, "Gulf forecast to see 81% rise in Chinese tourists by 2022," *Arabian Business*, December 19, 2018, https://www.arabianbusiness.com/travel-hospitality/409972-gulf-fore-cast-to-see-81-rise-in-chinese-tourists-by-2022.

104 "Chinese envoy sees KSA as a major tourist destination," *Arab News*, July 10, 2018, http://www.arabnews.com/node/1336756/saudi-arabia.

105 Travel & Tourism crucial to Saudi Arabia's economy," *World Travel & Tourism Council*, March 25, 2019, https://www.wttc.org/about/media-centre/press-releases/press-releases/2019/travel-and-tourism-crucial-to-saudi-arabias-economy/ .

106 Staff writer, "Saudi Arabia aims to attract 1.5m tourists by 2020," *Arabian Business*, June 5, 2016, https://www.arabianbusiness.com/saudi-arabia-aims-attract-1-5m-tourists-by-2020-634057.html.

107 "Chinese tourists travel more, spend more in 2018," *CGTN*, January 11, 2019, https://news.cgtn.com/news/3d3d774d3051544f31457a6333566d54/share_p.html.

2

Iran

1 "China, Iran Upgrade Ties to Carry Forward Millennia-Old Friendship," *Xinhua*, January 24, 2016, http://news.xinhuanet.com/english/china/2016-01/24/c_135039635.htm.

2 "Ahead of Saudi visit, China seeks 'deeper trust' with Iran," *Reuters*, February 19, 2019, https://www.reuters.com/article/us-china-iran/ahead-of-saudi-visit-china-seeks-deeper-trust-with-iran-idUSKCN1Q80PY.

3 Alex Vatanka, "China Courts Iran: Why One Belt, One Road Will Run Through Tehran," *Foreign Affairs*, November 1, 2017,

https://www.foreignaffairs.com/articles/china/2017-11-01/china-courts-iran.

4   Mohsen Shariatinia and Hamidreza Azizi, "Iran–China Cooperation in the Silk Road Economic Belt: From Strategic Understanding to Operational Understanding," *China & World Economy*, 25, (5), 2017, 46–61.

5   "Remarks by President Trump on the Joint Comprehensive Plan of Action," *The White House*, May 8, 2018, https://www.whitehouse.gov/briefings-statements/remarks-president-trump-joint-comprehensive-plan-action/.

6   "When the Sun Sets in the East: New Dynamics in China–Iran Trade Under Sanctions," *Bourse & Bazaar*, January 2, 2019, https://static1.squarespace.com/static/54db7b69e4b00a5e4 b11038c/t/5c4ad5ffc74c505f6368f1a8/1548408321766/ B%26B_Special_Report_China_Iran_Trade_v2.pdf.

7   Min Ye, "China and competing cooperation in Asia–Pacific: TPP, RCEP, and the New Silk Road," *Asian Security*, 11(3), 2015, 206–224.

8   "Vision and Actions on Jointly Building Silk Road Economic Belt and 21st-Century Maritime Silk Road," *National Development and Reform Commission, Ministry of Foreign Affairs, and Ministry of Commerce of the People's Republic of China*, March 28, 2015, http://en.ndrc.gov.cn/newsrelease/201503/t20150330_669367.html.

9   "President Xi meets Iran's Supreme Leader Khamenei," *Ministry of Foreign Affairs, the People's Republic of China*, January 25, 2016, https://www.fmprc.gov.cn/mfa_eng/sp/t1334695.shtml.

10   "China's desire for close Iran ties unchanged, Xi says ahead of Saudi prince's visit," *Reuters*, February 20, 2019, https://www.reuters.com/article/us-china-iran/chinas-desire-for-close-iran-ties-unchanged-xi-says-ahead-of-saudi-princes-visit-idUSKCN1Q A065.

11   "Vision and Actions on Jointly Building Silk Road Economic Belt and 21st-Century Maritime Silk Road," *National Development and Reform Commission, Ministry of Foreign Affairs, and Ministry of Commerce of the People's Republic of China*, March 28, 2015, http://en.ndrc.gov.cn/newsrelease/201503/t20150330_669367.html.

12   Mohsen Shariatinia and Hamidreza Azizi, "Iran–China Cooperation in the Silk Road Economic Belt: From Strategic Understanding to Operational Understanding," *China & World Economy*, 25, (5), 2017, 46–61.

13   Tristan Kenderdine, "China Eyes Iran As Important Belt And Road Hub," *Eurasia Review*, September 9, 2017, https://www.eurasiareview.com/09092017-china-eyes-iran-as-important-belt-and-road-hub/.

14   "First freight train from China arrives in Iran in 'Silk Road' boost: media," *Reuters*, February 16, 2016,

https://www.reuters.com/article/us-china-iran-railway-idUSKCN0VP0W8

15 "China's OBOR Developments with Iran & the Arab States," *Silk Road Briefing*, March 29, 2017, https://www.silkroadbriefing.com/news/2017/03/29/chinas-obor-developments-with-iran-the-arab-states/.

16 "1.7 Trillion Dollar Deal Signed with China for Electrification of Tehran-Mashhad Railway," *Tasnim News Agency*, July 25, 2017, https://www.tasnimnews.com/fa/news/1396/05/03/1474373.

17 "China Finances Tehran-Isfahan High-Speed Railroad," *Financial Tribune*, July 21, 2017, https://financialtribune.com/articles/economy-domestic-economy/68698/china-finances-tehran-isfahan-high-speed-railroad

18 Warren Reinsch, "Iran Ready to Join China's Belt and Road Initiative," *The Trumpet*, February 26, 2019, https://www.thetrumpet.com/18674-iran-ready-to-join-chinas-belt-and-road-initiative.

19 "Tehran-Mashhad railway electrification project to start within 45 days," *Tehran Times*, May 4, 2018, https://www.tehrantimes.com/news/423220/Tehran-Mashhad-railway-electrification-project-to-start-within.

20 Manoj JoshiI, "China and Iran: JCPOA and beyond," *ORF*, February18, 2019, https://www.orfonline.org/expert-speak/china-and-iran-jcpoa-and-beyond-48244/.

21 Ben Derudder, Xingjian Liu and Charles Kunaka, "Connectivity Along Overland Corridors of the Belt and Road Initiative," *The World Bank*, October 2018, http://documents.worldbank.org/curated/en/264651538637972468/pdf/130490-MTI-Discussion-Paper-6-Final.pdf.

22 Alex Vatanka, "China Courts Iran: Why One Belt, One Road Will Run Through Tehran". *Foreign Affairs*, November 1, 2017, https://www.foreignaffairs.com/articles/china/2017-11-01/china-courts-iran.

23 Israfil Abdullayev, "Reviving an Ancient Route? The Role of the Baku–Tbilisi–Kars Railway," *Modern Diplomacy*, December 1, 2017, http://www.ris.org.in/aagc/sites/default/files/Modren%20Diplomacy-01-12-2017-Reviving%20an%20Ancient%20Route%20The%20Role%20of%20the%20Baku%20%E2%80%93%0Tbilisi%20%E2%80%93%20Kars%20Railway.pdf.

24 Micha'el Tanchum, "Facing sanctions, Iran pioneers framework for cooperation with Russia, China and India: Analysis," *Hurriyet Daily News*, November 9, 2018, http://www.hurriyetdailynews.com/facing-sanctions-iran-pioneers-framework-for-cooperation-with-russia-china-and-india-138703.

25 Zheng Yanpeng, "New rail route proposed from Urumqi to Iran," *China Daily*, November 21, 2015, http://www.chinadaily.com.cn/china/2015-11/21/content_22506412. htm

26 "New freight train links Inner Mongolia and Iran," *Xinhua*, May 10, 2018, http://www.xinhuanet.com/english/2018-05/10/c_137170361.htm.

27 Mohsen Shariatinia and Hamidreza Azizi, "Iran–China Cooperation in the Silk Road Economic Belt: From Strategic Understanding to Operational Understanding," *China & World Economy*, Vol. 25, No. 5, 2017, 46–61.

28 "Vision and Actions on Jointly Building Silk Road Economic Belt and 21st-Century Maritime Silk Road," *National Development and Reform Commission, Ministry of Foreign Affairs, and Ministry of Commerce of the People's Republic of China*, March 28, 2015, http://en.ndrc.gov.cn/newsrelease/201503/t20150330_669367.html.

29 "Iran's Trade Partners in Three Seasons of the Year," *Donya-e Eghtesad*, April 17, 2017, http://www.donyae-eqtesad.com/fa/tiny/news-3342172.

30 Mohsen Shariatinia and Hamidreza Azizi, "Iran–China Cooperation in the Silk Road Economic Belt: From Strategic Understanding to Operational Understanding," *China & World Economy*, 25, (5), 2017, 46–61.

31 "Iran–China trade increases by 19pct," *AzerNews*, February 8, 2018, https://www.azernews.az/region/126825.html.

32 "China Customs Statistics: Imports and exports by country/region," *The Hong Kong Trade Development Council (HKTDC)*, May 27, 2019, http://china-trade-research.hktdc.com/business-news/article/Facts-and-Figures/China-Customs-Statistics/ff/en/1/1X39VTVQ/1X09N9NM.htm.

33 Ahmad Jamali, "8 Trillion Dollars of Foreign Investment were Attracted in 2017," *Tasnim News Agency*, 14 December 2017, https://www.tasnimnews.com/fa/news/1396/09/23/1601258.

34 "Biggest post-JCPOA Investors in Abadan Refinery," *Iranian Petro-Energy Information Network (SHANA)*, January 21, 2017, http://www.shana.ir/fa/newsagency/275727.

35 Manoj JoshiI, "China and Iran: JCPOA and beyond," *ORF*, February18, 2019, https://www.orfonline.org/expert-speak/china-and-iran-jcpoa-and-beyond-48244/.

36 Iran economy's recovery needs at least $500B in mid-term', *Azer News*, January 28, 2016, https://www.azernews.az/region/92174.html.

37 Mohsen Shariatinia and Hamidreza Azizi, "Iran–China Cooperation in the Silk Road Economic Belt: From Strategic Understanding to

Operational Understanding," *China & World Economy*, 25, (5), 2017, 46–61.

38 "China, Iran Agree to Expand Trade to $600 Billion in a Decade," *Bloomberg*, January 23, 2016,
www.bloomberg.com/news/articles/2016-01-23/china-iran-agree-to-expand-trade-to-600-billion-in-a-decade.

39 "Iran, China Sign $10 Billion Finance Deal," *Financial Tribune*, September 14, 2017,
https://financialtribune.com/articles/economy-business-and-markets/72363/iran-china-sign-10-billion-finance-deal.

40 "China gives billions to Iran," *News24*, September 16, 2017,
https://www.news24.com/World/News/china-gives-billions-to-iran-20170916.

41 Ellen R. Wald, "10 Companies Leaving Iran As Trump's Sanctions Close In," *Forbes*, June 6, 2019,
https://www.forbes.com/sites/ellenrwald/2018/06/06/10-companies-leaving-iran-as-trumps-sanctions-close-in/#542a960ac90f.

42 "EU, Russia, China rally behind Iran after Trump's move," *PressTV*, May 9, 2018,
https://www.presstv.com/DetailFr/2018/05/09/561113/France-Iran-JCPOA.

43 "When the Sun Sets in the East: New Dynamics in China–Iran Trade Under Sanctions," *Bourse & Bazaar*, January 2, 2019,
https://static1.squarespace.com/static/54db7b69e4b00a5e4b11038c/t/5c4ad5ffc74c505f6368f1a8/1548408321766/B%26B_Special_Report_China_Iran_Trade_v2.pdf.

44 Esfandyar Batmanghelidj, "Why China Isn't Standing By Iran," *Bloomberg*, March 27, 2019,
https://www.bloomberg.com/opinion/articles/2019-03-27/spooked-by-u-s-sanctions-china-isn-t-standing-by-iran.

45 Raymond Zhong, "Chinese Tech Giant on Brink of Collapse in New U.S. Cold War," *The New York Times*, May 9, 2018,
https://www.nytimes.com/2018/05/09/technology/zte-china-us-trade-war.html.

46 Lindsay Hughes," China in the Middle East: The Iran Factor," *Future Directions International*, October 25, 2018,
http://www.futuredirections.org.au/publication/china-in-the-middle-east-the-iran-factor/.

47 Zhao Hong, "China's Dilemma on Iran: Between Energy Security and a Responsible Rising Power," *Journal of Contemporary China* 23(87), 2014, 408–424.

48 Mohsen Shariatinia and Hamidreza Azizi, "Iran-China Cooperation in the Silk Road Economic Belt: From Strategic Understanding to Operational Understanding," *China & World Economy*, 25, (5), 2017, 46–61.

49   Debalina Ghoshal, "China Pivots to the Middle East and Iran," *Yale Global*, July 7, 2016,
https://yaleglobal.yale.edu/content/china-pivots-middle-east-and-iran.

50   "Iran's Oil Industry Needs 445 Trillion Dollars of Investment," *Iranian Petro-Energy Information Network (SHANA)*, February 2, 2017,
http://www.shana.ir/fa/newsagency/125796.

51   "China extends $1.3b for renovating Abadan refinery," *Iran Daily*, January 11, 2017,
http://www.iran-daily.com/News/175552.html.

52   Benoit Faucon, "China Offers Iran $3 Billion Oil-Field Deal as Europe Halts Iranian Crude Purchases," *The Wall Street Journal*, January 17, 2019,
https://www.wsj.com/articles/china-offers-iran-3-billion-oil-field-deal-as-europe-halts-iranian-crude-purchases-11547743480.

53   "China steady on Iran oilfields, to ditch South Pars project: Report," *PressTV*, December 12, 2018,
https://www.presstv.com/Detail/2018/12/12/582717/Iran-gas-China-CNPC-US-sanctions-oil-North-Azadegan.

54   "Iran: Total and NIOC sign contract for the development of phase 11 of the giant South Pars gas field," *Total*, July 3, 2017,
https://www.total.com/en/media/news/press-releases/iran-total-and-nioc-sign-contract-development-phase-11-giant-south-pars-gas-field.

55   "China's CNPC replaces Total in Iran's South Pars project: Iranian oil minister," *PressTV*, November 26, 2018,
https://www.presstv.com/DetailFr/2018/11/26/581160/Iran-China-CNPC-South-Pars.

56   "When the Sun Sets in the East: New Dynamics in China–Iran Trade Under Sanctions," *Bourse & Bazaar*, January 2, 2019,
https://static1.squarespace.com/static/54db7b69e4b00a5e4b11038c/t/5c4ad5ffc74c505f6368f1a8/1548408321766/B%26B_Special_Report_China_Iran_Trade_v2.pdf.

57   "China defends Iran business ties after Trump threat," *Reuters*, August 8, 2018,
https://in.reuters.com/article/us-iran-nuclear-china/china-says-its-business-ties-with-iran-are-transparent-lawful-idINKBN1KT0TU.

58   Chen Aizhu, "CNPC suspends investment in Iran's South Pars after U.S. pressure: sources," *Reuters*, December 12, 2018,
https://www.reuters.com/article/us-china-iran-gas-sanctions/cnpc-suspends-investment-in-irans-south-pars-after-u-s-pressure-sources-idUSKBN1OB0RU.

59   Chen Aizhu and Florence Tan, "Boxed in: $1 billion of Iranian crude sits at China's Dalian port," *Reuters*, April 30, 2019,
https://www.reuters.com/article/us-china-iran-oil-sanctions/boxed-in-1-billion-of-iranian-crude-sits-at-chinas-dalian-port-idUSKCN1S60HS.

60   Tsvetana Paraskova, "China's Sinopec Looks To Make Special

Arrangement For Iranian Oil Imports," *Oil Price*, October 31, 2018, https://oilprice.com/Latest-Energy-News/World-News/Chinas-Sinopec-Looks-To-Make-Special-Arrangement-For-Iranian-Oil-Imports.html.

61 Florence Tan, "Iran oil exports set to drop in August ahead of U.S. sanctions: data," *Reuters*, August 28, 2018, https://www.reuters.com/article/us-iran-crude/iran-oil-exports-set-to-drop-in-august-ahead-of-u-s-sanctions-data-idUSKCN1LD12M.

62 Josh Rogin, "China is reaping the rewards of undermining Trump's Iran strategy," *The Washington Post*, November 5, 2018, https://www.washingtonpost.com/news/josh-rogin/wp/2018/11/05/china-is-reaping-the-rewards-of-undermining-trumps-iran-strategy/?noredirect=on&utm_term=.c2e44eb8e843.

63 Chen Aizhu and Shu Zhang, "Exclusive: As U.S. sanctions loom, China's Bank of Kunlun to stop receiving Iran payments-sources," *Reuters*, October 23, 2018, https://www.reuters.com/article/us-china-iran-banking-kunlun-exclusive/exclusive-as-u-s-sanctions-loom-chinas-bank-of-kunlun-to-stop-receiving-iran-payments-sources-idUSKCN1MX1KA.

64 Chen Aizhu, "Exclusive: Sinopec, CNPC to skip Iran oil bookings for November as U.S. sanctions near," *Reuters*, October 24, 2018, https://www.reuters.com/article/us-china-iran-oil-exclusive/exclusive-sinopec-cnpc-to-skip-iran-oil-bookings-for-november-as-us-sanctions-near-idUSKCN1MY1C9.

65 Chen Aizhu and Florence Tan, "China's Iran oil imports to rebound in December as buyers use U.S. waivers," *Reuters*, December 7, 2018, https://af.reuters.com/article/commoditiesNews/idAFL4N1YA32E.

66 Jacopo Scita, "China-Iran: a Complex, Seesaw Relationship," *Italian Institute for International Political Studies (ISPI)*, February 8, 2019, https://www.ispionline.it/sites/default/files/pubblicazioni/commentary_s_cita_08.02.2018.pdf.

67 Chen Aizhu and Shu Zhang, "Exclusive: As U.S. sanctions loom, China's Bank of Kunlun to stop receiving Iran payments-sources," *Reuters*, October 23, 2018, https://www.reuters.com/article/us-china-iran-banking-kunlun-exclusive/exclusive-as-u-s-sanctions-loom-chinas-bank-of-kunlun-to-stop-receiving-iran-payments-sources-idUSKCN1MX1KA.

68 "Policy Change at China's Bank of Kunlun Cuts Iran Sanctions Lifeline," *Bourse & Bazaar*, January 2, 2019, https://www.bourseandbazaar.com/articles/2019/1/2/policy-change-at-chinas-bank-of-kunlun-cuts-sanctions-lifeline-for-iranian-industry.

69 Edward Wong, "U.S. Punishes Chinese Company Over Iranian Oil," *The New York Times*, July 22, 2019, https://www.nytimes.com/2019/07/22/world/asia/sanctions-china-iran-oil.html.

70   Sharon Cho and Alfred Cang, "China's Still Taking Iran Oil Weeks After U.S. Toughens Sanction," *Bloomberg*, July 26, 2019, https://www.bloomberg.com/news/articles/2019-07-26/china-s-still-taking-iran-oil-weeks-after-u-s-toughens-sanction.

71   Jacopo Scita, "China-Iran: A Complex, Seesaw Relationship," *Italian Institute for International Political Studies (ISPI)*, February 8, 2019, https://www.ispionline.it/sites/default/files/pubblicazioni/commentary_scita_08.02.2018.pdf.

72   "Vision and Actions on Jointly Building Silk Road Economic Belt and 21st-Century Maritime Silk Road," *National Development and Reform Commission, Ministry of Foreign Affairs, and Ministry of Commerce of the People's Republic of China*, March 28, 2015, http://en.ndrc.gov.cn/newsrelease/201503/t20150330_669367.html.

73   "China says Iran joins AIIB as founder member," *Reuters*, April 8, 2015, https://www.reuters.com/article/us-asia-aiib-iran/china-says-iran-joins-aiib-as-founder-member-idUSKBN0MZ08720150408.

74   "Iran AIIB Membership Unlocks Investment Potentials," *Financial Tribune*, February 12, 2017, https://financialtribune.com/articles/economy-business-and-markets/59465/iran-aiib-membership-unlocks-investment-potentials.

75   "China-led bloc keeps Iran at arm's length despite Russian backing," *Reuters*, June 23, 2016, https://www.reuters.com/article/us-uzbekistan-sco-idUSKCN0Z9213.

76   "China gives billions to Iran," *News24*, September 16, 2017, https://www.news24.com/World/News/china-gives-billions-to-iran-20170916.

77   "Iran accepts renminbi for crude oil," *Financial Times*, May 7, 2012, https://www.ft.com/content/63132838-732d-11e1-9014-00144feab49a.

78   "Tehran dumps the dollar for the yuan as reference currency," *Asia News*, August 23, 2018, http://www.asianews.it/news-en/Tehran-dumps-the-dollar-for-the-yuan-as-reference-currency-44731.html.

79   Anna Ahronheim,"Iran to Increase Naval Ties with China," *The Jerusalem Post*, April 23, 2019, https://www.jpost.com/Israel-News/Iran-to-increase-naval-ties-with-China-587680.

80   Joel Wuthnow, "China-Iran Military Relations at a Crossroads," *China Brief*, 15 (3), https://jamestown.org/program/china-iran-military-relations-at-a-crossroads/#.ViD-Kn6rTV0

81   "UN Register of Conventional Arms," *United Nations Office for Disarmament Affairs* www.un.org/disarmament/convarms/Register/.

82   Lindsay Hughes," China in the Middle East: The Iran Factor," *Future Directions International*, October 25, 2018,

http://www.futuredirections.org.au/publication/china-in-the-middle-east-the-iran-factor/.

83 Farzin Nadimi, "Iran and China Are Strengthening Their Military Ties," *The Washington Institute*, November 22, 2016, https://www.washingtoninstitute.org/policy-analysis/view/iran-and-china-are-strengthening-their-military-ties.

84 Dennis M. Gormley, Andrew S. Erickson, and Jingdong Yuan, *A Low-Visibility Force Multiplier: Assessing China's Cruise Missile Ambitions*. Washington, DC: NDU Press, 2014.

85 Farzin Nadimi, "Iran and China Are Strengthening Their Military Ties," *The Washington Institute*, November 22, 2016, https://www.washingtoninstitute.org/policy-analysis/view/iran-and-china-are-strengthening-their-military-ties.

86 Thomas Erdbrink and Chris Buckley, "China and Iran to Conduct Joint Naval Exercises in the Persian Gulf," *The New York Times*, September 21, 2014, https://www.nytimes.com/2014/09/22/world/middleeast/china-and-iran-to-conduct-joint-naval-exercises-in-the-persian-gulf.html.

87 "Iran and China conduct naval drill in Gulf," *Reuters*, June 18, 2017, https://www.reuters.com/article/us-iran-china-military-drill/iran-and-china-conduct-naval-drill-in-gulf-idUSKBN1990EF.

88 Anna Ahronheim,"Iran to Increase Naval Ties with China," *The Jerusalem Post*, April 23, 2019, https://www.jpost.com/Israel-News/Iran-to-increase-naval-ties-with-China-587680

89 "Navy Commander Eyes Closer Iran–China Military Cooperation," *Tasnim News Agency*, April, 21, 2019, https://www.tasnimnews.com/en/news/2019/04/21/1994044/navy-commander-eyes-closer-iran-china-military-cooperation.

90 Debalina Ghoshal, "China's Nuclear Opportunities in Iran," *The Globalist*, May 30, 2016, https://www.theglobalist.com/china-nuclear-opportunities-in-iran/.

91 Scott Harold and Alireza Nader, *China and Iran Economic, Political, and Military Relations*. Santa Monica, CA; Arlington, VA; Pittsburgh, PA: RAND Corporation, 2012, https://www.rand.org/content/dam/rand/pubs/occasional_papers/2012/RAND_OP351.pdf.

92 "China, Iran sign first contract for Arak redesign," *World Nuclear News*, 24 April 2017, http://www.world-nuclear-news.org/Articles/China,-Iran-sign-first-contract-for-Arak-redesign

93 Lee Jeong-ho, "China scales back Iran nuclear cooperation 'due to fears of US sanctions'," *South China Morning Post*, January 31, 2019, https://www.scmp.com/news/china/diplomacy/article/2184512/china-scales-back-iran-nuclear-cooperation-due-fears-us.

94 "Vision and Actions on Jointly Building Silk Road Economic Belt and 21st-Century Maritime Silk Road," *National Development and Reform Commission, Ministry of Foreign Affairs, and Ministry of Commerce of the People's Republic of China*, March 28, 2015, http://en.ndrc.gov.cn/newsrelease/201503/t20150330_669367.html.

95 Huang Zhiling, "10 new Confucius Institutes lift global total to 548, boosting ties," *China Daily*, December 5, 2018, http://www.chinadaily.com.cn/a/201812/05/WS5c07239da 310eff30328f182.html.

96 Mohsen Shariatinia and Hamidreza Azizi, "Iran-China Cooperation in the Silk Road Economic Belt: From Strategic Understanding to Operational Understanding," *China & World Economy*, 25, (5), 2017, 46–61.

97 Behzad Abdollahpour, "Iran a unique destination for Chinese tourists," *China Daily*, November 22, 2018, http://www.chinadaily.com.cn/a/201811/22/WS5bf62932a310eff 30328a698.html.

98 "Iran seeks to attract more Chinese tourists in the future," *China Outbound Tourism Research Institute (COTRI)*, February 15, 2016, https://china-outbound.com/2016/02/15/iran-seeks-to-attract-more-chinese-tourists-in-the-future/.

99 Hu Yuwei and Qu Xiangyu "Chinese enterprises trying to survive in Iran despite policy shifts, US bluffs," *Global Time*, January 10, 2019, http://www.globaltimes.cn/content/1135325.shtml.

100 "Iran Vying to Be Among China's Top 20 Destinations," *Financial Tribune*, January 23, 2018, https://financialtribune.com/articles/travel/80618/iran-vying-to-be-among-chinas-top-20-destinations.

3

Iran

1 "China, UAE agree to lift ties to comprehensive strategic partnership," *Xinhua*, July 21, 2018, http://www.xinhuanet.com/english/2018-07/21/c_137338423.htm.

2 Stanley Carvalho, "Xi's visit to UAE highlights China's rising interest in Middle East," *Reuters*, July 20, 2018, https://ca.reuters.com/article/topNews/idCAKBN1KA26K-OCATP.

3 "UAE vision," *United Arab Emirates: Ministry of Cabinet Affairs*, 2019, https://uaecabinet.ae/en/uae-vision.

4 Min Ye, "China and competing cooperation in Asia–Pacific: TPP, RCEP, and the New Silk Road," *Asian Security*, 11 (3), 2015, 206–224.

5 "China, UAE agree to lift ties to comprehensive strategic partnership," *Xinhua*, July 21, 2018, http://www.xinhuanet.com/english/2018-07/21/c_137338423.htm.

6   "Vision and Actions on Jointly Building Silk Road Economic Belt and 21st-Century Maritime Silk Road," *National Development and Reform Commission, Ministry of Foreign Affairs, and Ministry of Commerce of the People's Republic of China*, March 28, 2015, http://en.ndrc.gov.cn/newsrelease/201503/t20150330_669367.html.

7   Wei Min, "The Interests and Trends of Chinese Enterprises' Investment in the United Arab Emirates," *International Center for Risk Assessment*, May 4, 2016, http://icra.ae/article/the-interests-and-trends-of-chinese-enterprises-investment-in-the-study-by-ms-wei-min/.

8   Samir Salama, "UAE and China poised to take ties to next level, envoy says," *Gulf News*, July 13, 2018, https://gulfnews.com/uae/government/uae-and-china-poised-to-take-ties-to-next-level-envoy-says-1.2250794.

9   "China, UAE agree to lift ties to comprehensive strategic partnership," *Xinhua*, July 20, 2018, http://www.xinhuanet.com/english/2018-07/21/c_137338423.htm.

10 Sam Bridge, "UAE, China eye closer ties to drive $70bn trade in 2020," *Arabian Business*, April 27, 2019, https://www.arabianbusiness.com/politics-economics/418601-uae-china-eyes-deeper-ties-to-drive-70bn-trade-in-2020.

11 "Vision and Actions on Jointly Building Silk Road Economic Belt and 21st-Century Maritime Silk Road," *National Development and Reform Commission, Ministry of Foreign Affairs, and Ministry of Commerce of the People's Republic of China*, March 28, 2015, http://en.ndrc.gov.cn/newsrelease/201503/t20150330_669367.html.

12 Sarah Zheng, "China's President Xi Jinping wraps up UAE visit with series of deals to boost presence in Middle East," *South China Morning Post*, July 21, 2018, https://www.scmp.com/news/china/diplomacy-defence/article/2156291/chinas-president-xi-jinping-wraps-uea-visit-series.

13 Mordechai Chaziza, "The Significant Role of Oman in China's Maritime Silk Road Initiative," *Contemporary Review of the Middle East*, 6 (1), 2018, 1–14.

14 Jonathan Fulton, *China's Relations with the Gulf Monarchies*. New York: Routledge, 2019.

15 Fareed Rahman, "UAE set to play a big role in China's Silk Road project," *Gulf News*, July 21, 2018, https://gulfnews.com/business/markets/uae-set-to-play-a-big-role-in-chinas-silk-road-project-1.2254909.

16 "DP World, Zhejiang China Group sign deal for a new traders market," *Gulf News*, July 19, 2018, https://gulfnews.com/business/dp-world-zhejiang-china-group-sign-deal-for-a-new-traders-market-1.2254073.

17 Aarti Nagraj, "Dubai's DP World, Chinese group to open new Traders Market at JAFZA," *Gulf Business*, July 19, 2018, https://gulfbusiness.com/dubais-dp-world-chinese-group-open-new-traders-market-jafza/.

18 "China to set up financial firm in UAE's Abu Dhabi," *Xinhua*, July 20, 2018, http://www.xinhuanet.com/english/2018-07/21/c_137338432.htm.

19 "UAE's biggest industry zone signs agreement with China to boost trade," *Xinhua*, September 19, 2017, http://www.xinhuanet.com/english/2017-09/19/c_136621829.htm.

20 "Chinese firms plan $1bn investment in Abu Dhabi free zone," *Arabian Business*, April 20, 2018, https://www.arabianbusiness.com/banking-finance/394657-wkd-chinese-firms-plan-1bn-investment-in-abu-dhabi-free-zone.

21 "UAE free zone inks deal to promote trade ties with China," *Xinhua*, July 11, 2018, http://www.xinhuanet.com/english/2018-07/11/c_137317118.htm.

22 "UAE's Emirates SkyCargo, China's Alibaba join hands over cross-border logistics," *Xinhua*, June 13, 2018, http://www.xinhuanet.com/english/2018-06/14/c_137251849.htm.

23 Jonathan Fulton, *China's Relations with the Gulf Monarchies*. New York: Routledge, 2019.

24 Michael Fahy, "UAE on China's Silk Road map," *The National*, March 13, 2017, https://www.thenational.ae/business/uae-on-china-s-silk-road-map-1.638069.

25 Stanley Carvalho, "Chinese firms to invest $300 million in Abu Dhabi," *Reuters*, July 31, 2017, https://www.reuters.com/article/us-emirates-china-investment-idUSKBN1AG0UH?il=0.

26 Dania Saadi, "Khalifa Port to double container volumes in 2019, official says," *The National*, December 10, 2018, https://www.thenational.ae/business/economy/khalifa-port-to-double-container-volumes-in-2019-official-says-1.801010.

27 "China, UAE agree to lift ties to comprehensive strategic partnership," *Xinhua*, July 20, 2018, http://www.xinhuanet.com/english/2018-07/21/c_137338423.htm.

28 "Vision and Actions on Jointly Building Silk Road Economic Belt and 21st-Century Maritime Silk Road," *National Development and Reform Commission, Ministry of Foreign Affairs, and Ministry of Commerce of the People's Republic of China*, March 28, 2015, http://en.ndrc.gov.cn/newsrelease/201503/t20150330_669367.html.

29 Sultan bin Ahmed Sultan Al Jaber, "UAE–China ties a strategic priority for both," *China Daily*, July 12, 2018,

http://usa.chinadaily.com.cn/a/201807/12/WS5b4694b4a310796df4df 5ea3.html.

30   "China Customs Statistics: Imports and exports by country/region," *The Hong Kong Trade Development Council (HKTDC)*, May 27, 2019, http://china-trade-research.hktdc.com/business-news/article/Facts-and-Figures/China-Customs-Statistics/ff/en/1/1X39VTVQ/1X09N9NM.ht m.

31   Sam Bridge, "UAE–China trade forecast to hit $70bn by 2020 as ties grow," *Arabian Business*, 19 July, 2018, https://www.arabianbusiness.com/politics-economics/401134-china-uae-forecast-to-hit-70bn-by-2020-as-ties-grow.

32   "Mohammad Bin Rashid announces $3.4 billion UAE–China investment deals," *Gulf News*, April 26, 2019, https://gulfnews.com/uae/mohammad-bin-rashid-announces-34-billion-uae-china-investment-deals-1.1556286724883.

33   "Strategic shift in relations between the UAE, China, US$50 billion trade between two countries: UAE Ambassador to Beijing," *United Arab Emirates, Ministry of Foreign Affairs & International Cooperation*, July 15, 2018, https://www.mofa.gov.ae/EN/MediaCenter/News/Pages/15-07-2018-UAE-China.aspx#sthash.6H1L36Ly.dpuf.

34   Jonathan Fulton, *China's Relations with the Gulf Monarchies*. New York: Routledge, 2019.

35   Mohammad Al Asoomi, "The UAE can assume a strategic role in China's ambitions," *Gulf News*, July 11, 2018, https://gulfnews.com/business/analysis/the-uae-can-assume-a-strategic-role-in-chinas-ambitions-1.2249814.

36   Khaled bin Dhai, "UAE and China, how comprehensive strategic relations are built," *China Daily*, July 20, 2018, http://www.chinadaily.com.cn/a/201807/20/WS5b51a9f0a310796df 4df7be5.html.

37   Zhi Linfei, Tang Peipei, Su Xiaopo, "Xinhua Headlines: Xi's UAE visit showcases achievements, promises more Sino–Arab cooperation," *Xinhua*, July 21, 2018, http://www.xinhuanet.com/english/2018-07/21/c_137339974.htm.

38   Khaled bin Dhai, "UAE and China, how comprehensive strategic relations are built," *China Daily*, July 20, 2018, http://www.chinadaily.com.cn/a/201807/20/WS5b51a9f0a310796df 4df7be5.html.

39   Sam Bridge, "UAE–China trade forecast to hit $70bn by 2020 as ties grow," *Arabian Business*, 19 July, 2018, https://www.arabianbusiness.com/politics-economics/401134-china-uae-forecast-to-hit-70bn-by-2020-as-ties-grow.

40   Muhammad Zulfikar Rakhmat, "The UAE and China's Thriving Partnership," *Gulf State Analytics*, June 2015,

https://gallery.mailchimp.com/02451f1ec2ddbb874bf5daee0/files/
June_GSA_report.pdf.

41   Simeon Kerr and Lucy Hornby, "Chinese group eyes $10bn industrial investment in UAE," *Financial Times*, May 24, 2019, https://www.ft.com/content/1c93d350-7e2c-11e9-81d2-f785092ab560.

42   Khaled bin Dhai, "UAE and China, how comprehensive strategic relations are built," *China Daily*, July 20, 2018, http://www.chinadaily.com.cn/a/201807/20/WS5b51a9f0a310796df 4df7be5.html.

43   Muhammad Zulfikar Rakhmat, "The UAE and China's Thriving Partnership," *Gulf State Analytics*, June 2015, https://gallery.mailchimp.com/02451f1ec2ddbb874bf5daee0/ files/June_GSA_report.pdf.

44   "UAE–China sign major deal to boost Dubai's role as regional food hub," *Arabian Business*, September 10, 2017, https://www.arabianbusiness.com/uaepolitics-economics/378202-dubai-food-park-signs-367m-deal-to-create-china-uae-food-industrial-cluster.

45   "UAE to play big role in China's BRI: official," *Xinhua*, April 10, 2019, http://www.xinhuanet.com/english/2019-04/10/c_137966125.htm.

46   "Vision and Actions on Jointly Building Silk Road Economic Belt and 21st-Century Maritime Silk Road," *National Development and Reform Commission, Ministry of Foreign Affairs, and Ministry of Commerce of the People's Republic of China*, March 28, 2015, http://en.ndrc.gov.cn/newsrelease/201503/t20150330_669367.html.

47   "UAE becomes founding member of AIIB," *Gulf News*, June 29, 2015, https://gulfnews.com/business/banking/uae-becomes-founding-member-of-aiib-1.1542695.

48   "Spotlight: Fruitful China-UAE financial cooperation opens up possibilities for Gulf region," *Xinhua*, July 19, 2018, http://www.xinhuanet.com/english/2018-07/19/c_137336032.htm.

49   Muhammad Zulfikar Rakhmat, "The UAE and China's Thriving Partnership," *Gulf State Analytics*, June 2015, https://gallery.mailchimp.com/02451f1ec2ddbb874bf5daee0/files/ June_GSA_report.pdf.

50   "UAE, China to set up $10bn joint strategic investment fund," *Arabian Business*, December 14, 2015, https://www.arabianbusiness.com/uae-china-set-up-10bn-joint-strategic-investment-fund-615348.html?utm_source=Jarvis&utm_medi um=arabianbusiness.com&utm_campaign=recommended

51   Xi Jinping, "China and the UAE are both proud to have enterprising and creative people who never give up on their dreams," *The National*, July 17, 2018, https://www.thenational.ae/opinion/comment/china-and-the-uae-are-both-proud-to-have-enterprising-and-creative-people-who-never-give-up-on-their-dreams-1.751254.

52 John Calabrese, "China and the Persian Gulf: Energy and Security," *Middle East Journal*, 52 (3), 1998, 351–366; Steve Yetiv and Chunlong Lu, "China, Global Energy, and the Middle East", *Middle East Journal*, 61, (2), 2007, 199–218.

53 Daniel Workman, "Top 15 Crude Oil Suppliers to China," *World's Top Exports*, April 12, 2019, http://www.worldstopexports.com/top-15-crude-oil-suppliers-to-china/.

54 "United Arab Emirates," *U.S. Energy Information Administration (EIA)*, March 21, 2017, https://www.eia.gov/beta/international/analysis.php?iso=ARE.

55 B. Rajesh Kumar, "The UAE's Strategic Trade Partnership with Asia: A Focus on Dubai," *Middle East* Institute, August 19, 2013, https://www.mei.edu/publications/uaes-strategic-trade-partnership-asia-focus-dubai.

56 Andrew Scobell and Alireza Nader, *China in the Middle East: The Wary Dragon*. Santa Monica: RAND Corporation, 2016.

57 Lin, H. "'Yidai yilu' zou ru mitu" ("'One Belt, One Road' going astray"). http://forum.hkej.com/print/130698, Accessed on 27 March 2017.

58 Yiping Huang, "Understanding China's Belt & Road Initiative: Motivation, framework and assessment," *China Economic Review*, 40, 2016, 314–321.

59 Xu He, "China, UAE ties span a wide range," *China Daily*, July 19, 2018, http://www.chinadaily.com.cn/a/201807/19/WS5b4dcbc6a310796df4df6fd4.html.

60 Deena Kamel and Jennifer Gnana, "Adnoc and CNPC agree to explore partnership opportunities as emirate plans downstream expansion," *The National*, July 20, 2018, https://www.thenational.ae/business/energy/adnoc-and-cnpc-agree-to-explore-partnership-opportunities-as-emirate-plans-downstream-expansion-1.752415.

61 "China, UAE oil firms sign $330m worth oilfield development project," *China Daily*, May 18, 2015, http://europe.chinadaily.com.cn/business/2015-05/18/content_20745576.htm.

62 Mohammad Al Asoomi, "The UAE can assume a strategic role in China's ambitions," *Gulf News*, July 11, 2018, https://gulfnews.com/business/analysis/the-uae-can-assume-a-strategic-role-in-chinas-ambitions-1.2249814.

63 "Saudi ARAMCO and ADNOC sign MoU for participating in the Ratnagiri Refinery project in Maharashtra," *Press Information Bureau Government of India Ministry of Petroleum & Natural Gas*, June, 25, 2018, http://pib.nic.in/newsite/PrintRelease.aspx?relid=180158.

64 "Global Trends in Renewable Energy Investment 2018," *Frankfurt School of Finance & Management gGmbH*, 2018,

http://www.iberglobal.com/files/2018/renewable_trends.pdf.

65 Thani bin Ahmed Al Zeyoudi, "UAE and China: Towards a brighter and more sustainable future," *Arabian Business*, July 19, 2018, https://www.arabianbusiness.com/politics-economics/401068-uae-china-towards-brighter-more-sustainable-future.

66 "China's Silk Road Fund is investing in Dubai solar project, Acwa says," *The National*, June 16, 2018, https://www.thenational.ae/business/energy/china-s-silk-road-fund-is-investing-in-dubai-solar-project-acwa-says-1.740613.

67 "Feature: Hassyan Clean Coal project symbol of UAE–China green partnership," *Xinhua*, July 9, 2018, http://www.xinhuanet.com/english/2018-07/10/c_137313050.htm.

68 "Full text: UAE–China joint statement on strategic partnership," *Gulf News*, July 21, 2018, https://gulfnews.com/uae/government/full-text-uae-china-joint-statement-on-strategic-partnership-1.2254614.

69 "Abu Dhabi crown prince says committed to advancing UAE-China relations," *Xinhua*, March 22, http://www.xinhuanet.com/english/2019-03/22/c_137915785.htm.

70 "China's CSIC expands presence in UAE," *Jane's Defence Weekly*, February 21, 2019, https://www.janes.com/article/86729/china-s-csic-expands-presence-in-uae.

71 Teddy Ng and Liu Zhen, "China eyes bigger role in growing Middle East arms trade," *South China Morning Post*, February 24, 2019, https://www.scmp.com/news/china/military/article/2187436/china-eyes-bigger-role-growing-middle-east-arms-trade.

72 Natasha Turak, "Pentagon is scrambling as China 'sells the hell out of' armed drones to US allies," *CNBC*, February 21, 2019, https://www.cnbc.com/2019/02/21/pentagon-is-scrambling-as-china-sells-the-hell-out-of-armed-drones-to-americas-allies.html.

73 "Vision and Actions on Jointly Building Silk Road Economic Belt and 21st-Century Maritime Silk Road," *National Development and Reform Commission, Ministry of Foreign Affairs, and Ministry of Commerce of the People's Republic of China*, March 28, 2015, http://en.ndrc.gov.cn/newsrelease/201503/t20150330_669367.html.

74 Muhammad Zulfikar Rakhmat, "China and the UAE: New Cultural Horizons," *Middle East Institute*, March 19, 2015, https://www.mei.edu/publications/china-and-uae-new-cultural-horizons#_ftn5.

75 "UAEU a founding member of the Asian Universities Alliance (AUA) at the official launch in Beijing," *United Arab Emirates University*, May 8, 2017, https://www.uaeu.ac.ae/en/news/2017/may/aua.shtml

76 "Agreements strengthen China-UAE ties," *The National*, December 14, 2015,

https://www.thenational.ae/uae/agreements-strengthen-china-uae-ties-1.99839.

77 "China & UAE: Gulf Medical University & Sun Yat-Sen University Ink Alliance," *TrialSite News*, May 14, 2019, https://www.trialsitenews.com/china-uae-gulf-medical-university-sun-yat-sen-university-ink-alliance/.

78 Huang Zhiling, "10 new Confucius Institutes lift global total to 548, boosting ties," *China Daily*, December 5, 2018, http://global.chinadaily.com.cn/a/201812/05/WS5c07239da310eff30328f182.html.

79 "Confucius Institute/Classroom," Hanban, 2018, http://english.hanban.org/node_10971.htm.

80 Muhammad Zulfikar Rakhmat, "China and the UAE: New Cultural Horizons," *Middle East Institute*, March 19, 2015, https://www.mei.edu/publications/china-and-uae-new-cultural-horizons#_ftn5.

81 Daniel Bardsley, "China Honours Sheikh Zayed," *The National*, March 29, 2012, http://www.thenational.ae/news/uae-news/education/china-honours-sheikh-zayed.

82 Abdul Hannan Tago, "Over 40 Universities in China Teach Arabic," *Arab News*, February 23, 2014, http://www.arabnews.com/news/529946; Daniel Bardsley, "Arabic Studies Centre to Reopen in Beijing," *The National*, December 26, 2010, http://www.thenational.ae/news/world/south-asia/arabic-studies-centre-to-reopen-in-beijing.

83 Binsal Abdul Kader, "Over 1m Chinese tourists to visit UAE this year," *Gulf News*, September 18, 2018, https://gulfnews.com/world/asia/over-1m-chinese-tourists-to-visit-uae-this-year-1.2279920.

84 "Press Release: Chinese Delegation Visits Al Mushrif School," *Middle East business intelligence (MEED)*, March 8, 2012, http://www.meed.com/chinese-delegation-visits-al-mushrif-school/3128934.article.

85 "Chinese, UAE Universities Ink Deal to Boost Cooperation, Exchanges," *Global Times*, November 19, 2009, http://www.globaltimes.cn/content/486432.shtml.

86 Shreeja Ravindranathan, "7 places to celebrate Chinese New Year in the UAE," *Friday Magazine*, February 14, 2018, https://fridaymagazine.ae/life-culture/to-do/7-places-to-celebrate-chinese-new-year-in-the-uae-1.2173525.

87 Sami Zaatari, "UAE–China Week kicks off in Abu Dhabi," *Gulf News*, July 17, 2018,

https://gulfnews.com/entertainment/arts-culture/uae-china-week-kicks-off-in-abu-dhabi-1.2253125.

88 "UAE–China Week to be held annually," *The National*, July 28, 2018, https://www.thenational.ae/uae/government/uae-china-week-to-be-held-annually-1.754727.

89 Xi Jinping, "China and the UAE are both proud to have enterprising and creative people who never give up on their dreams," *The National*, July 17, 2018, https://www.thenational.ae/opinion/comment/china-and-the-uae-are-both-proud-to-have-enterprising-and-creative-people-who-never-give-up-on-their-dreams-1.751254.

90 Sam, Bridge, "Gulf forecast to see 81% rise in Chinese tourists by 2022," *Arabian Business*, December 19, 2018, https://www.arabianbusiness.com/travel-hospitality/409972-gulf-forecast-to-see-81-rise-in-chinese-tourists-by-2022.

91 "Chinese tourists make nearly 150 mln outbound trips in 2018," *Xinhua*, February 13, 2019, http://www.xinhuanet.com/english/2019-02/13/c_137818975.htm..

92 Xi Jinping, "China and the UAE are both proud to have enterprising and creative people who never give up on their dreams," *The National*, July 17, 2018, https://www.thenational.ae/opinion/comment/china-and-the-uae-are-both-proud-to-have-enterprising-and-creative-people-who-never-give-up-on-their-dreams-1.751254.

93 "Chinese tourists to Dubai up 12% in 2018: Report," *China Daily*, February 25, 2019, http://www.chinadaily.com.cn/a/201902/25/WS5c7359a4a3106c65c34eb38b.html.

4

Iraq

1 Li Xiaokun, "China and Iraq agree to build strategic partnership," *China Daily*, December 23, 2015, https://thediplomat.com/2015/12/china-and-iraq-announce-strategic-partnership/.

2 "China's Belt and Road Initiative: An Opportunity for Iraq," *Al-Bayan Centre for Planning and Studies Series of Publications*, 2018, http://www.bayancenter.org/en/wp-content/uploads/2018/04/867563522.pdf.

3 "Vision and Actions on Jointly Building Silk Road Economic Belt and 21st-Century Maritime Silk Road," *National Development and Reform Commission, Ministry of Foreign Affairs, and Ministry of Commerce of the People's Republic of China*, March 28, 2015, http://en.ndrc.gov.cn/newsrelease/201503/t20150330_669367.html.

4 "China, Iraq establish strategic partnership," *Xinhua*, December 22, 2015,
http://www.china.org.cn/world/2015-12/22/content_37376947.htm.

5 "Iraq and China sign five agreements and memoranda of understanding on economic, technological, military, diplomatic, and oil and energy cooperation," *Prime Minister's Media Office*, December 22, 2015, http://www.pmo.iq/pme/press2015en/22-12-20154en.htm.

6 "China, Iraq to deepen strategic partnership," *CGTN*, August 25, 2018, https://news.cgtn.com/news/3d3d774d7a4d7a4e79457a6333566d54/share_p.html.

7 "Spotlight: Iraq, China celebrate Silk Road initiative on 60th anniversary of bilateral ties," *Xinhua*, December 13, 2018, http://www.xinhuanet.com/english/2018-12/14/c_137672426.htm.

8 "China to contribute to the rebuilding of Iraq," *Kurdistan 24*, April 16, 2019, http://www.kurdistan24.net/en/news/2375d17c-7405-4f66-821b-e88d5fbd549e.

9 "Chinese ambassador presents credentials to Iraqi president," *Xinhua*, April 9, 2019, http://www.xinhuanet.com/english/2019-04/09/c_137960936.htm.

10 "China-Iraq trade exceeds 30 bln USD in 2018 amid increasing cooperation: Chinese ambassador," *Xinhua*, May 6, 2019, http://www.xinhuanet.com/english/2019-05/06/c_138036250.htm.

11 Tim Daiss, "China's Growing Oil Demand Has Created A Geopolitical Dilemma,"*Oil Price*, May 2, 2018, https://oilprice.com/Energy/Crude-Oil/Chinas-Growing-Oil-Demand-Has-Created-A-Geopolitical-Dilemma.html.

12 John Calabrese, "China and the Persian Gulf: Energy and Security," *Middle East Journal* 52 (3), (1998), pp. 351–366; Steve Yetiv and Chunlong Lu, "China, Global Energy, and the Middle East", *Middle East Journal* 61, (2) (2007), pp. 199–218.

13 Daniel Workman, "Top 15 Crude Oil Suppliers to China," *World's Top Exports*, April 12, 2019, http://www.worldstopexports.com/top-15-crude-oil-suppliers-to-china/.

14 "Country Analysis Executive Summary: Iraq," *U.S. Energy Information Administration (EIA)*, January 7, 2019, https://www.eia.gov/beta/international/analysis_includes/countries_long/Iraq/iraq_exe.pdf.

15 en Lando, "Iraq oil exports steady in June though federal revenues fall," Iraq Oil Report, July 2, 2018, https://www.iraqoilreport.com/news/iraqi-oil-exports-steady-in-june-though-federal-revenues-fall-31164/

16 Richard Wachman, "China pushes for bigger role in Iraqi reconstruction," *Arab News*, March 3, 2018, http://www.arabnews.com/node/1257811/business-economy.

17 "China, Iraq ink economic, military agreements during Abadi visit," *The Brics Post*, December 23, 2015, https://www.thebricspost.com/china-iraq-ink-economic-military-agreements-during-abadi-visit/.

18 Wang Jin, "Opinion: China-Iraq Ties in the New Era," *CGTN*, August 26, 2018, https://news.cgtn.com/news/3d3d414e31557a4e79457a6333566d54/share_p.html.

19 Wei Li, "An Analysis of Current Political Situation and Oil and Gas Investment Prospect in Iraq" [in Chinese] *Sino-Global Energy*, no. 3 (March 2016): 10; Eberling, G. George, *China's Bilateral Relations With Its Principal Oil Suppliers*. Lanham: Lexington, 2017

20 "Iraq Signs Deal with China's Zhenhua Oil as Exxon Mobil Agreement Stalls," *Asharq Al-Awsat*, 26 December, 2017, https://aawsat.com/english/home/article/1124441/iraq-signs-deal-china%E2%80%99s-zhenhua-oil-exxon-mobil-agreement-stalls.

21 "China's CNPC interested in Iraq's Majnoon oilfield -oil officials," *Reuters*, December 27, 2017, https://www.reuters.com/article/us-iraq-oil-majnoon/chinas-cnpc-inter-ested-in-iraqs-majnoon-oilfield-oil-officials-idUSKBN1DR186.

22 Chen Aizhu and Rania El Gamal, "China's Zhenhua Oil to sign oil deals with Iraq, Saudi at Shanghai expo-sources," *Reuters*, November 3, 2018, https://uk.reuters.com/article/uk-china-iraq-zhenhua/chinas-zhenhua-oil-to-sign-oil-deals-with-iraq-saudi-at-shanghai-expo-sources-idUKKCN1N806Z.

23 "Iraq signs contract with PowerChina, Norinco to build Fao oil refinery," *Reuters*, April 29, 2018, https://www.reuters.com/article/iraq-oil-refining-china/iraq-signs-contract-with-powerchina-norinco-to-build-fao-oil-refinery-idUSL8N1S60M3.

24 "Iraq to build oil refinery in Fao with Chinese firms, plans three others," *Reuters*, January 29, 2018, https://www.reuters.com/article/us-iraq-oil-refining/iraq-to-build-oil-refinery-in-fao-with-chinese-firms-plans-three-others-idUSKBN1FI0I0.

25 Richard Wachman, "China pushes for bigger role in Iraqi reconstruction," *Arab News*, March 3, 2018, http://www.arabnews.com/node/1257811/business-economy.

26 Shunsuke Tabeta, "China looks to Iraq to secure oil supply," *Nikkei Asian Review*, June 15, 2018, https://asia.nikkei.com/Business/Companies/China-looks-to-Iraq-to-secure-oil-supply.

27 "Iraq to Boost China Oil Sales by 60% as OPEC Giant Eyes Asia," *Bloomberg News*, November 6, 2018, https://www.bloomberg.com/news/articles/2018-11-06/iraq-to-boost-china-oil-sales-by-60-as-opec-giant-eyes-asia.

28   "UPDATE 1-Iraq signs deal with China's CNOOC for seismic surveys of two oil blocks," *Reuters*, January 31, 2019, https://www.reuters.com/article/iraq-oil-exploration/update-1-iraq-signs-deal-with-chinas-cnooc-for-seismic-surveys-of-two-oil-blocks-id USL5N1ZV48N.

29   "Country Analysis Executive Summary: Iraq," *U.S. Energy Information Administration (EIA)*, January 7, 2019, https://www.eia.gov/beta/international/analysis_includes/countries_long/Iraq/iraq_exe.pdf.

30   "Chinese oil, gas contractor inks deal to construct gas plant in Iraq," *Xinhua*, February 27, 2019, http://www.xinhuanet.com/english/2019-02/27/c_137855433.htm.

31   Shatha Khalil, "Al-Hareer Road . . . An economic belt linking Iraq with China," *Rawabet Center for Research and Strategic Studies*, December 14, 2017, https://rawabetcenter.com/en/?p=4650.

32   "Interview: Iraq to reap from BRI through active participation: analyst," *Xinhua*, January 29, 2019, http://www.xinhuanet.com/english/2019-01/29/c_137782280.htm.

33   "China's Belt and Road Initiative: An Opportunity for Iraq," *Al-Bayan Centre for Planning and Studies Series of Publications*, 2018, http://www.bayancenter.org/en/wp-content/uploads/2018/04/867563522.pdf.

34   "Vision and Actions on Jointly Building Silk Road Economic Belt and 21st-Century Maritime Silk Road," *National Development and Reform Commission, Ministry of Foreign Affairs, and Ministry of Commerce of the People's Republic of China*, March 28, 2015, http://en.ndrc.gov.cn/newsrelease/201503/t20150330_669367.html.

35   "Iraq discusses possibility of joining Asian Infrastructure Investment Bank," *Xinhua*, March 4, 2019, http://www.xinhuanet.com/english/2019-03/04/c_137866422.htm.

36   Ben Van Heuvelen and Samya Kullab, "Iraq and China to sign massive financing deal," *Iraq Oil Report*, March 13, 2019, https://www.iraqoilreport.com/news/iraq-and-china-to-sign-massive-financing-deal-38041/.

37   "Vision and Actions on Jointly Building Silk Road Economic Belt and 21st-Century Maritime Silk Road," *National Development and Reform Commission, Ministry of Foreign Affairs, and Ministry of Commerce of the People's Republic of China*, March 28, 2015, http://en.ndrc.gov.cn/newsrelease/201503/t20150330_669367.html.

38   "China Customs Statistics: Imports and exports by country/region," *The Hong Kong Trade Development Council (HKTDC)*, May 27, 2019, http://china-trade-research.hktdc.com/business-news/article/Facts-and-Figures/China-Customs-Statistics/ff/en/1/1X39VTVQ/1X09N9NM.htm.

39   "China–Iraq trade exceeds 30 bln USD in 2018 amid increasing cooper-
     ation: Chinese ambassador," *Xinhua*, May 6, 2019,
     http://www.xinhuanet.com/english/2019-05/06/c_138036250.htm.

40   "China, Iraq to deepen strategic partnership," *CGTN*, August 25, 2018,
     https://news.cgtn.com/news/3d3d774d7a4d7a4e79457a6333566d54/sh
     are_p.html.

41   Maher Chmaytelli and Ahmed Hagagy, "Allies promise Iraq $30 billion,
     falling short of Baghdad's appeal," *Reuters*, February 14, 2018,
     https://www.reuters.com/article/us-mideast-crisis-iraq-reconstruction-
     ku/allies-promise-iraq-30-billion-falling-short-of-baghdads-appeal-idU
     SKCN1FY0TX.

42   "China to actively participate in reconstruction of Iraq: ambassador,"
     Xinhua, February 14, 2018,
     http://www.xinhuanet.com/english/2018-02/15/c_136976540.htm.

43   "China vows active role in Iraqi post-war reconstruction," *Xinhua*, April
     24, 2017,
     http://www.xinhuanet.com//english/2017-04/24/c_136232659.htm.

44   "Chinese company wins bidding for power station construction in Iraq,"
     Xinhua Silk Road Information Service, February 21, 2019,
     https://en.imsilkroad.com/p/131156.html.

45   "Iraqi governor calls for Chinese investment, expertise for reconstruc-
     tion," *Xinhua*, January 27, 2109,
     http://www.xinhuanet.com/english/2019-01/28/c_137779710.htm.

46   "Iraq + China MOU Establishes Long Term Oil & Gas Partnership," *Oil
     and Gas360*, December 23, 2015,
     https://www.oilandgas360.com/iraq-china-mou-establishes-long-term-
     oil-gas-partnership/.

47   "China, Iraq ink economic, military agreements during Abadi visit," *The
     Brics Post*, December 23, 2015,
     https://www.thebricspost.com/china-iraq-ink-economic-military-agree-
     ments-during-abadi-visit/.

48   Richard A. Bitzinge, "Arms to Go: Chinese Arms Sales to the Third
     World," *International Security*, Vol. 17, No. 2 (Fall, 1992), pp. 84–111.

49   Arnaud Delalande, "Iraq's Chinese-Made Killer Drones Are Actually
     Pretty Good," *War is Boring*, February 21, 2018,
     https://warisboring.com/iraqs-chinese-made-killer-drones-are-actually-
     pretty-good/.

50   Adam Rawnsley, "Meet China's Killer Drones, *Foreign Policy Magazine*,
     January 14, 2016,
     https://foreignpolicy.com/2016/01/14/meet-chinas-killer-drones/.

51   "Are China And Iraq Working On A Huge Arms Deal?," *21st Century
     Asian Arms Race*, January 1, 2017,
     https://21stcenturyasianarmsrace.com/2017/01/01/are-china-and-iraq-
     working-on-a-huge-arms-deal/.

5

Kuwait

1 Khizar Niazi, "Kuwait Looks towards the East: Relations with China," *The Middle East Institute Policy Brief*, no. 26, September 2009, https://www.files.ethz.ch/isn/106361/No_26_Kuwait_looks_towards_th e_east.pdf.

2 "China Focus: China, Kuwait agree to establish strategic partnership," *Xinhua*, July 9, 2018, http://www.xinhuanet.com/english/2018-07/10/c_137312795.htm.

3 Christopher Layne, "The US-Chinese power shift and the end of the Pax Americana," *International Affairs*, 94 (1), 2018, 89–111.

4 Imad K. Harb, "Self-preservation and Strategic Hedging in the Gulf Cooperation Council," *Policy brief*, no. 23, June 26, 2018, http://ams.hi.is/wp-content/uploads/2018/06/Self-Preservation-and-Strategic-Hedging-in-the-GCC-2.pdf.

5 Giorgio Cafiero and Daniel Wagner, "What the Gulf States Think of 'One Belt, One Road'," *The Diplomat*, May 245, 2017, https://thediplomat.com/2017/05/what-the-gulf-states-think-of-one-belt-one-road/.

6 Sumedh Lokhande, "China's One Belt One Road Initiative and the Gulf Pearl Chain", *China Daily*, June 5, 2017, http://www.chinadaily.com.cn/opinion/2017beltandroad/2017-06/05/content_29618549.htm.

7 Robert Anderson, "China and the GCC: Rebuilding the Silk Road," *Gulf Business*, December 15, 2018, https://gulfbusiness.com/china-gcc-rebuilding-silk-road/.

8 "Kuwait National Development Plan," *New Kuwait*, January 30, 2017, http://www.newkuwait.gov.kw/image/NewKuwait_CampaignLaunch Event.pdf.

9 "Govt launches ambitious 'New Kuwait' 2035 strategy," *Kuwait Times*, January 31, 2017, https://news.kuwaittimes.net/website/govt-launches-ambitious-new-kuwait-2035-strategy/.

10 Jasim Ali, "Revival of mega projects heralds positives for Kuwait," *Gulf News*, July 14, 2018, https://gulfnews.com/business/analysis/revival-of-mega-projects-heralds-positives-for-kuwait-1.2251117.

11 Faten Omar, "Kuwait woos foreign investments, details progress on Vision 2035," *Kuwait Times*, March 20, 2018, https://news.kuwaittimes.net/website/kuwait-woos-foreign-investments-details-progress-on-vision-2035/.

12 "Changing times calls for new GCC relations with China, Russia," *Oxford Business Group*, 2019, https://oxfordbusinessgroup.com/analysis/east-meets-middle-east-changing-times-calls-new-relations-china-and-russia.

13 Min Ye, "China and competing cooperation in Asia–Pacific: TPP, RCEP, and the New Silk Road," *Asian Security*, 11 (3), 2015, 206–224.

14 "Vision and Actions on Jointly Building Silk Road Economic Belt and 21st-Century Maritime Silk Road," *National Development and Reform Commission, Ministry of Foreign Affairs, and Ministry of Commerce of the People's Republic of China*, March 28, 2015, http://en.ndrc.gov.cn/newsrelease/201503/t20150330_669367.html.

15 Samah Ibrahim, "Kuwait as a Gateway for Chinese Influence in the Arabian Gulf," *Future Directions International*, August 29, 2018, http://www.futuredirections.org.au/publication/kuwait-as-a-gateway-for-chinese-influence-in-the-arabian-gulf/

16 Weida Li, "China and Kuwait agree to establish strategic partnership," *GB Times*, July 10, 2018, https://gbtimes.com/china-and-kuwait-agree-to-establish-strategic-partnership

17 Mordechai Chaziza, "The Significant Role of Oman in China's Maritime Silk Road Initiative," *Contemporary Review of the Middle East*, 6 (1), 2018, 1–14.

18 Robert Anderson, "China and the GCC: Rebuilding the Silk Road," *Gulf Business*, December 15, 2018, https://gulfbusiness.com/china-gcc-rebuilding-silk-road/.

19 "Island projects to attract international investments," *Times Kuwait*, October 30, 2018, http://www.timeskuwait.com/Times_Island-projects-to-attract-international-investments.

20 Habib Toumi, "Kuwait, China sign 10 cooperation accords," *Gulf News*, June 4, 2014, https://gulfnews.com/world/gulf/kuwait/kuwait-china-sign-10-cooperation-accords-1.1342938.

21 "Kuwait, China sign MoU on finding mechanism for Silk City, 5 islands," *Kuwait News Agency (KUMA)*, November 18, 2018, https://www.kuna.net.kw/ArticleDetails.aspx?id=2760010&language=en.

22 Sam Bridge, "Kuwait, China ink deal to move forward with Silk City project," *Arabian Business*, November 24, 2018, https://www.arabianbusiness.com/politics-economics/408347-kuwait-china-ink-deal-to-move-forward-with-silk-city-project.

23 Naser Al Wasmi, "Kuwait and China push forward on Silk City development plan," *The National*, November 18, 2018, https://www.thenational.ae/world/gcc/kuwait-and-china-push-forward-on-silk-city-development-plan-1.793180.

24 "Kuwait, Huawei sign MoU to implement smart cities strategy," *Kuwait News Agency (KUMA)*, July 18, 2018, https://www.kuna.net.kw/ArticleDetails.aspx?id=2736348&language=en.

25   "Kuwait is spending its way to a new direction," *Financial Times*, September 10, 2018, https://www.ft.com/content/b8e6079e-4e32-11e8-ac41-759eee1efb74.

26   "Vision and Actions on Jointly Building Silk Road Economic Belt and 21st-Century Maritime Silk Road," *National Development and Reform Commission, Ministry of Foreign Affairs, and Ministry of Commerce of the People's Republic of China*, March 28, 2015, http://en.ndrc.gov.cn/newsrelease/201503/t20150330_669367.html.

27   "China Focus: China, Kuwait agree to establish strategic partnership," *Xinhua*, July 9, 2018, http://www.xinhuanet.com/english/2018-07/10/c_137312795.htm.

28   "China, Kuwait agree to establish strategic partnership," *Xinhua*, July 9, 2018, http://www.xinhuanet.com/english/2018-07/10/c_137312795.htm.

29   Philip Gater-Smith, "Qatar Crisis Impacts China's Ambitious Foreign Policy," International Institute for Middle-East and Balkan studies, June 13, 2017, http://www.ifimes.org/en/9426.

30   "What countries are the top producers and consumers of oil?," *U.S. Energy Information Administration (EIA)*, December 3, 2018, https://www.eia.gov/tools/faqs/faq.php?id=709&t=6.

31   "Kuwait," *U.S. Energy Information Administration (EIA)*, November 2, 2016, https://www.eia.gov/beta/international/country.php?iso=KWT.

32   Tim Daiss, "China's Growing Oil Demand Has Created A Geopolitical Dilemma," *Oil Price*, May 2, 2018, https://oilprice.com/Energy/Crude-Oil/Chinas-Growing-Oil-Demand-Has-Created-A-Geopolitical-Dilemma.html.

33   "Is the Chinese oil consumption growing faster than the US oil production?," *Newropeans Magazine*, March 23, 2018, http://www.newropeans-magazine.org/en/2018/03/27/is-the-chinese-oil-consumption-growing-faster-than-the-us-oil-production/.

34   "World Energy Outlook 2017," *International Energy Agency's (IEA)*, 14 November 2017, https://www.iea.org/weo2017/#section-1-5.

35   John Calabrese, "China and the Persian Gulf: Energy and Security," *Middle East Journal*, 52 (3), 1998, 351–366; Steve Yetiv and Chunlong Lu, "China, Global Energy, and the Middle East", *Middle East Journal*, 61 (2), 2007, 199–218.

36   Daniel Workman, "Top 15 Crude Oil Suppliers to China," *World's Top Exports*, April 1, 2018, http://www.worldstopexports.com/top-15-crude-oil-suppliers-to-china/.

37   "Interview: Development of win-win Kuwait-China ties contributes to better well-being, common progress: Kuwaiti emir," *Xinhua*, July 7, 2018,

http://www.xinhuanet.com/english/2018-07/08/c_137309006.htm.

38 Muhamad S. Olimat, *China and the Gulf Cooperation Council Countries: Strategic Partnership in a Changing World.* Maryland: Lexington Books, 2016.

39 "Kuwait to boost oil exports to China to 500,000 bpd in three years," *Gulf News*, August 23, 2014, https://gulfnews.com/business/energy/kuwait-to-boost-oil-exports-to-china-to-500000-bpd-in-three-years-1.1375610.

40 "China becomes one of the biggest oil drilling contractors in Kuwait: report," *Global Times*, July 16, 2017, http://www.globaltimes.cn/content/1056580.shtml.

41 "Kerui wins drilling rigs contract from Kuwait AREC," *Pipeline Oil and Gas News*, July 19, 2018, https://www.pipelineoilandgasnews.com/regionalinternational-news/regional-news/2018/july/kerui-wins-drilling-rigs-contract-from-kuwait-arec/?utm_source=web&utm_medium=&utm_term=&utm_content=&utm_campaign=.

42 Asma Alsharif, "Kuwait signs agreement with Sinopec to build Chinese refinery," *Reuters*, October 25, 2018, https://www.reuters.com/article/kuwait-sinopec-corp/kuwait-signs-agreement-with-sinopec-to-build-chinese-refinery-idUSC6N1JG02J.

43 "PetroChina agrees 2019 annual crude supply deals with Saudi Aramco, Kuwait," *Reuters*, November 7, 2018, https://af.reuters.com/article/commoditiesNews/idAFB9N1X603U; "China's Sinopec signs 2019 annual crude oil supply deal with Kuwait," *Reuters*, November 8, 2018, https://af.reuters.com/article/commoditiesNews/idAFB9N1XG001; "China's Sinochem raises 2019 term oil supply from Saudi Aramco, Kuwait," *Today*, November 9, 2018, https://www.todayonline.com/world/chinas-sinochem-raises-2019-term-oil-supply-saudi-aramco-kuwait.

44 "Vision and Actions on Jointly Building Silk Road Economic Belt and 21st-Century Maritime Silk Road," *National Development and Reform Commission, Ministry of Foreign Affairs, and Ministry of Commerce of the People's Republic of China*, March 28, 2015, http://en.ndrc.gov.cn/newsrelease/201503/t20150330_669367.html.

45 "Government releases New Kuwait 2035 strategic plan," *The Economist Intelligence Unit*, February 3, 2017, http://country.eiu.com/article.aspx?articleid=1675084151.

46 "Xi Jinping Holds Talks with Kuwaiti Emir Sheikh Sabah Al-Ahmad Al-Jaber Al-Sabah," *Ministry of Foreign Affairs, the People's Republic of China*, July 9, 2018, https://www.fmprc.gov.cn/mfa_eng/wjb_663304/zzjg_663340/xybfs_663590/xwlb_663592/t1575565.shtml.

47 "China continues to be Kuwait's top trade partner," *Kuwait News Agency (KUMA)*, September 4, 2017,

https://www.kuna.net.kw/ArticleDetails.aspx?id=2631683&language=en.

48 "China Customs Statistics: Imports and exports by country/region," *The Hong Kong Trade Development Council (HKTDC),* May 27, 2019, http://china-trade-research.hktdc.com/business-news/article/Facts-and-Figures/China-Customs-Statistics/ff/en/1/1X39VTVQ/1X09N9NM.htm.

49 "Interview: Development of win-win Kuwait-China ties contributes to better well-being, common progress: Kuwaiti emir," *Xinhua,* July 7, 2018, http://www.xinhuanet.com/english/2018-07/08/c_137309006.htm.

50 "Kuwaiti-Sino construction deals surge to $8.2bln in '17," *Kuwait News Agency (KUNA),* November 27, 2017, https://www.kuna.net.kw/ArticleDetails.aspx?id=2662355&language=en.

51 "Kuwaiti, Chinese officials discuss expanding strategic cooperation," *Xinhua,* July 12, 2018, http://www.xinhuanet.com/english/2017-07/13/c_136439230.htm

52 "Kuwait calls for increased investment from China," *Xinhua,* March 20, 2018, http://www.xinhuanet.com/english/2018-03/21/c_137053484.htm.

53 Jaber Ali, "Kuwait, China ink several agreements, MoUs to boost ties," *Middle East Confidential,* July 9, 2018, https://me-confidential.com/19899-kuwait-china-ink-several-agreements-mous-to-boost-ties.html.

54 "Vision and Actions on Jointly Building Silk Road Economic Belt and 21st-Century Maritime Silk Road," *National Development and Reform Commission, Ministry of Foreign Affairs, and Ministry of Commerce of the People's Republic of China,* March 28, 2015, http://en.ndrc.gov.cn/newsrelease/201503/t20150330_669367.html.

55 "Interview: China–Kuwait cooperation enters fast tracks under BRI: Chinese envoy," *Xinhua,* April 24, 2019, http://www.xinhuanet.com/english/2019-04/25/c_138006314.htm.

56 Sam, Bridge, "Gulf forecast to see 81% rise in Chinese tourists by 2022," *Arabian Business,* December 19, 2018, https://www.arabianbusiness.com/travel-hospitality/409972-gulf-forecast-to-see-81-rise-in-chinese-tourists-by-2022.

57 "Kuwait launches Chinese center for cultural exchanges", *Xinhua,* March 4, 2018, http://www.xinhuanet.com/english/2018-03/04/c_137014119.htm.

58 Laura Zhou, "Chinese private investment in belt and road projects may be losing steam," *South China Morning Post,* 15 November, 2018, https://www.scmp.com/news/china/diplomacy/article/2173467/chinese-private-investment-belt-and-road-projects-may-be-losing.

59 ZHU Weilie, "Middle East Terrorism, Global Governance and China's

Anti-terror Policy," *Journal of Middle Eastern and Islamic Studies (in Asia)*, Vol. 5, No. 2, 2011, 1–16.

6
Qatar

1   "China now Qatar's third-largest trading partner, says top MCI official," *Gulf-Times*, November 7, 2018, https://www.gulf-times.com/story/612174/China-now-Qatar-s-third-largest-trading-partner-sa.

2   Santhosh V. Perumal, "Qatar seen playing a key role in China's Belt and Road plan," *Gulf-Times*, November 26, 2018, https://www.gulf-times.com/story/614255/Qatar-seen-playing-a-key-role-in-China-s-Belt-and-.

3   "Qatar National Vision 2030," *General Secretariat For Development Planning*, July 2008, https://www.gco.gov.qa/wp-content/uploads/2016/09/GCO-QNV-English.pdf.

4   "Chinese FM: Qatar a key partner to promote 'Belt and Road' initiative," *CCTV.com*, December 5, 2016, http://english.cctv.com/2016/05/12/VIDENMyddtTBNQUM9zSt LhAV160512.shtml.

5   "Vision and Actions on Jointly Building Silk Road Economic Belt and 21st-Century Maritime Silk Road," *National Development and Reform Commission, Ministry of Foreign Affairs, and Ministry of Commerce of the People's Republic of China*, March 28, 2015, http://en.ndrc.gov.cn/newsrelease/201503/t20150330_669367.html.

6   "China, Qatar announce strategic partnership," *China Daily*, November 11, 2014, http://www.chinadaily.com.cn/world/2014-11/04/content_18863364.htm.

7   Haifa Said and Du Chao, "Qatar and China: Developing a Comprehensive Strategic Partnership," *China Today*, November 8, 2018, http://www.chinatoday.com.cn/ctenglish/2018/ii/201808/t20180811_800138032.html.

8   "China, Qatar agree to deepen strategic partnership," *Ministry of Foreign Affairs, the People's Republic of China*, January 31, 2019, https://www.fmprc.gov.cn/mfa_eng/zxxx_662805/t1634698.shtml.

9   "Chinese FM: Qatar a key partner to promote 'Belt and Road' initiative," *CCTV.com*, December 5, 2016, http://english.cctv.com/2016/05/12/VIDENMyddtTBNQUM9zSt LhAV160512.shtml.

10 "Qatar Chamber Sign Agreements with China's Trade Promotion Council," *Qatar Chamber*, April 3, 2017,

https://qatarchamber.com/qatar-chamber-sign-agreements-with-chinas-trade-promotion-council/.

11 "China Signs Port Investment MoU with Qatar," *Port Technology*, November 9, 2018, https://www.porttechnology.org/news/china_signs_port_investment_mou_with_qatar.

12 Anne Barnard and David D. Kirkpatrick, "5 Arab Nations Move to Isolate Qatar, Putting the U.S. in a Bind," *The New York Times*, June 5, 2017, https://www.nytimes.com/2017/06/05/world/middleeast/qatar-saudi-arabia-egypt-bahrain-united-arab-emirates.html.

13 Jonathan Fulton, *China's Relations with the Gulf Monarchies*, New York: Routledge, 2019.

14 Philip Gater-Smith, "Qatar Crisis Impacts China's Ambitious Foreign Policy," *International Policy Digest*, June 13, 2017, https://intpolicydigest.org/2017/06/13/qatar-crisis-impacts-china-s-ambitious-foreign-policy/.

15 "Vision and Actions on Jointly Building Silk Road Economic Belt and 21st-Century Maritime Silk Road," *National Development and Reform Commission, Ministry of Foreign Affairs, and Ministry of Commerce of the People's Republic of China*, March 28, 2015, http://en.ndrc.gov.cn/newsrelease/201503/t20150330_669367.html.

16 "Spotlight: Qatari emir's visit to China shows positive signals," *Xinhua*, February 3, 2019, http://www.xinhuanet.com/english/2019-02/03/c_137797580.htm.

17 "China's top legislator meets Qatari emir," *Xinhua*, January 31, 2019, http://www.xinhuanet.com/english/2019-01/31/c_137790222.htm.

18 "China now Qatar's third-largest trading partner, says top MCI official," *Gulf-Times*, November 7, 2018, https://www.gulf-times.com/story/612174/China-now-Qatar-s-third-largest-trading-partner-sa.

19 "China is Qatar's key trading partner; trade volume at QR38.6bn," *The Peninsula*, November 8, 2018, https://thepeninsulaqatar.com/article/08/11/2018/China-is-Qatar%E2%80%99s-key-trading-partner-trade-volume-at-QR38.6bn.

20 "China Customs Statistics: Imports and exports by country/region," *The Hong Kong Trade Development Council (HKTDC)*, May 27, 2019, http://china-trade-research.hktdc.com/business-news/article/Facts-and-Figures/China-Customs-Statistics/ff/en/1/1X39VTVQ/1X09N9NM.htm.

21 "Qatar–China trade jumps 27% to $13.5bn in 2018, says Kuwari," *Qatar Tribune*, February 1, 2019, http://www.qatar-tribune.com/news-details/id/153980.

22 "Chinese Investments & Contracts in Qatar (2013–2018)," *China Global Investment Tracker*, 2019,

https://www.aei.org/china-global-investment-tracker/.

23   Santhosh V. Perumal, "Qatar seen playing a key role in China's Belt and Road plan," *Gulf-Times*, November 26, 2018, https://www.gulf-times.com/story/614255/Qatar-seen-playing-a-key-role-in-China-s-Belt-and-.

24   "China Harbour and Engineering wins Doha port deal," *Construction Week Online* 15 March, 2011, https://www.constructionweekonline.com/article-11395-china-harbour-and-engineering-wins-doha-port-deal.

25   "Direct Service between Hamad Port and Shanghai launched," *Gulf-Times*, January 28 2017, https://www2.gulf-times.com/story/530771/Direct-Service-between-Hamad-Port-and-Shanghai-lau.

26   "Hamad Port development Phase II to start by early 2019," *The Peninsula*, November 9, 2018, https://www.thepeninsulaqatar.com/article/09/11/2018/Hamad-Port-development-Phase-II-to-start-by-early-2019.

27   "China Railway to build iconic Lusail Stadium for Qatar's World Cup," *Global Construction Review*, November 29, 2016, http://www.globalconstructionreview.com/news/china-railway-build-iconic-lus7ail-stadi7um-qa7ar/.

28   "China's Huawei becomes one of first fully-owned tech firms in Qatar," *Xinhua*, September 19, 2018, http://www.xinhuanet.com/english/2018-09/19/c_137479605.htm.

29   "With world's first 5G, Qatar leads in communication tech," *Qatar-Tribune*, July 2, 2018, http://www.qatar-tribune.com/news-details/id/130696.

30   "Interview: China Int'l Import Expo boosts Qatar–China cooperation under Belt and Road Initiative," *Xinhua*, November 3, http://www.xinhuanet.com/english/2018-11/03/c_137579551.htm.

31   Haifa Said and Du Chao, "Qatar and China: Developing a Comprehensive Strategic Partnership," *China Today*, November 8, 2018, http://www.chinatoday.com.cn/ctenglish/2018/ii/201808/t20180811_800138032.html

32   "Qatar sets up US$10bn fund to invest in China," *The Economist Intelligence Unit*, November 7, 2014, http://country.eiu.com/article.aspx?articleid=182473202&Country=Qatar&topic=Economy&subtopic=Fore_11.

33   Dinesh Nair and Manuel Baigorri, "Qatar Fund Is Near Investment in China's Top Online Lender," *Bloomberg*, September 18, 2018, https://www.bloomberg.com/news/articles/2018-09-17/qatar-fund-said-to-near-investment-in-china-s-top-online-lender

34   Li Wenfang and Zhu Wenqian, "Qatar Airways buys stake in China Southern," *China Daily*, September 5, 2019,

http://global.chinadaily.com.cn/a/201901/05/
WS5c2fee84a31068606745efe2.html.

35   "Vision and Actions on Jointly Building Silk Road Economic Belt and 21st-Century Maritime Silk Road," *National Development and Reform Commission, Ministry of Foreign Affairs, and Ministry of Commerce of the People's Republic of China*, March 28, 2015, http://en.ndrc.gov.cn/newsrelease/201503/t20150330_669367.html.

36   "Chinese FM: Qatar a key partner to promote 'Belt and Road' initiative," *CCTV.com*, December 5, 2016, http://english.cctv.com/2016/05/12/VIDENMyddtTBNQUM9zSt LhAV160512.shtml.

37   Cary Huang, "57 nations approved as founder members of China-led AIIB," *South China Morning Post*, April 27, 2015, https://www.scmp.com/news/china/diplomacy-defence/article/1766970/ 57-nations-approved-founder-members-china-led-aiib.

38   "China, Qatar agree to deepen strategic partnership," *Xinhua*, January 31, 2019, http://www.xinhuanet.com/english/2019-01/31/c_137790332.htm.

39   Andrew Torchia and Tom Finn, "Qatar's $300 billion conundrum: how liquid are its reserves?," *Reuters*, July 19, 2017, https://www.reuters.com/article/us-gulf-qatar-reserves/qatars-300- billion-conundrum-how-liquid-are-its-reserves-idUSKBN1A415X.

40   Muhammad Zulfikar Rakhmat, "China, Qatar, and RMB Internationalization," *The Diplomat*, June 6, 2015, https://thediplomat.com/2015/06/china-qatar-and-rmb- internationalization/.

41   Esther Teo, "More Middle East countries using the yuan," *The Straits Times*, February 5, 2016, https://www.straitstimes.com/asia/east- asia/more-middle-east-countries-using-the-yuan.

42   Haifa Said and Du Chao, "Qatar and China: Developing a Comprehensive Strategic Partnership," *China Today*, November 8, 2018, http://www.chinatoday.com.cn/ctenglish/2018/ii/201808/t20180811_80 0138032.html.

43   "Qatar–China ties promise economic partnerships and advanced stages of integration," *Gulf Times* January 30, 2019, https://www.gulf- times.com/story/620770/Qatar-China-ties-promise-economic-partnersh ips-and

44   Jessica Jaganathan, "Australia grabs world's biggest LNG exporter crown from Qatar in November," *Reuters*, December 10, 2018, https://www.reuters.com/article/us-australia-qatar-lng/australia-grabs- worlds-biggest-lng-exporter-crown-from-qatar-in-nov-idUSKBN1O90 7N.

45   "Qatar–China trade jumps 27% to $13.5 bn in 2018, says Kuwari," *Qatar Tribune*, February 1, 2019,

http://www.qatar-tribune.com/news-details/id/153980.

46 "Natural Gas Weekly Update," *U.S. Energy Information Administration (EIA)*, December 5, 2018, https://www.eia.gov/naturalgas/weekly/archivenew_ngwu/2018/12_06/.

47 Satyendra Pathak, "Qatar–China trade volume jumps 50% on LNG exports," *Qatar Tribune*, November 19, 2017, http://www.qatar-tribune.com/news-details/id/96747.

48 "Qatar," *U.S. Energy Information Administration (EIA)*, October 20, 2015, https://www.eia.gov/beta/international/analysis.php?iso=QAT#note.

49 Hassan E. Alfadala and Mahmoud M. El-Halwagi, "Qatar's Chemical Industry: Monetizing Natural Gas," *AIChE*, February 2017, https://www.aiche.org/resources/publications/cep/2017/february/qatars-chemical-industry-monetizing-natural-gas.

50 Haifa Said and Du Chao, "Qatar and China: Developing a Comprehensive Strategic Partnership," *China Today*, November 8, 2018, http://www.chinatoday.com.cn/ctenglish/2018/ii/201808/t20180811_800138032.html.

51 Zheng Xin, "US LNG exports to China are declining," *China Daily*, August 22, 2018, http://www.chinadaily.com.cn/a/201808/22/WS5b7cc6fea310add14f3871b2_2.html.

52 Andrew Torchia, "Qatargas agrees on 22-year LNG supply deal with China," *Reuters*, September 10, 2018, https://www.reuters.com/article/us-usa-china-trade-analysis/trump-wont-soften-hardline-on-china-to-make-trade-deal-advisers-idUSKCN1PH02I.

53 Rania El Gamal, "Qatar Petroleum signs five-year LPG supply deal with China," *Reuters*, October 16, 2018, https://in.reuters.com/article/qatar-petroleum-china/qatar-petroleum-signs-five-year-lpg-supply-deal-with-china-idINKCN1MQ0NI.

54 Anas Iqtait, "China's rising interests in Qatar," *The Interpreter*, June 8, 2018, https://www.lowyinstitute.org/the-interpreter/china-s-rising-interests-qatar.

55 John Calabrese, "China and the Persian Gulf: Energy and Security," *Middle East Journal*, 52 (3), 1998, 351–366; Steve Yetiv and Chunlong Lu, "China, Global Energy, and the Middle East", *Middle East Journal*, 61(2), 2007, 199–218.

56 Daniel Workman, "Top 15 Crude Oil Suppliers to China," *World's Top Exports*, April 12, 2019, http://www.worldstopexports.com/top-15-crude-oil-suppliers-to-china/.

57 Brahim Saidy, "Qatar and Rising China: An Evolving Partnership," *China Report*, 53, 4 (2017): 447–466.

58 Samuel Ramani, "China's Growing Security Relationship with Qatar," *The Diplomat*, November 16, 2017,

https://thediplomat.com/2017/11/chinas-growing-security-relationship-with-qatar/.

59 Christopher Layne, "The US-Chinese power shift and the end of the Pax Americana," *International Affairs*, 94 (1), 2018, 89–111.

60 Imad K. Harb, "Self-preservation and Strategic Hedging in the Gulf Cooperation Council," *Policy brief*, no. 23, June 26, 2018, http://ams.hi.is/wp-content/uploads/2018/06/Self-Preservation-and-Strategic-Hedging-in-the-GCC-2.pdf.

61 Samuel Ramani, "China's Growing Security Relationship with Qatar," *The Diplomat*, November 16, 2017, https://thediplomat.com/2017/11/chinas-growing-security-relationship-with-qatar/.

62 Camilla Hodgson, Qatar has boosted spending by 282% to become the world's 3rd biggest weapons importer," *Business Insider*, August 10, 2017, https://www.businessinsider.com/qatar-becomes-worlds-third-biggest-weapons-importer-in-two-years-2017-8.

63 Julia Hollingsworth, "Why Qatar matters to China, in spite of Gulf isolation," *South China Morning Post*, June 12, 2017, https://www.scmp.com/news/china/diplomacy-defence/article/2097206/why-qatar-matters-china-spite-gulf-isolation.

64 Giorgio Cafiero and Daniel Wagner, "What the Gulf States Think of 'One Belt, One Road'," *The Diplomat*, May 24, 2017, https://thediplomat.com/2017/05/what-the-gulf-states-think-of-one-belt-one-road/.

65 Anas Iqtait, "China's rising interests in Qatar," *The Interpreter*, June 8, 2018, https://www.lowyinstitute.org/the-interpreter/china-s-rising-interests-qatar.

66 Matthew Lee, "Pompeo signs off on al-Udeid Air Base expansion, but says Qatar diplomatic crisis 'has dragged on too long'," *Military Times*, January 13, 2019, https://www.militarytimes.com/flashpoints/2019/01/13/pompeo-signs-off-on-al-udeid-air-base-expansion-but-says-qatar-diplomatic-crisis-has-dragged-on-too-long/.

67 Theodore Karasik and Giorgio Cafiero, "Why China Sold Qatar The SY-400 Ballistic Missile System," *Lobe Log* December 21, 2017, https://lobelog.com/why-china-sold-qatar-the-sy-400-ballistic-missile-system/.

68 Giorgio Cafiero and Muhammad Zulfikar Rakhmat, "China Eyes Qatar in its Quest to Build a New Silk Road," *The National Interest*, June 2, 2016, https://nationalinterest.org/blog/the-buzz/china-eyes-qatar-its-quest-build-new-silk-road-16437?nopaging=1.

69 Theodore Karasik and Giorgio Cafiero, "Why China Sold Qatar The

SY-400 Ballistic Missile System," *Lobe Log* December 21, 2017, https://lobelog.com/why-china-sold-qatar-the-sy-400-ballistic-missile-system/.

70 "Qatar Displays Chinese Missile," *Arms Control Association*, March 1, 2018, https://www.armscontrol.org/act/2018-03/news-briefs/qatar-displays-chinese-missile

71 "Vision and Actions on Jointly Building Silk Road Economic Belt and 21st-Century Maritime Silk Road," *National Development and Reform Commission, Ministry of Foreign Affairs, and Ministry of Commerce of the People's Republic of China*, March 28, 2015, http://en.ndrc.gov.cn/newsrelease/201503/t20150330_669367.html.

72 "China, Qatar agree to deepen strategic partnership," *Ministry of Foreign Affairs, the People's Republic of China*, January 31, 2019, https://www.fmprc.gov.cn/mfa_eng/zxxx_662805/t1634698.shtml

73 Sam, Bridge, "Gulf forecast to see 81% rise in Chinese tourists by 2022," *Arabian Business*, December 19, 2018, https://www.arabianbusiness.com/travel-hospitality/409972-gulf-forecast-to-see-81-rise-in-chinese-tourists-by-2022.

74 "45,000 Chinese tourists visited Qatar in '17: Envoy," *The Peninsula*, July 3, 2018, https://www.thepeninsulaqatar.com/article/03/07/2018/45,000-Chinese-tourists-visited-Qatar-in-%E2%80%9917-Envoy.

75 "Qatar sees 38% growth in Chinese arrivals," *The Peninsula*, May 3, 2019, https://www.thepeninsulaqatar.com/article/03/03/2019/Qatar-sees-38-growth-in-Chinese-arrivals.

76 "Qatar's tourism industry takes measures to attract more Chinese tourists," *China Daily*, April 13, 2018, http://www.chinadaily.com.cn/a/201804/13/WS5ad05bffa3105cdcf_651827b.html.

77 Haifa Said and Du Chao, "Qatar and China: Developing a Comprehensive Strategic Partnership," *China Today*, November 8, 2018, http://www.chinatoday.com.cn/ctenglish/2018/ii/201808/t20180811_800138032.html.

78 "China-Qatar visa exemption agreement to take effect later this month," *Xinhua*, December 12, 2018, http://www.xinhuanet.com/english/2018-12/12/c_137669098.htm.

79 Ailyn Agonia, "Chinese Embassy marks 30th anniversary of Qatar–China diplomatic ties in style," *Qatar Tribune*, July 6, 2018, http://www.qatar-tribune.com/news-details/id/131203.

80 Jure Snoj, "Population of Qatar by nationality-2017 report," *Priya DSouza Communications*, February 7, 2017, http://priyadsouza.com/population-of-qatar-by-nationality-in-2017/.

81   Muhammad Zulfikar Rakhmat, "China-Qatar Relations: Media, Culture, Education, and People," *HuffPost*, May 18, 2017, https://www.huffingtonpost.com/muhammad-zulfikar-rakhmat/chinaqatar-relations-medi_b_10006408.html.

82   "Luxury Chinese Travel to the Middle East Hots Up; Chinese Travellers Seek New Silk Road Adventure," *The Luxury Conversation*, February 17, 2018, http://luxuryconversation.com/chinese-travellers-seek-new-silk-road-adventure-as-luxury-chinese-travel-to-the-middle-east-hots-up/.

83   "Memorandum of Understanding Signed by Translation and Interpreting Institute and the Chinese Embassy in Qatar," *Qatar Foundation*, February 22, 2015, https://www.qf.org.qa/news/tii-mou-chinese-embassy.

84   Wang Yue, "Delegation from Qatar University visits PKU," *Peking University*, November 24, 2014, http://newsen.pku.edu.cn/News_Events/News/Global/11776.htm.

85   "Qatar, China agree on 'strategic partnership'," *Gulf Times*, November 4, 2014, https://www.gulf-times.com/story/414942/Qatar-China-agree-on-strategic-partnership.

86   Lesley Walker, "Qatar–China Year of Culture to kick off with exhibits, festival in 2016," *Doha News*, December 30, 2015, https://dohanews.co/qatar-china-year-culture-kick-off-exhibits-festival-2016/.

87   Haifa Said and Du Chao, "Qatar and China: Developing a Comprehensive Strategic Partnership," *China Today*, November 8, 2018, http://www.chinatoday.com.cn/ctenglish/2018/ii/201808/t20180811_80 0138032.html.

7

Oman

1   "Oman and China strategic partners," *Times of Oman*, September 8, 2018, https://timesofoman.com/article/140883.

2   Giorgio Cafiero and Daniel Wagner, "What the Gulf States Think of 'One Belt, One Road'," *The Diplomat*, May 24, 2017, https://thediplomat.com/2017/05/what-the-gulf-states-think-of-one-belt-one-road/.

3   Sumedh A. Lokhande, "China's One Belt One Road Initiative and the Gulf Pearl Chain," *China Daily*, June 5, 2017, http://www.chinadaily.com.cn/opinion/2017beltandroad/2017-06/05/content_29618549.htm.

4   "China, Oman announce establishment of strategic partnership," *CGTN*, May 25, 2018,

https://news.cgtn.com/news/3d3d414f35676a4e77457a6333566d54/share_p.html.

5   "Oman 9ᵗʰ Five-Year Development Plan and the Strategic Economic Sectors (2016–2020)," *The Supreme Council of Planning in the Sultanate of Oman*, July 7, 2017, http://obfaoman.com/wp-content/uploads/2017/09/2.-Oman-Uk-comm-July17-V1-1.pdf.

6   Alfred Strolla and Phaninder Peri, "Oman 20/20 Vision," *A Middle East Point of View*, 2013, https://www2.deloitte.com/content/dam/Deloitte/xe/Documents/About-Deloitte/mepovdocuments/mepov12/dtme_mepov12_Oman2020vision.pdf.

7   Amar Diwakar, "Vision 2040: Oman's ambitious strategy towards a post-oil economy," *Al-Araby*, April 16, 2019, https://www.alaraby.co.uk/english/indepth/2019/4/16/vision-2040-omans-ambitious-strategy-towards-a-post-oil-economy.

8   Min Ye, "China and competing cooperation in Asia–Pacific: TPP, RCEP, and the New Silk Road," *Asian Security*, 11 (3), 2015, 206–224.

9   "Vision and Actions on Jointly Building Silk Road Economic Belt and 21st-Century Maritime Silk Road," *National Development and Reform Commission, Ministry of Foreign Affairs, and Ministry of Commerce of the People's Republic of China*, March 28, 2015, http://en.ndrc.gov.cn/newsrelease/201503/t20150330_669367.html.

10 Sumedh A. Lokhande, "China's One Belt One Road Initiative and the Gulf Pearl Chain," *China Daily*, June 5, 2017, http://www.chinadaily.com.cn/opinion/2017beltandroad/2017-06/05/content_29618549.htm.

11 Giorgio Cafiero and Daniel Wagner, "What the Gulf States Think of 'One Belt, One Road'," *The Diplomat*, May 24, 2017, https://thediplomat.com/2017/05/what-the-gulf-states-think-of-one-belt-one-road/.

12 "Oman is a Key Regional Partner in the Belt and Road Initiative," *The Sirius Report*, June 7, 2018, https://www.thesiriusreport.com/geopolitics/oman-china-bri/.

13 "Oman's Duqm, a New Port City for the Middle East?," *Belt & Road News*, February 11, 2019, https://www.beltandroad.news/2019/02/11/omans-duqm-a-new-port-city-for-the-middle-east/.

14 Jonathan Schanzer and Nicole Salter, "Oman in the Middle: Muscat's Balancing Act Between Iran and America," *The Foundation for Defense of Democracies (FDD)*, May 9, 2019, https://www.fdd.org/analysis/2019/05/09/oman-in-the-middle/.

15 Alfred Strolla and Phaninder Peri, "Oman: 20/20 Vision," *World Finance Review*, May 2016, https://islamicmarkets.com/publications/oman-vision-2020.

16 Han Guo and Zhou Zhou, "China's Strategic Vision: Five Years on and Looking Ahead," *ICAS BULLETIN: Institute for China–America Studies,* November 1, 2017, https://chinaus-icas.org/bulletin/chinas-strategic-vision-five-years-on-and-looking-ahead/.

17 "Oman Stands to benefit from China-Arab Belt and Road Initiative: HE FULONG," *Muscat Daily,* July 16, 2018, https://muscatdaily.com/Archive/Oman/Oman-stands-to-benefit-from-China-Arab-Belt-and-Road-initiative-H-E-Fulong-5a0p.

18 "Vision and Actions on Jointly Building Silk Road Economic Belt and 21st-Century Maritime Silk Road," *National Development and Reform Commission, Ministry of Foreign Affairs, and Ministry of Commerce of the People's Republic of China,* March 28, 2015, http://en.ndrc.gov.cn/newsrelease/201503/t20150330_669367.html.

19 "Oman among top four Arab trading partners of China," *Times of Oman,* March 11, 2018, https://timesofoman.com/article/129848.

20 "China, Oman announce establishment of strategic partnership," *CGTN,* May 25, 2018, https://news.cgtn.com/news/3d3d414f35676a4e77457a6333566d54/share_p.html.

21 "China, Oman issue joint statement on establishment of strategic partnership," *Xinhua,* May 26, 2018, http://www.xinhuanet.com/english/2018-05/26/c_137206872.htm.

22 "China and Oman Sign the Memorandum of Understanding on Jointly Building the 'Belt and Road'," *Permanent Mission of the People's Republic of China to the UN,* May 15, 2018, http://www.china-un.org/eng/zgyw/t1560128.htm.

23 "Belt and Road Initiative aims to achieve mutual benefits for all: Omani officials," *Xinhua,* December 4, 2018, http://www.xinhuanet.com/english/2018-12/05/c_137650958.htm.

24 Tim Daiss, "China's Growing Oil Demand Has Created A Geopolitical Dilemma," *Oil Price,* May 2, 2018, https://oilprice.com/Energy/Crude-Oil/Chinas-Growing-Oil-Demand-Has-Created-A-Geopolitical-Dilemma.html.

25 John Calabrese, "China and the Persian Gulf: Energy and Security," *Middle East Journal,* 52 (3), 1998, 351–366; Steve Yetiv and Chunlong Lu, "China, Global Energy, and the Middle East," *Middle East Journal,* 61 (2), 2007, 199–218.

26 Daniel Workman, "Top 15 Crude Oil Suppliers to China," *World's Top Exports,* April 12, 2019, http://www.worldstopexports.com/top-15-crude-oil-suppliers-to-china/.

27 "Oman-Overview," *US Energy Information Administration (EIA),* January 7, 2019, https://www.eia.gov/beta/international/analysis.php?iso=OMN.

28 "Annual Report 2017," *Central Bank of Oman*, June 2018, https://cbo.gov.om/sites/assets/Documents/English/Publications/AnnualReports/AnnualReport2017eng.pdf.

29 Mordechai Chaziza, "The Significant Role of Oman in China's Maritime Silk Road Initiative," *Contemporary Review of the Middle East*, 6 (1), 2018, 1–14.

30 Mahmoud Ghafouri, "China's Policy in the Persian Gulf," *Middle East Policy Council*, 16 (2), 2009, 80–92.

31 "Exploring the China and Oman Relationship," *The Diplomat*, May 10, 2014, https://thediplomat.com/2014/05/exploring-the-china-and-oman-relationship/.

32 "China remains largest buyer of Oman's crude in December: report," *Xinhua*, January 16, 2019, http://www.chinadaily.com.cn/a/201901/16/WS5c3ec328a3106c65c34e4cc7.html.

33 "China remains biggest importer of Omani oil," *Times of Oman*, July 15, 2018, https://timesofoman.com/article/138149.

34 "Oman-China Trade ties to deepen Further," *Muscat Daily*, January 13, 2019, https://muscatdaily.com/Archive/Business/Oman-China-trade-ties-to-deepen-further-5cpn.

35 "China, Oman issue joint statement on establishment of strategic partnership," *Xinhua*, May 26, 2018, http://www.xinhuanet.com/english/2018-05/26/c_137206872.htm.

36 "Vision and Actions on Jointly Building Silk Road Economic Belt and 21st-Century Maritime Silk Road," *National Development and Reform Commission, Ministry of Foreign Affairs, and Ministry of Commerce of the People's Republic of China*, March 28, 2015, http://en.ndrc.gov.cn/newsrelease/201503/t20150330_669367.html.

37 "China Customs Statistics: Imports and exports by country/region," *The Hong Kong Trade Development Council (HKTDC)*, May 27, 2019, http://china-trade-research.hktdc.com/business-news/article/Facts-and-Figures/China-Customs-Statistics/ff/en/1/1X39VTVQ/1X09N9NM.htm.

38 "China, Oman issue joint statement on establishment of strategic partnership," *Xinhua*, May 26, 2018, http://www.xinhuanet.com/english/2018-05/26/c_137206872.htm.

39 "Oman Stands to benefit from China-Arab Belt and Road Initiative: HE FULONG," *Muscat Daily*, July 16, 2018, https://muscatdaily.com/Archive/Oman/Oman-stands-to-benefit-from-China-Arab-Belt-and-Road-initiative-H-E-Fulong-5a0p.

40 Oman-China Trade ties to Deepen Further," *Muscat Daily*, January 13, 2019,

https://muscatdaily.com/Archive/Business/Oman-China-trade-ties-to-deepen-further-5cpn.

41 "Oman-China trade topped $19bn in 2018," *Times of Oman* April 27, 2019,
https://timesofoman.com/article/1204030.

42 "Oman important partner in building Belt and Road: Chinese envoy," *Times of Oman*, April 30, 2019,
https://timesofoman.com/article/1219648.

43 Wade Shepard, "Why China is Building A New City Out in the Desert of Oman," *Forbes*, September 8, 2017,
https://www.forbes.com/sites/wadeshepard/2017/09/08/why-china-is-building-a-new-city-out-in-the-desert-of-oman/#6d3249316b2f.

44 James Kynge, Chris Campbell, Amy Kazmin & Farhan Bokhari, "How China rules the waves." *Financial Times*, January 12, 2017,
https://ig.ft.com/sites/china-ports/.

45 "Oman Wanfang plans 25 new projects in Duqm," *Times of Oman*. August 12, 2017,
http://timesofoman.com/article/114777/Business/Oman-Wanfang-plans-25-new-projects-at-Duqm.

46 "Oman's 2020 vision," Arabian Business, March 10, 2010,
http://www.arabianbusiness.com/oman-s-2020-vision-89986.html.

47 Nawied Jabarkhyl, "Oman counts on Chinese billions to build desert boomtown," *Reuters*, September 5, 2017,
https://www.reuters.com/article/us-oman-china-investment/oman-counts-on-chinese-billions-to-build-desert-boomtown-idUSKCN1BG1WJ.

48 "Oman among top four Arab trading partners of China," *Times of Oman*, March 11, 2018,
https://timesofoman.com/article/129848.

49 "Vision and Actions on Jointly Building Silk Road Economic Belt and 21st-Century Maritime Silk Road," *National Development and Reform Commission, Ministry of Foreign Affairs, and Ministry of Commerce of the People's Republic of China*, March 28, 2015,
http://en.ndrc.gov.cn/newsrelease/201503/t20150330_669367.html.

50 "China, Oman issue joint statement on establishment of strategic partnership," *Xinhua*, May 26, 2018,
http://www.xinhuanet.com/english/2018-05/26/c_137206872.htm.

51 "Oman signs pact as founding member of Asian Infrastructure Investment Bank," *Times of Oman*, October 26, 2014,
https://timesofoman.com/article/42316.

52 "Oman hosts AIIB delegation," *Muscat Daily*, March 4, 2019,
https://muscatdaily.com/Archive/Business/Oman-hosts-AIIB-delegation-5dbs.

53 "UPDATE 1-Oman signs $3.55 billion loan with Chinese banks," *Reuters*, August 3, 2017,

https://www.reuters.com/article/oman-loan/update-1-oman-signs-3-55-billion-loan-with-chinese-banks-idUSL5N1KP2XX.

54 "Vision and Actions on Jointly Building Silk Road Economic Belt and 21st-Century Maritime Silk Road," *National Development and Reform Commission, Ministry of Foreign Affairs, and Ministry of Commerce of the People's Republic of China*, March 28, 2015, http://en.ndrc.gov.cn/newsrelease/201503/t20150330_669367.html.

55 "China, Oman issue joint statement on establishment of strategic partnership," Xinhua, May 26, 2018, http://www.xinhuanet.com/english/2018-05/26/c_137206872.htm.

56 Liu Xi and Yang Yuanyong, "Spotlight: China, Oman establish industrial park to boost bilateral cooperation," *Xinhua*, December 19, 2018, http://www.xinhuanet.com/english/2018-12/19/c_137683272.htm.

57 "Oman and China strategic partners," *Times of Oman*, September 8, 2018, https://timesofoman.com/article/140883.

58 Sam Bridge, "Gulf forecast to see 81% rise in Chinese tourists by 2022," *Arabian Business*, December 19, 2018, https://www.arabianbusiness.com/travel-hospitality/409972-gulf-forecast-to-see-81-rise-in-chinese-tourists-by-2022.

59 "Oman-China trade topped $19bn in 2018," *Times of Oman*, April 27, 2019, https://timesofoman.com/article/1204030.

60 "Oman important partner in building Belt and Road: Chinese envoy," *Times of Oman*, April 30, 2019, https://timesofoman.com/article/1219648.

61 Marc M. Valeri, *Simmering Unrest and Succession Challenges in Oman.* Washington, DC: Carnegie Endowment for International Peace, 2015.

62 Zhibin Han and Xiaoqian Chen, "Historical Exchanges and Future Cooperation between China and Oman Under the 'Belt & Road' Initiative," *International Relations and Diplomacy*, 6 (1), 2018, 1–15.

63 Neeta Lal, "India, China Jockey for Influence in Oman," *Asia Sentinel*, February 21, 2018, https://www.asiasentinel.com/politics/india-china-jockey-influence-oman/.

64 Kenneth Katzman, "Oman: Reform, Security, and U.S. Policy," *Congressional Research Service*, March 8, 2018, https://fas.org/sgp/crs/mideast/RS21534.pdf.

65 Richard J. Schmierer, "The Sultanate of Oman and the Iran Nuclear Deal," *Middle East Policy*, 22 (4), 2015, 113–120.

8

Bahrain

1   Muhammad Zulfikar Rakhmat, "China and Bahrain: Undocumented Growing Relations," *Fair Observer*, May 22, 2014, https://www.fairobserver.com/region/middle_east_north_africa/china-and-bahrain-undocumented-growing-relations-66107/.

2   "Bahrain Strengthens Economic Ties with China, Signs 8 Landmark MoUs," *Asharq Al-Awsat*, November 19, 2018, https://aawsat.com/english/home/article/1469476/bahrain-strengthens-economic-ties-china-signs-8-landmark-mous.

3   "Bahrain has played an important role in consolidating relations between China and the rest of the Gulf States," *VAAJU.COM*, July 9, 2018, https://vaaju.com/lebanon/bahrain-has-played-an-important-role-in-consolidating-relations-between-china-and-the-rest-of-the-gulf-states/.

4   "The Economic Vision 2030," *Kingdom of Bahrain*, September 11, 2017, https://www.bahrain.bh/wps/portal/!ut/p/a1/jdDfE4FAEAfwv8VDr-3qqHg7TSlTwyByLybmHKY6k8ifLzz5Efbtdj7f2d0DBhGwLD7vRF zsZBYntzfTl-4Q9aZmagOchg7S4aTl-rZLcGxUYPEECL EroBsjY9bRdBP_y6MWWE2vVYEgQKRmb-xPHQuxT_7M1x T9OX_CM5gDe2HvV9zBtzUfoH6PATCRyNX9Txc0WxFTAMv5h uc8V0951d4WxeHYVVDBsixVIaVIuLqWqYKfIlt5LCB6lnBIwzC6e Pt2cvYpbTSuTGJy6Q!!/dl5/d5/L2dBISEvZ0FBIS9nQSEh/.

5   "Bahrain: Market Profile," *The Hong Kong Trade Development Council (HKTDC)*, February 8, 2019, file:///C:/Users/moti/Downloads/hktdc_1X0K7WJT_en.pdf.

6   "Doing Business 2018: Reforming to Create Jobs," *The World Bank*, October 31, 2017, http://www.doingbusiness.org/content/dam/doingBusiness/media/Annual-Reports/English/DB2018-Full-Report.pdf.

7   "The Global Competitiveness Report 2017–2018," *World Economic Forum*, September 26, 2017, http://www3.weforum.org/docs/GCR2017-2018/05FullReport/TheGlobalCompetitivenessReport2017%E2%80%932018.pdf.

8   "Bahrain GDP and Economic Data," *Global Finance Magazine*, October 29, 2018, https://www.gfmag.com/global-data/country-data/bahrain-gdp-country-report.

9   "Bahrain GCC's Fastest Growing Economy with 3.9 Percent in 2017," *Albawaba*, May 6, 2018, https://www.albawaba.com/business/bahrain-gcc%E2%80%99s-fastest-growing-economy-39-percent-2017-1126870.

10 Giorgio Cafiero and Daniel Wagner, "What the Gulf States Think of 'One Belt, One Road'," *The Diplomat*, May 24, 2017, https://thediplomat.com/2017/05/what-the-gulf-states-think-of-one-belt-one-road/.

11   Sumedh Anil Lokhande, "China's One Belt One Road Initiative and the Gulf Pearl Chain," China Daily, June 5, 2017, http://www.chinadaily.com.cn/interface/flipboard/158870/2017-06-05/cd_29618549.html.

12   "Changing times calls for new GCC relations with China, Russia," *Oxford Business Group*, 2019, https://oxfordbusinessgroup.com/analysis/east-meets-middle-east-changing-times-calls-new-relations-china-and-russia.

13   Giorgio Cafiero and Daniel Wagner, "What the Gulf States Think of 'One Belt, One Road'," *The Diplomat*, May 24, 2017, https://thediplomat.com/2017/05/what-the-gulf-states-think-of-one-belt-one-road/.

14   Min Ye, "China and competing cooperation in Asia-Pacific: TPP, RCEP, and the New Silk Road," *Asian Security*, 11 (3), 2015, 206–224.

15   "Vision and Actions on Jointly Building Silk Road Economic Belt and 21st-Century Maritime Silk Road," *National Development and Reform Commission, Ministry of Foreign Affairs, and Ministry of Commerce of the People's Republic of China*, March 28, 2015, http://en.ndrc.gov.cn/newsrelease/201503/t20150330_669367.html.

16   Habib Toumi, "King Hamad's visit to boost Bahrain-China relations," *Gulf News*, September 13, 2013, https://gulfnews.com/world/gulf/bahrain/king-hamads-visit-to-boost-bahrain-china-relations-1.1230640.

17   "Xi Jinping Holds Talks with King of Bahrain Sheikh Hamad bin Isa Al-khalifa Stressing to Build China-Bahrain Friendly Cooperative Relations of Long-term Stability," *Ministry of Foreign Affairs, the People's Republic of China*, September 9, 2013, https://www.fmprc.gov.cn/mfa_eng/wjb_663304/zzjg_663340/xybfs_663590/gjlb_663594/2803_663606/2805_663610/t1078070.shtml.

18   Qi Zhenhong, "Join Hands To Push China–Bahrain Relations," Embassy of the People's Republic of China in the Kingdom of Bahrain, May, 9, 2018, http://bh.china-embassy.org/eng/xwdt/t1558049.htm.

19   Ola Aboukhsaiwan, "China in Bahrain: building shared interests," *Wamda*, February 22, 2017, https://www.wamda.com/2017/02/china-bahrain-building-shared-interests-entrepreneurship.

20   Khalifa Bin Salman Port," Ministry of Transportation and Telecommunications Kingdom of Bahrain, 2019, http://www.transportation.gov.bh/content/khalifa-bin-salman-port.

21   "Investing in Bahrain," *The Bahrain Economic Development Board*, 2019, https://www.bahrainbay.com/wp-content/uploads/2016/08/Investing-In-Bahrain-Brochure-09-CS3.pdf .

22   "Ambassador Qi Zhenhong's Speech on the 2016 Chinese National Day Reception," *Embassy of the People's Republic of China in the Kingdom of Bahrain*, September 21, 2016,

http://bh.china-embassy.org/eng/zbgx/t1399255.htm.

23 "China's 'One Belt, One Road' is a 'win-win' for GCC – Bahrain Minister," *Gulf Insider*, May 13, 2018, https://www.gulf-insider.com/chinas-one-belt-one-road-win-win-gulf-countries-bahrain-minister/.

24 "China, Bahrain ink MOU to promote Belt and Road Initiative," *Xinhua*, July 10, 2018, http://www.xinhuanet.com/english/2018-07/10/c_137312832.htm.

25 "Vision and Actions on Jointly Building Silk Road Economic Belt and 21st-Century Maritime Silk Road," *National Development and Reform Commission, Ministry of Foreign Affairs, and Ministry of Commerce of the People's Republic of China*, March 28, 2015, http://en.ndrc.gov.cn/newsrelease/201503/t20150330_669367.html.

26 "Bahrain Delegation to visit China to fortify economic and trade ties between the two nations," *EDS Bahrain*, November 11, 2018, https://bahrainedb.com/latest-news/bahrain-delegation-to-visit-china-to-fortify-economic-and-trade-ties-between-the-two-nations/.

27 "Huawei to accelerate 5G ecosystem in Bahrain," *Technical Review Middle East*, August 12, 2018, http://www.technicalreviewmiddleeast.com/it/communication/huawei-to-accelerate-5g-ecosystem-in-bahrain.

28 "China Customs Statistics: Imports and exports by country/region," *The Hong Kong Trade Development Council (HKTDC)*, May 27, 2019, http://china-trade-research.hktdc.com/business-news/article/Facts-and-Figures/China-Customs-Statistics/ff/en/1/1X39VTVQ/1X09N9NM.htm.

29 Han Lu, "Bahraini business environment gives it edge," *China Daily*, May 30, 2018, http://www.chinadaily.com.cn/cndy/2018-05/30/content_36295733.htm.

30 "The 2019 Index of Economic Freedom: Bahrain," *The Heritage Foundation*, 2019, https://www.heritage.org/index/country/bahrain.

31 Han Lu, "Bahraini business environment gives it edge," *China Daily*, May 30, 2018, http://www.chinadaily.com.cn/cndy/2018-05/30/content_36295733.htm.

32 Ahmed Al-Masri and Kevin Curran, *Smart technologies and innovation for a sustainable future: proceedings of the 1st American University in the Emirates International Research Conference – Dubai, UAE 2017*. Cham, Switzerland: Springer, 2019.

33 James Reardon-Anderson, *The Red Star and the Crescent: China and the Middle East*, New York: Oxford University Press, 2018.

34 Muhammad Zulfikar Rakhmat, "China and Bahrain: Undocumented Growing Relations," *Fair Observer*, May 22, 2014,

https://www.fairobserver.com/region/middle_east_north_africa/china-and-bahrain-undocumented-growing-relations-66107/.

35 "Celebrating Strong Ties," *Bahrain this Month,* October 1, 2018, https://www.bahrainthismonth.com/magazine/interviews/chinese-ambassador-celebrating-strong-ties.

36 Han Lu, "Bahraini business environment gives it edge," *China Daily,* May 30, 2018, http://www.chinadaily.com.cn/cndy/2018-05/30/content_36295733.htm.

37 "Bahrain to host Mideast's largest Chinese trade expo," *Trade Arabia,* December 25, 2018, http://www.tradearabia.com/news/IND_349105.html.

38 Nyshka Chandran, "Bahrain sees 'growing interest' from Chinese tech firms," *CNBC,* September, 20 2018, https://www.cnbc.com/2018/09/20/bahrain-sees-growing-interest-from-chinese-tech-firms.html

39 Bernd Debusmann Jr ,"Bahrain's Investcorp makes first foray into China," *Arabian Business,* September 20, 2018, https://www.arabianbusiness.com/banking-finance/404734-wknd-bahrains-investcorp-makes-first-foray-into-china

40 "A high-level Bahraini delegation is visiting China to further strengthen trade and economic ties," *StartUp Bahrain,* November 12, 2018, https://startupbahrain.com/a-high-level-bahraini-delegation-is-visiting-china-to-further-strengthen-trade-and-economic-tie/

41 "Bahrain signs eight landmark agreements to deepen economic ties with Shenzhen," *PR Newswire,* November 16, 2018, https://www.prnewswire.com/news-releases/bahrain-signs-eight-land-mark-agreements-to-deepen-economic-ties-with-shenzhen-300751963.html.

42 "China's Provincial Economies: Growing Together or Pulling Apart?," Moody's, January 2019, https://www.moodysanalytics.com/-/media/article/2019/china-provin-cial-economies.pdf.

43 "Bahrain signs key business deals with China," *TradeArabia,* November 22, 2018, http://www.tradearabia.com/news/BANK_347879.html.

44 "Bahrain signs more agreements with China as economic ties deepen," *The National,* November 20, 2018, https://www.thenational.ae/business/economy/bahrain-signs-more-agreements-with-china-as-economic-ties-deepen-1.793952.

45 "Bahrain EDB seals strategic agreements with China," *Trade Arabia,* November 20, 2018, http://www.tradearabia.com/news/BANK_347823.html.

46 "Vision and Actions on Jointly Building Silk Road Economic Belt and 21st-Century Maritime Silk Road," *National Development and Reform*

Commission, Ministry of Foreign Affairs, and Ministry of Commerce of the People's Republic of China, March 28, 2015, http://en.ndrc.gov.cn/newsrelease/201503/t20150330_669367.html.

47   Sam Bridge, "Gulf forecast to see 81% rise in Chinese tourists by 2022," *Arabian Business*, December 19, 2018, https://www.arabianbusiness.com/travel-hospitality/409972-gulf-forecast-to-see-81-rise-in-chinese-tourists-by-2022.

48   "International tourism, number of arrivals – Bahrain," The *World Bank Group*, 2019, https://data.worldbank.org/indicator/ST.INT.ARVL?locations=BH.

49   Aarti Nagraj, "Bahrain, China sign visa exemption for diplomatic, special passports," *Gulf Business*, October 17, 2018, https://gulfbusiness.com/bahrain-china-sign-visa-exemption-diplomatic-special-passports/.

50   "Arabian Travel Market Series: GCC Source Market China," *Colliers International*, January 2018, http://www.shamalcomms.com/sites/default/files/Colliers%20-%20ATM%20Knowledge%20Partner%20-%20China%20%20-%20English.pdf.

51   "Celebrating Strong Ties," *Bahrain this Month*, October 1, 2018, https://www.bahrainthismonth.com/magazine/interviews/chinese-ambassador-celebrating-strong-ties.

52   "Bahrain takes part in Arab Arts Festival in China," *Arab Today*, September 13, 2014, https://www.arabstoday.net/en/75/bahrain-takes-part-in-arab-arts-festival-in-china.

53   "4th Arabic Arts Festival Opens in City," *Go Chengdu*, July 16, 2018, http://www.gochengdu.cn/news/Highlights/4th-arabic-arts-festival-opens-in-city-a7585.html.

54   "The Confucius Institute at University of Bahrain," *University of Bahrain*, 2016, http://www.uob.edu.bh/en/index.php/administration/centers/confucius-institute.

55   Huang Zhiling, "10 new Confucius Institutes lift global total to 548, boosting ties," *China Daily*, December 5, 2018, http://global.chinadaily.com.cn/a/201812/05/WS5c07239da310eff_30328f182.html.

56   "The Confucius Institute at University of Bahrain," *University of Bahrain*, 2016, http://www.uob.edu.bh/en/index.php/administration/centers/confucius-institute.

57   "Chinese Government Scholarship Open for Application," *Embassy of the People's Republic of China in the Kingdom of Bahrain*, January 16, 2019, http://bh.china-embassy.org/eng/xwdt/t1528121.htm.

58   Muhammad Zulfikar Rakhmat, "China and Bahrain: Undocumented

Growing Relations," Fair Observer, May 22, 2014, https://www.fairobserver.com/region/middle_east_north_africa/china-and-bahrain-undocumented-growing-relations-66107/.

Conclusion: Challenges and Prospects

1 Xuming Qian and Jonathan Fulton, "China–Gulf Economic Relationship under the 'Belt and Road' Initiative, "*Asian Journal of Middle Eastern and Islamic Studies*, 11(3), 2017, 12–21.

2 Daniel Workman, "Top 15 Crude Oil Suppliers to China," *World's Top Exports*, June 7, 2019, http://www.worldstopexports.com/top-15-crude-oil-suppliers-to-china/.

3 Rania El Gamal, "UPDATE 3-Saudi Arabia announces rise in oil reserves after external audit," *Reuters*, January 9, 2019, https://www.reuters.com/article/saudi-oil-reserves/update-3-saudi-arabia-announces-rise-in-oil-reserves-after-external-audit-idUSL8N1Z93WO.

4 "The State of Persian Gulf Oil Reserves," *The Globalist*, September 12, 2017, https://www.theglobalist.com/gulf-oil-reserves-saudi-arabia-iran/.

5 Daniel Workman, "Petroleum Gas Exports by Country," *World's Top Exports*, May 21, 2019, http://www.worldstopexports.com/petroleum-gas-exports-country/.

6 Yitzhak Shichor, "China's Middle East strategy: In search of wells and power," In L. Dittmer and G. T. Yu (eds.), *China, the Developing World, and the New Global Dynamic* (pp. 157–175). Boulder and London: Lynne Rienner Publishers, 2010.

7 "The Role of Energy within BRI," *EURObiz*, January 4, 2019, https://www.eurobiz.com.cn/the-role-of-energy-within-bri/.

8 "Chinese Investments & Contracts in the Gulf states (2013 – 2018)," *China Global Investment Tracker*, 2019, https://www.aei.org/china-global-investment-tracker/.

9 "China Customs Statistics: Imports and exports by country/region," *The Hong Kong Trade Development Council (HKTDC)*, May 27, 2019, http://china-trade-research.hktdc.com/business-news/article/Facts-and-Figures/China-Customs-Statistics/ff/en/1/1X39VTVQ/1X09N9NM.htm.

10 Xuming Qian and Jonathan Fulton, "China-Gulf Economic Relationship under the "Belt and Road" Initiative, *Asian Journal of Middle Eastern and Islamic Studies*, 11(3), 2017, 12–21.

11 "DP World, Zhejiang China Group sign deal for a new traders market," *Gulf News*, July 19, 2018, https://gulfnews.com/business/dp-world-zhejiang-china-group-sign-deal-for-a-new-traders-market-1.2254073.

12 James Kynge, Chris Campbell, Amy Kazmin & Farhan Bokhari, "How China rules the waves." *Financial Times*, January 12, 2017, https://ig.ft.com/sites/china-ports/.

13 Jonathan Fulton, *China's Relations with the Gulf Monarchies*. New York: Routledge, 2019.
14 "Remarks by President Trump on the Joint Comprehensive Plan of Action," *The White House*, May 8, 2018, https://www.whitehouse.gov/briefings-statements/remarks-president-trump-joint-comprehensive-plan-action/.
15 Liu Haiquan, "The Security Challenges of the 'One Belt, One Road' Initiative and China's Choices," *CIRR*, XXIII (78), 2017, 129–147.
16 Jeffrey S. Payne, "The G.C.C. and China's One Belt, One Road: Risk or Opportunity?," *Middle East Institute*, August 11, 2016, https://www.mei.edu/publications/gcc-and-chinas-one-belt-one-road-risk-or-opportunity.
17 Liu Haiquan, "The Security Challenges of the 'One Belt, One Road' Initiative and China's Choices," *CIRR*, XXIII (78), 2017, 129–147.
18 Liu Li and Wang Zesheng,"Belt and Road Initiative in the Gulf Region: Progress and Challenges," *China Institute of International Studies*, September 11, 2017, http://www.ciis.org.cn/english/2017-11/09/content_40063037.htm.
19 Mordechai Chaziza, "China's Counter-Terrorism Policy in the Middle East," In M. Clarke (ed.), *Terrorism and Counter-Terrorism in China: Domestic and Foreign Policy Dimensions* (pp. 141–156). New York: Oxford University Press, 2018.
20 Mathieu Duchatel, "China's foreign fighter's problem," *War on the Rocks*, January 25, 2019, https://warontherocks.com/2019/01/chinas-foreign-fighters-problem/.
21 "Position Paper of the People's Republic of China At the 71st Session of the United Nations General Assembly," *Ministry of Foreign Affairs, the People's Republic of China*, September 7, 2016, https://www.fmprc.gov.cn/mfa_eng/wjdt_665385/2649_665393/t1395489.shtml
22 Giorgio Cafiero and Daniel Wagner, "What the Gulf States Think of 'One Belt, One Road'," *The Diplomat*, May 24, 2017, https://thediplomat.com/2017/05/what-the-gulf-states-think-of-one-belt-one-road/.
23 Robert D. Kaplan, "Center Stage for the 21st Century: Power Plays in the Indian Ocean," *Foreign Affairs*, 88(2), 2009, 16–33.
24 "China's Xi pledges to 'fight corruption' at Belt and Road summit," *Al-Jazeera*, April 26, 2019, https://www.aljazeera.com/news/2019/04/china-xi-pledges-fight-corruption-belt-road-summit-190426063632664.html.
25 Yoel Guzansky and Shmuel Even, "The Challenge of the Oil Market to the Gulf States," *INSS Insight No. 926*, May 10, 2017, https://www.inss.org.il/publication/challenge-oil-market-gulf-states/.
26 "Corruption Perceptions Index 2018," *Transparency International*, 2019, https://www.transparency.org/cpi2018.

27 "China's Xi pledges to 'fight corruption' at Belt and Road summit," *Al-Jazeera*, April 26, 2019, https://www.aljazeera.com/news/2019/04/china-xi-pledges-fight-corruption-belt-road-summit-190426063632664.html.

28 Liu Li and Wang Zesheng,"Belt and Road Initiative in the Gulf Region: Progress and Challenges," *China Institute of International Studies*, September 11, 2017, http://www.ciis.org.cn/english/2017-11/09/content_40063037.htm.

29 "The Belt and Road Initiative Progress, Contributions and Prospects," *Belt and Road Portal*, April 22, 2019, https://eng.yidaiyilu.gov.cn/zchj/qwfb/86739.htm.

30 Sumedh Anil Lokhande, "China's One Belt One Road Initiative and the Gulf Pearl chain," *China Daily*, June 5, 2017, http://www.chinadaily.com.cn/opinion/2017beltandroad/2017-06/05/content_29618549.htm.

31 Liu Li and Wang Zesheng,"Belt and Road Initiative in the Gulf Region: Progress and Challenges," *China Institute of International Studies*, September 11, 2017, http://www.ciis.org.cn/english/2017-11/09/content_40063037.htm.

32 Sumedh Anil Lokhande, "China's One Belt One Road Initiative and the Gulf Pearl chain," *China Daily*, June 5, 2017, http://www.chinadaily.com.cn/opinion/2017beltandroad/2017-06/05/content_29618549.htm.

33 Liu Li and Wang Zesheng,"Belt and Road Initiative in the Gulf Region: Progress and Challenges," *China Institute of International Studies*, September 11, 2017, http://www.ciis.org.cn/english/2017-11/09/content_40063037.htm.

34 Mordechai Chaziza, "China's Economic Diplomacy Approach in the Middle East Conflicts," *China Report*, 55(1), 2019, 24–39.

35 Mordechai Chaziza, "China's Mediation Efforts in the Middle East and North Africa: Constructive Conflict Management," *Strategic Analysis*, 42 (1), 2018, 29–41.

36 Liu Li and Wang Zesheng,"Belt and Road Initiative in the Gulf Region: Progress and Challenges," *China Institute of International Studies*, September 11, 2017, http://www.ciis.org.cn/english/2017-11/09/content_40063037.htm.

37 Yitzhak Shichor, "Gains and Losses: Historical Lessons of China's Middle East Policy for Its OBOR Initiative," *Asian Journal of Middle Eastern and Islamic Studies*, 12 (2), 2018, 127–141.

38 Jonathan Fulton, "The G.C.C. Countries and China's Belt and Road Initiative (BRI): Curbing Their Enthusiasm?," *Middle East Institute*, October 17, 2017, https://www.mei.edu/publications/gcc-countries-and-chinas-belt-and-road-initiative-bri-curbing-their-enthusiasm.

39 Liu Li and Wang Zesheng, "Belt and Road Initiative in the Gulf Region:

Progress and Challenges," *China Institute of International Studies*, September 11, 2017, http://www.ciis.org.cn/english/2017-11/09/content_40063037.htm.

40 "Vision and Actions on Jointly Building Silk Road Economic Belt and 21st-Century Maritime Silk Road," *National Development and Reform Commission, Ministry of Foreign Affairs, and Ministry of Commerce of the People's Republic of China*, March 28, 2015, http://en.ndrc.gov.cn/newsrelease/201503/t20150330_669367.html.

41 Liu Li and Wang Zesheng,"Belt and Road Initiative in the Gulf Region: Progress and Challenges," *China Institute of International Studies*, September 11, 2017, http://www.ciis.org.cn/english/2017-11/09/content_40063037.htm.

42 "Vision and Actions on Jointly Building Silk Road Economic Belt and 21st-Century Maritime Silk Road," *National Development and Reform Commission, Ministry of Foreign Affairs, and Ministry of Commerce of the People's Republic of China*, March 28, 2015, http://en.ndrc.gov.cn/newsrelease/201503/t20150330_669367.html.

43 Liu Li and Wang Zesheng, "Belt and Road Initiative in the Gulf Region: Progress and Challenges," *China Institute of International Studies*, September 11, 2017, http://www.ciis.org.cn/english/2017-11/09/content_40063037.htm.

44 "Vision and Actions on Jointly Building Silk Road Economic Belt and 21st-Century Maritime Silk Road," *National Development and Reform Commission, Ministry of Foreign Affairs, and Ministry of Commerce of the People's Republic of China*, March 28, 2015, http://en.ndrc.gov.cn/newsrelease/201503/t20150330_669367.html.

45 Liu Li and Wang Zesheng,"Belt and Road Initiative in the Gulf Region: Progress and Challenges," *China Institute of International Studies*, September 11, 2017, http://www.ciis.org.cn/english/2017-11/09/content_40063037.htm.

46 "Vision and Actions on Jointly Building Silk Road Economic Belt and 21st-Century Maritime Silk Road," *National Development and Reform Commission, Ministry of Foreign Affairs, and Ministry of Commerce of the People's Republic of China*, March 28, 2015, http://en.ndrc.gov.cn/newsrelease/201503/t20150330_669367.html.

47 Liu Li and Wang Zesheng,"Belt and Road Initiative in the Gulf Region: Progress and Challenges," *China Institute of International Studies*, September 11, 2017, http://www.ciis.org.cn/english/2017-11/09/content_40063037.htm.

48 "Vision and Actions on Jointly Building Silk Road Economic Belt and 21st-Century Maritime Silk Road," *National Development and Reform Commission, Ministry of Foreign Affairs, and Ministry of Commerce of the People's Republic of China*, March 28, 2015, http://en.ndrc.gov.cn/newsrelease/201503/t20150330_669367.html.

49 Liu Li and Wang Zesheng,"Belt and Road Initiative in the Gulf Region:

Progress and Challenges," *China Institute of International Studies,* September 11, 2017, http://www.ciis.org.cn/english/2017-11/09/content_40063037.htm.

Bibliography

Al-Masri, Ahmed and Curran, Kevin. *Smart technologies and innovation for a sustainable future: Proceedings of the 1st American University in the Emirates International Research Conference – Dubai, UAE 2017*. Cham, Switzerland: Springer, 2019.

Alterman, Jon B., and Garver, John. *The Vital Triangle: China, the United States, and the Middle East*. Washington: Center for Strategic and International Studies, 2008.

Alterman, Jon B. "China's Soft Power in the Middle East," in C. Mcgiffert (ed.), *Chinese Soft Power and Its Implications for the United States* (pp. 63–76). Washington, DC: Center for Strategic and International Studies, 2009.

Anoushiravan, Ehteshami and Horesh, Niv. *China's presence in the Middle East: the implications of the One Belt, One Road Initiative*. London; New York: Routledge, Taylor & Francis Group, 2018.

Armijo, Jacqueline. "China and the Gulf: The Social and Cultural Implications of Their Rapidly Developing Economic Ties," In T. Niblock and M. Malik (eds.), *Asia–Gulf Economic Relations in the 21st Century: The Local to Global Transformation* (pp.141–156). Berlin: Gerlach Press, 2013.

Bin Huwaidin, Mohamed. *China's Relations with Arabia and the Gulf, 1949–1999*. London: Routledge, 2011.

Bitzinge, Richard A. "Arms to Go: Chinese Arms Sales to the Third World," *International Security*, 17 (2), 1992, 84–111.

Blanchard, Jean-Marc F., and Flint, Colin. "The Geopolitics of China's Maritime Silk Road Initiative," *Geopolitics*, 22 (2), 2017, 223–225.

Cai, Peter. *Understanding China's Belt and Road Initiative*. Sydney: Lowy Institute for International Policy, 2017.

Calabrese, John. "China and the Persian Gulf: Energy and Security," *Middle East Journal*, 52 (3), 1998, 351–366.

Chaziza, Mordechai. "China's Counter-Terrorism Policy in the Middle East," In M. Clarke (ed.), *Terrorism and Counter-Terrorism in China: Domestic and Foreign Policy Dimensions* (pp. 141–156). New York: Oxford University Press, 2018.

Chaziza, Mordechai. "China's Mediation Efforts in the Middle East and North Africa: Constructive Conflict Management," *Strategic Analysis*, 42 (1), 2018, 29–41.

Chaziza, Mordechai. "The Significant Role of Oman in China's Maritime Silk Road Initiative," *Contemporary Review of the Middle East*, 6 (1), 2018, 1–14.

Chaziza, Mordechai. "China's Economic Diplomacy Approach in the Middle East Conflicts," *China Report*, 55(1), 2019, 24–39.

Chaziza, Mordechai. "Six Years After the Arab Spring: China Foreign Policy in the Middle East-North Africa," In C. Çakmak and A. O. Özçelik (eds.), *The World Community and Arab Spring* (pp.185–204). Cham, Switzerland: Palgrave Macmillan, 2019.

Cheng, Joseph Y. S. "China's Relations with the Gulf Cooperation Council States: Multilevel Diplomacy in a Divided Arab World," *China Review*, 16 (1), 35–64.

Dorsey, James M. *China and the Middle East: Venturing into the Maelstrom*. Cham, Switzerland: Palgrave Macmillan, 2019.

Duchâtel, Mathieu, Oliver, Bräuner, and Zhou, Hang. "Protecting China's Overseas Interests: The Slow Shift Away from Non-Interference," *SIPRI, Policy Paper 41*, Stockholm, Sweden: Stockholm International Peace Research Institute, 2014.

Eberling, George, G. *China's Bilateral Relations With Its Principal Oil Suppliers*. Lanham: Lexington, 2017.

Fallon, Theresa. "The New Silk Road: Xi Jinping's Grand Strategy for Eurasia," *American Foreign Policy Interests*, 37 (3), 2015, 140–147.

Fardella, Enrico. "China's Debate on the Middle East and North Africa: A Critical Review," *Mediterranean Quarterly*, 26, (1), 2015, 5–25.

Feng, Chaoling. "Embracing Interdependence: The Dynamics of China and the Middle East," *Policy Briefing*. Doha, Brookings Doha Center, 2015.

Ferdinand, Peter. "Westward ho – the China dream and 'one belt, one road': Chinese foreign policy under Xi Jinping," *International Affairs*, 92 (4), 2016, 941–957.

Fulton, Jonathan. "China's Presence in the Middle East: The Implications of the One Belt, One Road Initiative/The Red Star and the Crescent: China and the Middle East," *The Middle East Journal*, 72 (2), 2018, 341–343.

Fulton, Jonathan and Li-Chen, Sim. *External Powers and the Gulf Monarchies*. London, Oxon; New York, NY: Routledge, 2019.

Fulton, Jonathan. *China's Relations with the Gulf Monarchies*. Abingdon, Oxon; New York, NY: Routledge, 2019.

Ghafouri, Mahmoud. "China's Policy in the Persian Gulf," *Middle East Policy Council*, 16 (2), 2009, 80–92.

Goh, Evelyn. *Meeting the China Challenge: The United States in Southeast Asian Regional Security Strategies*. Washington: East-West Center, 2005.

Goldstein, Avery. *Rising to the Challenge: China's Grand Strategy and International Security*. Stanford: Stanford University Press, 2005.

Gormley, Dennis M., Erickson, Andrew S., and Yuan, Jingdong. *A Low-Visibility Force Multiplier: Assessing China's Cruise Missile Ambitions*. Washington, DC: NDU Press, 2014.

Han, Zhibin and Chen, Xiaoqian. "Historical Exchanges and Future Cooperation between China and Oman Under the "Belt & Road" Initiative," *International Relations and Diplomacy*, 6 (1), 2018, 1–15.

Horesh, Niv. *Toward Well-Oiled Relations? China's Presence in the Middle East Following the Arab Spring*. London: Palgrave Macmillan UK: Imprint: Palgrave Macmillan, 2016.

Huang, Yiping. "Understanding China's Belt & Road Initiative: Motivation, framework and assessment," *China Economic Review*, 40, 2016, 314–321.

Hudson, Michael and Kirk, Mimi. *Gulf Politics and Economics in a Changing World*. Middle East Institute, Washington DC, 2014.

Jalal, Mohammed N, The China-Arab States Cooperation Forum: Achievements, Challenges and Prospects," *Journal of Middle Eastern and Islamic Studies (in Asia)*, 8 (2), 2014, 1–21.

Kaiser-Cross, Sarah and Mao, Yufeng. "China's Strategy in the Middle East and the Arab World," In J. Eisenman and E. Heginbotham (eds.), *China Steps Out: Beijing's Major Power Engagement with the Developing World* (pp. 170–192). New York: Routledge, 2018.

Kaplan, Robert D. "Center Stage for the 21st Century: Power Plays in the Indian Ocean," *Foreign Affairs*, 88(2), 2009, 16–33.

Kumaraswamy, P. R., and Quamar, Md. Muddassir. *India's Saudi Policy: Bridging the Gulf*. Singapore: Palgrave Macmillan, 2019.

Lanteinge, Marc. *Chinese Foreign Policy: An Introduction*. London: Routledge, 2013.

Layne, Christopher. "The US-Chinese power shift and the end of the Pax Americana," *International Affairs*, 94 (1), 2018, 89–111.

Liu, Haiquan. "The Security Challenges of the "One Belt, One Road" Initiative and China's Choices," *CIRR*, XXIII (78), 2017, 129–147.

Liu, Zhongmin. "Historical evolution of relationship between China and the Gulf Region." *Journal of Middle Eastern and Islamic Studies (in Asia)* 10(1), 2016, 1–25.

Min, Ye. "China and competing cooperation in Asia-Pacific: TPP, RCEP, and the New Silk Road," *Asian Security*, 11 (3), 2015, 206–224.

Miller, Tom. *China's Asian Dream*. London: Zed Books, 2017.

Mo, Chen. "Exploring Economic Relations between China and the GCC States," *Journal of Middle Eastern and Islamic Studies (in Asia)*, 5 (4), 2011, 88–105.

Niblock, Tim and Yang, Guang. *Security Dynamics of East Asia in the Gulf region*. Berlin: Gerlach Press, 2014.

Niu, Xinchun and Haibing, Xing. "China's Interest in and Influence Over the Middle East," *Contemporary International Relations*, 24, (1), 2014, 37–58.

Olimat, Muhamad S. *China and the Middle East: From Silk Road to Arab Spring*. London: Routledge, 2013.

Olimat, Muhamad S. *China and the Middle East since World War II: A Bilateral Approach*. Lanham: Lexington Books, 2014.

Olimat, Muhamad S. *China and the Gulf Cooperation Council Countries: Strategic Partnership in a Changing World*. Maryland: Lexington Books, 2016.

Qian, Xuewen, "The New Silk Road in West Asia under "the Belt and Road"

Initiative," *Journal of Middle Eastern and Islamic Studies (in Asia)*, 10 (1), 2016, 26–55.

Qian, Xuming and Fulton, Jonathan. "China–Gulf Economic Relationship under the "Belt and Road" Initiative, "*Asian Journal of Middle Eastern and Islamic Studies*, 11(3), 2017, 12–21.

Qian, Xuming, "The Belt and Road Initiatives and China–GCC Relations," *International Relations and Diplomacy*, 5(11), 2017, 687–693.

Reardon-Anderson, James. *The Red Star and the Crescent: China and the Middle East*. New York: Oxford University Press, 2018.

Schmierer, Richard J. "The Sultanate of Oman and the Iran Nuclear Deal," *Middle East Policy*, 22 (4), 2015, 113–120.

Scobell, Andrew and Nader Alireza. *China in the Middle East: The Wary Dragon*. Santa Monica, Calif.: RAND, 2016.

Scobell, Andrew "Why the Middle East matters to China," In A. Ehteshami and N. Horesh (eds.), *China's Presence in the Middle East: The Implications of the One Belt, One Road Initiative* (pp. 9–23). New York: Routledge, 2018.

Sevilla, Henelito A Jr. "China's New Silk Route Initiative: Political and Economic Implications for the Middle East and Southeast Asia," *Journal of Middle Eastern and Islamic Studies (in Asia)*, 11 (1), 83–106.

Shariatinia, Mohsen and Azizi, Hamidreza. "Iran–China Cooperation in the Silk Road Economic Belt: From Strategic Understanding to Operational Understanding," *China & World Economy*, 25, No. (5), 2017, 46–61.

Shichor, Yitzhak. *The Middle East in China's Foreign Policy: 1949–1977*. Cambridge: Cambridge University Press, 1979.

Shichor, Yitzhak. "China's Middle East strategy: In search of wells and power," In L. Dittmer and G. T. Yu (eds.), *China, the Developing World, and the New Global Dynamic* (pp. 157–175). Boulder and London: Lynne Rienner Publishers, 2010.

Shichor, Yitzhak. "Vision, provision and supervision: The politics of China's OBOR and AIIB and their implications for the Middle East', In A. Ehteshami, N. Horesh (eds.), *China's Presence in the Middle East: Implications for One Belt, One Road Initiative* (pp. 38–53). London: Routledge, 2017.

Shichor, Yitzhak. "Gains and Losses: Historical Lessons of China's Middle East Policy for Its OBOR Initiative," *Asian Journal of Middle Eastern and Islamic Studies*, 12 (2), 2018, 127–141.

Struver, Georg. "China's partnership diplomacy: International alignment based on interests of ideology," *The Chinese Journal of International Politics*, 10(1), (2017), 31–65.

Sun, Degang and Yahia H. Zoubir. "China's Economic Diplomacy Towards the Arab Countries: Challenges Ahead?," *Journal of Contemporary China*, 24 (95), 2015, 903-21.

Tessman, Brock, F. "System structure and state strategy: Adding hedging to the Menu," *Security Studies* 21(2), 2012, 192–231.

Valeri, Marc M. *Simmering Unrest and Succession Challenges in Oman.* Washington, DC: Carnegie Endowment for International Peace, 2015.

Wu, Bingbing. "Strategy and Politics in the Gulf as Seen from China," In B. Wakefield and S. L. Levenstein (eds.), *China and the Persian Gulf: Implications for the United States* (pp.10–26). Washington: Woodrow Wilson International Center for Scholars, 2011.

Wu Sike, "Constructing 'One Belt and One Road' to Enhancing China and GCC Cooperation," *Arab World Studies*, 2, 2015, pp. 4–13.

Wu, Sike, "The Strategic Docking between China and Middle East Countries under the "Belt and Road" Framework," *Journal of Middle Eastern and Islamic Studies (in Asia)*, 9(4), 2015, 1–13.

Yang, Guang. *China-Middle East Relations.* UK: Paths International Ltd, 2013.

Yetiv Steven A., and Chunlong Lu, "China, Global Energy, and the Middle East", *Middle East Journal*, 61 (2), 2007, 199–218.

Yetiv Steven A. *Challenged Hegemony: The United States, China, and Russia in the Persian Gulf.* Stanford, California: Stanford University Press, 2018.

Yu-Shek Cheng, Joseph. "China's Relations with the Gulf Cooperation Council States: Multilevel Diplomacy in a Divided Arab World," *The China Review*, 16 (1), 2016, 35–64.

Zambelis, Chris. "China and the Quiet Kingdom: An Assessment of China–Oman Relations," *China Brief*, XV (22), 2015, 11–15.

Zhao, Hong. "China's Dilemma on Iran: Between Energy Security and a Responsible Rising Power," *Journal of Contemporary China* 23(87), 2014, 408–424.

Index